Insuring Security

Insurance is the world's largest economic industry, providing a form of security that more than triples global defence expenditure. However, little is known about the form of security insurance provides. This book offers a genealogical interrogation of the relationship between security and risk through its materialization in insurance.

This work seeks to argue that insurance practices ascribe value to life and in so doing produce a form of security central to the understanding of contemporary liberal governance and security. Lobo-Guerrero theorizes insurance as a biopolitical effect that results from the continuous interaction of an 'entrepreneurial form of power' and traditional forms of sovereign security. Through rich empirical cases and a unique theorization, the book breaks apart the traditional division between security studies, political economy and political theory. The author explores this theory in relation to specific issues such as the use of life insurance in the molecular age, the use of insurance to securitize against environmental catastrophic risk, and specialist products such as kidnap and ransom insurance, as well as the use of insurance to counter maritime piracy in the twenty-first century.

Providing an important and original contribution to the study of the biopolitics of security, this work will be of great interest to all scholars of security studies, international relations and international political economy.

Luis Lobo-Guerrero is Lecturer in International Relations at Keele University, UK. He has published widely on the biopolitics of security, insurance as a liberal security technology and the relationship between security, risk and liberal governance.

Interventions

Edited by Jenny Edkins, Aberystwyth University, and Nick Vaughan-Williams, University of Warwick

> "As Michel Foucault has famously stated, 'knowledge is not made for understanding; it is made for cutting'. In this spirit The Edkins–Vaughan-Williams Interventions series solicits cutting edge, critical works that challenge mainstream understandings in international relations. It is the best place to contribute post disciplinary works that think rather than merely recognize and affirm the world recycled in IR's traditional geopolitical imaginary."
>
> Michael J. Shapiro, University of Hawai'i at Mãnoa, USA

The series aims to advance understanding of the key areas in which scholars working within broad critical post-structural and post-colonial traditions have chosen to make their interventions, and to present innovative analyses of important topics.

Titles in the series engage with critical thinkers in philosophy, sociology, politics and other disciplines and provide situated historical, empirical and textual studies in international politics.

Critical Theorists and International Relations
Edited by Jenny Edkins and Nick Vaughan-Williams

Ethics as Foreign Policy
Britain, the EU and the Other
Dan Bulley

Universality, Ethics and International Relations
A grammatical reading
Véronique Pin-Fat

The Time of the City
Politics, philosophy, and genre
Michael J. Shapiro

Governing Sustainable Development
Partnership, protest and power at the World Summit
Carl Death

Foucault and International Relations
New critical engagements
Edited by Nicholas J. Kiersey and Doug Stokes

International Relations and Non-Western Thought
Imperialism, colonialism and investigations of global modernity
Edited by Robbie Shilliam

Insuring Security
Biopolitics, security and risk
Luis Lobo-Guerrero

Insuring Security

Biopolitics, security and risk

Luis Lobo-Guerrero

First published 2011
by Routledge
2 Park Square, Milton Park, Abingdon, Oxon OX14 4RN

Simultaneously published in the USA and Canada
by Routledge
711 Third Avenue, New York, NY 10017

Routledge is an imprint of the Taylor & Francis Group, an informa business

First issued in paperback 2011

Typeset in Times New Roman by Prepress Projects Ltd, Perth, UK

British Library Cataloguing in Publication Data
A catalogue record for this book is available from the British Library

Library of Congress Cataloging in Publication Data
Lobo-Guerrero, Luis.
Insuring security: biopolitics, security, and risk / Luis Lobo-Guerrero.
p. cm. – (Interventions)
Includes bibliographical references.
ISBN 978-0-415-58343-5 (hardback) – ISBN 978-0-203-84589-9 (e-book)
1. Risk (Insurance) 2. Risk management. 3. Life insurance. 4. Disaster insurance. 5. Marine insurance. I. Title.
HG3054.5.L63 2010
368--dc22
2010013219

ISBN: 978-0-415-58343-5 (hbk)
ISBN: 978-0-415-52285-4 (pbk)

To Mick and Nadine

Contents

Preface and acknowledgements

Following a Foucauldian tradition, this book is intended as a contribution to the history of an emergent present. While offering some analytical and theoretical reflections on the ways in which security is insured, the book aims to further develop a way of thinking of security away from the history of the security of institutions. The security that insurance secures is the security of ways of being in the world, which, as emergent, can be analysed through the instruments that make it possible.

Insuring Security provides elements to understand what is so particular about the kind of security produced through insurance and consumed by the richest 14 per cent of the world's population. OECD countries buy 88 per cent of the world's insurance premium volume. The conclusion offered in this book is that insurance operates a security technology that, while ascribing value to life, capitalizes livelihoods and promotes lifestyles. This form of security is central to the development of a liberal way of life within and beyond advanced liberal economies.

This book is the beginning of a wider scholarly analysis on the relationship between security and risk. It arises out of curiosity to understand how technologies of risk are employed in securing ways of living. I have been particularly interested in exploring why there is such a significant difference in the ways risks are understood and dealt with in advanced liberal economies compared with emerging markets. With a life experience divided between South America and Europe, it became evident to me from an early age that security was more than the quest for the legitimate monopoly of violence by a state. It was also clear that cultural and socio-economic issues were as important as geopolitical ones for understanding how individuals and societies managed to negotiate difference and prevent violent conflict. However, it was not clear to me why security studies scholarship, within the wider discipline of international relations, had not developed elements from which to understand how risks became the objects of those representations of danger. During my masters and doctoral studies I began to engage with what I consider a fascinatingly promiscuous body of literature on risk, security and liberal governance, involving the philosophy of science, the social studies of finance, sociology and criminology, socio-legal studies, medieval economics, as well as so-called post-structuralist approaches to international politics. The result of that experience was my doctoral thesis on which this book is based.

Although an individual enterprise, through writing this book I have had the pleasure of having established a deep intellectual and academic interaction with many colleagues in various parts of the world. Many of them have read various chapters in various stages. The end result is a significant revision to the original thesis based on the comments of two extraordinary anonymous reviewers and the editors of this series, to whom I am greatly indebted. All inaccuracies and shortcomings remain my own.

I also want to acknowledge the continuous enthusiasm and endless source of inspiration from my doctoral supervisor and friend, to whom I dedicate the book. Peter Burgess has also contributed a critical eye to various parts of this project, Pat O'Malley has gone through the pain of reading earlier versions of most of my work and has proved to be an inexhaustible source of useful ideas, and Marieke de Goede, Louise Amoore, David Campbell, Mark Lacy and Aaron Doyle have acted as discussants of many of the ideas included here. I am grateful to all of them.

At Lancaster I had the fortune of being able to debate early ideas of this project with Cindy Weber, Mark Duffield, Paolo Palladino, Paul Fletcher and Brian Wynne. Oliver Westall introduced me to the world of insurance in the UK and also shared with me part of his personal library. Funding for this project was provided by the Department of Politics and International Relations, the Peel Trust and County College at Lancaster University. Funding from the Wellcome Trust for the project 'Underwriting health and security: insurance as health-enabler in a molecular age', which arose out of my doctoral proposal and resulted in Chapter 3 of this book, was central to the completion of the thesis. Participants of two workshops organized through that grant provided me with an insight into the life and health insurance business in the UK. Alan Tyler has remained a constant source of information and advice. I also thank Ronnie Lippens, Tim Doyle, Peter Adey and Barry Godfrey at Keele University for their intellectual and institutional support. My loveliest thanks go to Nadine, who has endured the constant rewriting of this book.

Parts of this book have been presented at various International Studies Association (ISA) and British International Studies Association (BISA) conferences, as well as at conferences, seminars and keynotes at Carleton University, Newcastle University, Queen's University Belfast, Keele University, the London School of Economics, University of Amsterdam, the Norwegian School of Management, Sciences-Po, Universidad Javeriana (Bogotá) and Osmania University (Hyderabad). I am thankful to participants of those events for useful and constructive comments. Parts of Chapter 5 were first published by Sage as 'Biopolitics of Specialized Risk: An Analysis of Kidnap and Ransom Insurance', *Security Dialogue*, 38(3), 2007. Parts of Chapter 6 first appeared as '"Pirates", Stewards, and the Securitization of Global Circulation', *International Political Sociology*, 1(2), 2008, published by Wiley-Blackwell.

This is the first book of a trilogy I am writing on the relationship between insurance and security. The second volume will explore the relationship between insurance and war in the modern period, and the third one will be dedicated to the analysis of life insurance in relation to the capitalization of life hypothesis introduced in this book. However, rather than anchoring these relationships within established disciplinary and interdisciplinary debates, I have wanted to explore them as constituting problem spaces of their own. In that respect no formal respects will be paid to established bodies of literature and particular frameworks for analysis. This book and the following volumes concentrate instead on opening up a field of study that can be problematized in multiple ways. In that spirit I hope the book will be enjoyed more through the thought it provokes than for the ideas it portrays.

Luis Lobo-Guerrero
Keele, Staffordshire

Introduction

The importance of insurance as a global security technology cannot be overstated. In 2007, over $US4 trillion was spent on insurance premiums worldwide.[1] That figure corresponded to 9 per cent of the gross domestic product (GDP) of industrialized countries and 7.5 per cent of the world's GDP. It was more than three times the global defence expenditure for the same year.[2] In the case of the European Union (EU) the insurance–defence expenditure ratio was 6.7. With $US18.5 trillion of assets under management, or 11 per cent of global financial assets, the insurance industry is the world's largest economic industry.[3]

However, insurance is not a worldwide security technology. Of all policies sold in 2007, 88 per cent were sold in OECD countries, 70 per cent in the G7 countries and 38.5 per cent in the EU. These figures compare starkly with Africa's share of the world market of 1.3 per cent, 2.2 per cent for Latin America and the Caribbean and 4.4 per cent for South and East Asia.

Based on these figures, and on the importance of insurance in providing a technology for the management of uncertainty for individuals and collectivities, it is surprising that insurance has, as yet, not attracted the devoted attention of security studies scholarship. Moreover, insurance has scarcely figured in the analysis of international relations and international political economy.[4] Regardless of the importance of insurance in shaping the behaviour of institutions and individuals, and of the myriad of power relations that take place within insurance operations, insurance has not been a concern for political theory either.

This book is intended as a critical introduction to the study of insurance as an empirical site from which to interrogate security as a problem space. The problem of security, as will be argued below, relates in this case not to referent objects such as the state, as the disciplined study of international relations has traditionally understood it, but to lives and forms of life in continuous need of promotion and protection. As such, the study of insurance as a problem demands moving away from the curious division of labour between security studies, political economy and political theory. It also entails taking a distance from traditional categories of thought such as the political, the social, the economical and the human. Taking life and forms of life as its referents, this book explores different forms in which insurance is employed in promoting and protecting livelihoods and lifestyles. In the process it characterizes ways of life in the form of specific populations that have historically demanded and consumed different types of insurance.

Insurance as a technology of risk

Insurance, as Ewald introduced it, is an application of a technology of risk.[5] Risk, as a wider tradition of Foucauldian scholarship has noted, is a rationality of governance.[6] It is 'a way of representing events in a certain form so they might be made governable in particular ways, with particular technologies and for particular goals'.[7] In this respect, there is nothing natural about risk. As historians of ideas have documented, the modern concept of risk emerged in the late seventeenth century with the application of probabilities as a way of measuring uncertainty.[8] Although aleatory contracts, as described by Daston, were already operating a form of risk since the medieval Renaissance (see Chapter 1), and such contracts worked on the premise of ensuring equality of terms between all parties, the problem of measuring uncertainty remained. 'How should the (certain) price of an uncertain gain be assessed in order to preserve the rule of equity?'[9]

The use of probabilities as an instrument for measuring risk, however, was not as objective as it might appear. Hacking documented, for example, how seventeenth-century probability had a dual character. On the one hand, it was statistical, 'concerning itself with stochastic laws of chance and processes'. On the other, it was epistemological, 'dedicated to assessing reasonable degrees of belief in propositions quite devoid of statistical background'.[10] Probabilities therefore arose as a way of reckoning uncertainty, a problem that mattered greatly particularly in commercial relations where the possibility of establishing the price of an uncertain gain could determine the legality and morality of those practices. The modern concept of risk began to be developed when probabilities started to be employed for the measurement of uncertainty in late seventeenth-century Europe.

However, and particularly relevant to the understanding of insurance, the concept of uncertainty is quite complex and relates to the problem of identifying a reference from which to make judgements or calculations. In 1921, Knight expressed this idea in the following way:

> The practical difference between the two categories, risk and uncertainty, is that in the former the distribution of the outcome in a group of instances is known (either through calculation *a priori* or from statistics of past experience), while in the case of uncertainty this is not true, the reason being in general that it is impossible to form a group of instances, because the situation dealt with is in a high degree unique.[11]

The instances which Knight referred to are the categories into which reality is classified according to *certain* criteria. The certainty of classification depends not on mathematical precision but rather on authoritative *decisions*. Whoever decides what is to be observed, in which way, and how those observations should be recorded, is already exercising a form of power that operates as a referent for the reckoning of uncertainty. In this respect, uncertainty does not exist in the abstract, at least not when thinking about technologies of risk and insurance. Uncertainty matters in relation to ways of being in the world exercised through forms of power.

Making uncertainty matter, however, is already the manifestation of a particular way of thinking and of being in the world. When compared with alternative imaginaries, for example, in the world of divine providence promoted by the Church in thirteenth-century Europe, uncertainty did not make much sense. For a form of life characterized by an acquisitive spirit, in contrast, uncertainty mattered a great deal in so far as the livelihood and lifestyle of merchants depended to an extent on the mechanisms through which assets and merchandise could be protected from unwanted contingencies. Even when God wanted a storm to destroy a ship and its cargo, merchants still wanted to have some basic level of economic protection from such a catastrophe.

Histories of insurance, as the chapters of this book illustrate, indicate a constant tension between ways of imagining the world and ways of making uncertainty matter. These tensions do not result from preformed social categories such as social classes, as some Marxist readings would have it. They result instead from the continuous requirement to promote and protect ways of being in the world expressed as forms of life which are never a terminated project. Forms of life constantly adapt to the environments in which they operate and are simultaneously actors and subjects of power that seek to shape their conditions of existence. In this respect, forms of life cannot be objectified in so far as their determining features can be considered to be under constant emergence. However, they can be identified based on the instruments developed for the promotion and protection of livelihoods and lifestyles. For example, the development of the third-party form of insurance is explored in Chapter 1 in relation to the form of life of a thirteenth-century Italian merchant population, the emergence of actuarial life insurance is analysed in Chapter 2 in relation to the lifestyle of a landless gentlemen population in eighteenth-century England, debates around the use of predictive genetic testing for life and health insurance in twenty-first-century Britain are explored in Chapter 3 in relation to the lifestyle of a population genetically at risk, parametric environmental insurance schemes are analysed in Chapter 4 in relation to populations at risk of environmental hazard in emerging economies, kidnap and ransom insurance instruments are analysed in Chapter 5 in relation to a population of expatriate workers in countries of heightened kidnap risk, and the role of an insurance market institution is analysed in Chapter 6 in relation to a global capitalist population. A central claim of this book is that insurance products are 'emerging securities' developed to promote and protect the livelihood and lifestyles of populations.

As securities that promote and protect forms of life, insurance performs a technological role. This is not a new idea. It was introduced by Ewald in the late 1980s when he noted that insurance technology 'takes a certain form in certain institutions, thanks to the contribution of a certain imaginary'. This is not a natural process either. Instead, technologies of insurance

> were built up gradually out of multiple practices which they reflected and rationalized, practices of which they were more effects than causes, and it would be wrong to imagine that they have now assumed a definite shape. Existing in economic, moral and political conjunctures which continually alter, the practice of insurance is always reshaping its techniques.[12]

Rather than seeking to theorize the technological role of insurance, this book concentrates on exploring the technological effect of insurance.[13] This effect consists in transforming uncertainty into something amenable to be exchanged, something tradable. Something amenable to trade is usually referred to as a commodity. The role of insurance, as we know it in its modern actuarial form, is to transform uncertainty into the commodity we call, after the seventeenth century, risk. This transformation of uncertainty into risk, however, is not a natural phenomenon and should not be taken for granted. It is the result, instead, of a complex process through which, as analysed in Chapter 1, *insurance renders uncertainty fungible*. The process involves continuous negotiation between political imaginaries and livelihoods, the development of metrics for calculation, the evolution of knowledge regimes, the production and use of actuarial tables and other instruments, as well as a permanent understanding of how livelihoods and lifestyles change as the referents of protection and promotion of insurance practices. As constantly evolving and adapting, the technological role of insurance resists a general theorization. Instead of seeking to theorize a general role of insurance as a security technology, the technological role of insurance is approached in this book, chapter by chapter, in relation to the form of life it is expected to protect.

Insurance and the capitalization of life

It is possible to make, however, a general observation on the technological role of insurance as a security technology. In the cases dealt with in the book an outcome of insurance practices is, in one way or another, the capitalization of life. This claim involves three central elements that help constitute a political economy of security out of the capitalization of lives.

First, insurance, through underwriting practices, engages in processes of valuation. The life and lifestyle of the individual to be insured, or the lives and lifestyles of collectivities for which protection is sought, are assessed in relation to their future capacity to generate revenue. This is a particular characteristic of life insurance ever since the assurance of lives became an actuarial practice in eighteenth-century Britain, as shown in Chapter 2. In today's terms, and based on actuarial tables, the life of a man aged 65 will differ in value from that of a man in his mid-30s in relation to this individual's projected economic capacity. It is more likely that the 30-year-old client will be in a better position to use his life as collateral for a mortgage through the agency of a life insurance policy. What insurance does in this case is to value the lives of clients in relation to their capacity to obtain credit for capital investment. This technological role of insurance supports today the observation made by Dodson in 1753 when he noted that '[t]he values of the possessions, and the reversions, of much of the greatest part of the real estates of this kingdoms, will, one way or another, depend on the value of lives'.[14]

A second element that characterizes the insurantial function of capitalizing life is the idea of providing a financial resource to protect against the loss of capital. As explored in Chapter 4 through cases in which parametric insurance has been used to protect populations from environmental hazard, pushing the limits of insurability to encompass otherwise catastrophic risks, such as earthquakes, hurricanes and drought, provides a form of financial protection for property and infrastructure required to support livelihoods and lifestyles affected by these events. In the absence of these mechanisms, or when they provide very limited financial cover, as was the case of the Haitian earthquake of January 2010, populations lose all material investment in the form of assets and infrastructure that would facilitate their prompt material recovery after catastrophic events. Whereas insurance against natural or man-made catastrophic events is usually presented as a form of reparation of damage on buildings and infrastructure, its real effect is on the protection and promotion of forms of life.

The capitalization of life through insurance implies also an understanding of capital, not solely in the form of assets, lives and infrastructure, but also in the conditions of possibility of ways of life. In the case of capitalist forms of life, these conditions of possibility are the ones that make trade and exchange possible. In particular, these conditions relate to *circulation* and *connectivity* as essential features for *being* commercial.[15] The value of lives, goods, ideas and services depends on their continuous capacity to connect and circulate. This capacity depends on the existence of material enablers such as physical infrastructure whose function is to enable the connection of flows. It also depends in a crucial way on the contingent capacity of entrepreneurial leaders to creatively employ forms of power to mobilize circulation where the connectivity of flows has been interrupted. This is clearly shown in Chapter 6 through the analysis of the agency of the Joint War Committee (JWC) of the Lloyd's Market Association in re-establishing maritime circulation through the Strait of Malacca in 2005, at a time of heightened maritime piracy in the region. By means of suggesting a higher price on marine insurance for vessels sailing those waters, the JWC influenced the decision of regional governments to coordinate naval operations to patrol the waters of the Strait. The result was a reduction in the negative effects of piracy on the safe circulation of vessels.

The capitalization of lives is also manifest in a third example analysed in Chapter 5 through the role of kidnap and ransom insurance. In this case, life is capitalized as a productive asset by insuring it against the risk of abduction when operating in countries and regions of high personal and corporate security risk. What is being protected here is the circulation of an asset that is required for a particular economic activity. In this respect, kidnap risk is analysed as an operational risk against which an insurance product can be used to provide the financial means to recover the life, if and when it is taken out of circulation. The life of the individual, as a productive asset, matters for the employer in as much as the individual is capable of performing the activities for which he or she was hired.

The life of the individual, in the case of the kidnapper, matters as an asset which has been taken out of circulation. The human dimension to this atrocious practice is exploited as a means to challenge the economy of exchange instituted between kidnapper and ransom. The ethical analysis of the use of kidnap and ransom insurance, however, is used to highlight a controversial, if common, practice on the insurantial capitalization of life that enables commercial and productive operations in areas of high security risk.

The third element of the technological agency of insurance in capitalizing life is the dimension of life as investment. A commercial form of life and its liberal derivatives in the modern period is premised on the idea of capital accumulation. When lifestyles develop they demand the generation of higher incomes which in turn sponsor the continuous development of lifestyles. Higher incomes and higher lifestyles demand higher forms of financial protection. Failing to protect incomes and lifestyles opens up the possibility for partial or complete capital loss, which would impact on the capacity of the individual and his or her dependants to recover after negative events. Lifestyles develop as an effect of education, experience, training, tradition, social recognition, prestige and reputation, all immaterial values that perform a role in qualifying the standing of lives. As values, they are invested in progressing social, cultural, material and political conditions. Damage to these intangible values represents a loss of investment in life with repercussions on livelihoods and lifestyles. Insurance practices perform a technological role that provides a form of security that protects life, as invested capital, and presents it in a form amenable for further investment: insurable life. In this respect, insurance protects lifestyles by promoting livelihoods. The reparational form of security that results from this process has clear implications in the ways security is to be understood and theorized in relation to life. In short, and as elaborated in Chapter 7, the form of power exercised by insurance performs a biopolitical security effect.

Securing life by embracing risk

Baker and Simon have coined the term risk-embracing to 'evoke and distinguish the idea of "spreading risk" that has been so influential over the last century'.[16] For them, the term encompasses two related cultural trends, one that involves understanding social problems in terms of risk and the other which moves away from risk-spreading strategies and practices and holds the individual accountable for risk itself. Taking risks, then, 'increasingly becomes what one does with risk'.[17] The idea of risk-embracing highlights a distinction between forms of spreading risks which is usually ascribed to the public–private divide. However, this idea transcends this situation, as will be shown below.

The practice of risk-spreading, as the work of Baker and Simon and that of Ewald analysed, has been generally understood as the practice of distributing risks over populations.[18] These practices can be premised on two different principles which are not necessarily mutually exclusive but have in reality been combined to provide an instrument for social cohesion in liberal societies. On the one hand, risk-spreading has operated a principle of solidarity whereby stakeholders of society contribute and benefit from constituting a universal risk pool used to provide the means to repair lives and livelihoods under adverse circumstances. This is the world of social insurance as the technology to operate welfare state systems. On the other hand, risk-spreading has operated under a principle of mutuality whereby only a selected membership contributes towards the constitution of an insurantial pool used to promote and protect livelihoods and lifestyles of those assured. Whereas the former operates a public rationality of insurance, the latter operates an actuarial private form of insurance.

In a subsequent article, Baker revised the embracing risk claim in light of phenomena such as 'destructive competition' and catastrophic risks. '[W]hen insurance companies compete by "cream-skimming" the good risks and shutting out the bad risks' destroying 'the safety net that insurance is supposed to provide', and in a context in which societies must cope with catastrophic risks such as those dealt with during 9/11 and Hurricane Katrina, the risk-embracing position had to be qualified.[19] His suggestion was then to understand the risk-embracing claim in relation to the sharing of responsibility. Moving away from a principle of solidarity and universally engaging a principle of mutuality when employing technologies of risk to cope with uncertainty would not allow for risk-taking in light of these phenomena. The revised approach was one in which individuals embrace risk but share the responsibility of universal hazards through the agency of governments,[20] state insurance pools or some other mechanisms. 'Embrace risks when it is socially responsible to do so. Spread risks over to areas in which people do not have control, and do not leave it only to the market to sort that out'.[21]

The different chapters of this book, however, illustrate ways in which life is secured by embracing risks without always making a clear distinction between a mutual or a solidarity approach. Chapters 1 and 2 indicate an evolution of the necessary conditions for the development of the role of insurance in both mutual and solidarity forms (the emergence of the third-party form of insurance and the development of the principle of insurable interest). Chapter 3 presents a case in which the principle of mutuality operating under market conditions clashes with the state's responsibility to protect the life of individuals. The case highlights the difficulty in separating a principle of mutuality from one of solidarity when the protection of life itself is at stake. Whereas the role of insurance when dealing with lives adopts a form of capitalization as a strategy for protecting livelihoods and promoting lifestyles, the role of the state in its sovereign function adopts a form of regulation within the context of a neoliberal form of governance. The governmental pressure over individuals for taking responsibility in managing their own risks clashes with the sovereign responsibility to protect when deterministic readings of science are dramatized in the form of necessary biological exclusions. The chapter shows, however, that the use of insurance to secure life requires not necessarily the regulation of the state but the implementation of a principle of transparency and accountability in evidence-based underwriting. The use of private life insurance in the securing of liberal life remains an instrument for the embracing of risk as a way of promoting capitalist lifestyles.

Chapter 4 brings the two principles of mutuality and solidarity together to transfer risk as a private–public risk-embracing strategy. The chapter illustrates how uncertainty in relation to environmental hazard is translated as risk through public/private insurance schemes supported by financial securitization instruments. By blending the two principles in one, the emerging form of security that results from the process is one which combines the entrepreneurial agency of commercial insurers, and the sovereign state responsibility to protect. The effect of these schemes is a curious ensemble of security where the livelihoods to be protected and the lifestyles to be promoted become the referent of financial derivatives. The biopolitical security economy resulting from the process is one where the capacity of individuals to recover from environmental catastrophic events depends on the performance of a global financial market.

It is worth noting in passing that the biopolitical security economy analysed in Chapter 4 provides elements to engage in dialogue with Duffield's claim that development is 'a regime of biopolitics that generically divides humankind into developed and underdeveloped species-life'.[22] In his work, the 'distinction between life that is "insured" as opposed to "non-insured" provides a fertile metaphor for distinguishing the different but connected biopolitical strategies that constitute "developed" and "underdeveloped" populations respectively.'[23] The strategies described and analysed in the chapter openly challenge Duffield's distinction by illustrating how, in a global economy of insurance and risk management, uninsured populations are always the condition of possibility for insurance growth. Analysing this phenomenon away from an Agambean position that takes biopolitics as a function of sovereign power (discussed in Chapter 7),[24] it is possible to observe instead a productive element of parametric environmental insurance schemes that makes lives live in a globalized market environment.

Chapter 5 offers an illustration of how the use of kidnap and ransom insurance, as a commercial instrument for embracing risk, contributes to the constitution of an economy of security that in fact erodes the idea of social cohesion in the societies where it is employed. Based on a principle of mutuality, the use of this form of insurance would barely stand public scrutiny in advanced liberal economies. However, its wide use is tolerated by states and societies of regions of heightened security risks. Seen as an instrument that enables foreign investment and commercial enterprise, it is commonly presented in debates as countering the principle of solidarity that supports the existence and operation of state armed forces charged with responsibility for promoting law and order within a constitutional territory. By operating a market economy of risk management, the use of kidnap and ransom insurance has been presented as stimulating kidnapping practice and contributing towards the privatization of security in emerging and developing economies. This chapter illustrates a case in which insurantial technology is employed to commercially embrace risk outside the borders of what could be understood as a western liberal security community.

Chapter 6 deals with a case in which risk-embracing is exercised to stimulate the management of piracy risk in the Strait of Malacca by sovereign means. The use of maritime insurance to compensate against losses incurred as a result of acts of piracy is restricted by the charging of higher premiums as a means to stimulate a reaction from the littoral governments. The result, as noted before, and as elaborated in the chapter, was a combined naval effort to patrol and guard the Strait. In this case, and for the interest of the debate between risk-embracing and risk-spreading, the role of the JWC was to act as an agent in spreading the risk of piracy through non-insurantial means, in this case through naval force. This mutually beneficial relationship between a form of security provided through insurance and a form of security provided through the sovereign use of force is part of a wider symbiotic relationship which is not explored in this book in great detail but will constitute the subject of subsequent work.

Sovereign power, 'entrepreneurial power' and biopower

Adapting a concept from the history and philosophy of science, insurance instruments in this book are researched as 'epistemic objects'. Epistemic objects are here understood as instruments constituted through practices of power. As noted by Knorr-Cetina, these objects are open-ended projections lacking fixed qualities.[25] As open projections, they open up the possibility for novel and critical responses to specific problematizations. The concept was coined by Rheinberger in 1997 to refer to research objects, or scientific objects.[26] He defined them, while studying the notion of 'experimental system', as 'material entities or processes – physical structures, chemical reactions, biological functions – that constitute the object of enquiry. One of their features is that 'they present themselves in a characteristic irreducible vagueness'.[27] This vagueness is inevitable because, paradoxically, epistemic things embody what one does not yet know.[28] As he noted:

> [s]cientific objects have the precarious status of being absent in their experimental presence; they are not simply hidden things to be brought to light through sophisticated manipulations. A mixture of hard and soft, like Serres's veils, they are 'object, still, sign, already; sign, still, object, already'.[29]

Insurance instruments, approached as 'object, still, sign, already; sign, still, object, already', open up the possibility of observing novelties in the power interactions that generate these epistemic objects. In such spirit, it is possible to think insurance *politically*, as a security problem that brings together the sovereign, the juridical, the economical and the social. Although insurance is studied in this book in relation to forms of life, the question for insurance as an epistemic object is not what forms of life it promotes and protects, but what happens in the process of doing so. This is the guiding question that underlies the different chapters of the book. Insurance instruments are therefore analysed as having biopolitical effects. These biopolitical effects materialize in forms of capitalizing lives as a strategy to protect livelihoods and promote lifestyles. As described in later chapters, these biopolitical security effects result from a mutual interaction between what is here referred to as 'entrepreneurial power' and well-known practices of sovereign power.

The concept of entrepreneurial power is introduced in this book to understand how practices of insurance are made possible. It refers, specifically, to the effects of the agency of entrepreneurial people concerned with extracting revenue from insurantial technologies employed in protecting populations against undesired events. Inventors and developers of novel insurance products and practices have historically characterized themselves by operating at, and beyond, the margins of tolerated normality. Seeking to secure against the uncertain, they venture into areas for which knowledge is patchy, at best, and chart the spaces that were until then considered uninsurable or catastrophic. By means of exploring and adopting novel forms of knowledge, speculating about possible and imagined futures, engineering financial manoeuvres, shaping the behaviour of individuals and collectivities (instantiating moral economies) and exploiting the legal opportunities arising from existing orders of governance, insurers always seek to insure the uninsurable and generate a profit from doing so.

As entrepreneurs, insurers do not assume insurance as a ready-made security. They instead develop and operate technologies of insurance to generate insurance products as securities aimed at specific markets with expected economic returns. When doing so insurers exercise a form of power that differs from the sovereign power of sovereign monarchs and states. It is a form of power that seeks to secure forms of life through the material incentive of making a profit. It seeks 'to make live' whilst capitalizing lives as subjects of wealth. It is a form of power exercised to promote livelihoods and protect lifestyles by generating products whose profitability depends on their success in securing. In this respect, it is a form of power supported not by tradition and right, but by security effects. Insurers are so, in so far as they manage to insure.

Because of the precarious base that supports insurance, namely the necessity to generate profit, insurers are required to constantly employ their entrepreneurial power to shape and profit from markets of security. This entrepreneurial activity has historically operated, in various ways, in interaction with the sovereign forms of power of monarchs and states. As noted in the various chapters, insurers have constantly negotiated with orders of governance resulting from Church institutions, governments and states. They have always required, for example, the rule of law provided through sovereign institutions in order to legitimize their practice and enforce insurance contracts. Other forms of interaction are described throughout the book and analysed in some detail in Chapter 7.

Although interaction between the entrepreneurial form of power of insurers and the sovereign power of states is usually productive, it is also haunted by governmentalizing attempts to bring insurance and insurers under the regulation of states. Insurers have historically resisted these processes and fought for the right to underwrite. The narratives of the following chapters illustrate such cases. However, this productive tension and the products that result from them highlight a form of biopolitics that has, as yet, escaped the analysis of what can now be referred to as established biopolitical traditions based on the work of Foucault, Agamben, Hardt and Negri, Virno and Esposito.[30]

The biopolitical effect of insurance, analysed in this book as the capitalization of lives, opens up the analysis of biopolitics at the intersection between security studies, political economy and political theory. Based on a Foucauldian tradition, it focuses on the analysis of the ways in which ways of being in the world, as forms of life, are secured. In so doing it takes a distance from Hardt and Negri's focus on the transformations of productive labour and their analysis of the multitude as productive class. It also moves away from Virno's attempt to define a multitude as the middle space between the individual and the collective in an attempt of making sense of the blurring of binary categories such as the public–private and local–global.[31] This book does not assume forms of life in the abstract but analyses them in relation to livelihoods to be protected and lifestyles to be promoted. Livelihoods and lifestyles are describable features of forms of life which are historically located and can be analysed by interrogating the instruments through which they are secured. A particular contribution of this book is therefore its focus on insurance as a technology that produces securities aimed at securing forms of life. It does not assume biopolitics as a form of oppression. Nor is it the result of strategies to subjectify populations as objects of sovereign control as readings of Agamben's work might suggest. It is instead a form of biopolitics that results from the interaction between entrepreneurial efforts to capitalize life and sovereign efforts to protect populations. Biopolitics, it is here suggested, is the result of the interaction between entrepreneurial and sovereign power.

What unfolds from the analysis of insurance as an epistemic security object offered in this book is that there is no sovereign, but only governmentalizing practices; that there is no entrepreneurial, but only practices of capitalization; and that there is no life and no preformed ways of life, but only emerging ways of being in the world for which forms of security in the form of insurance are constantly developed. The biopolitics that results from the interaction between entrepreneurial and sovereign exercises of power influences the subjectivities that result from employing insurance practices and products to secure life and forms of life. These ideas are developed further in Chapter 7.

Some notes on methodology

In what follows, the book is structured through seven chapters that deal with seven different problems in the history of insurance. They are, however, not intended as a chronological narrative of how insurance emerged in the thirteenth century and developed into what we recognize of it in the twenty-first. The cases used in each chapter have instead been chosen as spaces from which to interrogate the biopolitics of security that results from insurance practices and products. They are used to explore a genealogy of insurance from the perspective of the event that is being insured.

As noted in Chapter 7, insurance belongs to the contingent, it operates a continuous present, even if its effects seem to create and shape a future. In reality, insurance always seeks to protect the possibility of a present. In that respect, a genealogy of insurance must highlight elements of novelty in the ways in which insurance secures life in present time. The aims of such genealogy are not to produce a general theory of insurance as a biopolitical security technology but rather to locate, describe, analyse and problematize specific issues that contribute to the understanding of the ways in which forms of life are the subjects of insurantial security. A genealogical approach to insurance is not intended to unearth ontological conditions for the operation of insurantial technologies. Instead, it is used to understand how and why insurance has adopted particular forms in specific periods of time in relation to emerging forms of life.

In that logic, each of the chapters of this book is offered as a problematization of a particular insurantial event. Chapter 1 is used to explore the emergence of the third-party form of insurance in the thirteenth century as a process through which uncertainty is rendered fungible. Chapter 2 moves on to analyse the incorporation of the principle of insurable interest and the emergence of the actuarial form of life insurance in eighteenth-century Britain. Chapter 3 analyses what happened when the hype on genetic determinism in twenty-first-century Britain threatened the insurer's 'right to underwrite'. Chapter 4 explores the use of parametric forms of insurance to secure populations against catastrophic environmental risks in the mid-2000s. Chapter 5 offers an analysis of the use of kidnap and ransom insurance as an instrument that enables the operation of foreign businesses in regions of heightened personal and corporate security risk. Chapter 6 analyses the role of the JWC of the Lloyd's Market Association in securing global circulation in a new age of maritime piracy. Finally, Chapter 7 is offered as a reflection of the major themes arising from previous chapters and analyses, in the form of conclusions to the book, the relationship between processes of valuation of life, the creation of subjectivities through insurance practices and products and the insurance of security that results from the interaction between entrepreneurial and sovereign forms of power.

Readers who are not interested in understanding the complex process through which uncertainty was rendered insurable through third-party forms of insurance in thirteenth-century Italy can proceed directly to Chapter 2. All chapters can be read independently from each other.

1 Making uncertainty fungible

In the *quaestio* concerning insurance (*contractus assecurationis*), the Spanish Dominican priest and theologian Domingo de Soto (1495–1560) offered a social argument in favour of *assecuratio* while asserting that 'trade is a fundamental factor of the common good'.[1] De Soto argued that the process of sharing risks with insurers 'allow[ed] many merchants to start businesses that they would never even have considered because of the dangers of long-distance maritime travel'. He then went on to argue that '*assecuratio* is a necessary instrument of commerce, a financial practice that generates common good'.[2] Ceccarelli, writing on this issue, noted that

> de Soto [was] not concerned with the religious implications that derive[d] from the economic exploitation of random events. God's absolute power and his foreknowledge of the future [were] not threatened by the fact that some types of contracts [were] based on future events humanly unknowable.[3]

For de Soto, writing in the 1550s, the *liceity* of insurance was clear enough as there was already a well-established theological tradition that recognized it as such.[4] Liceity is here referred to as the lawfulness of insurance in moral and religious terms.[5]

The well-established theological tradition that supported de Soto's defence of *assecuratio* was, however, the result of a complex tension that took place during the medieval Renaissance in northern Italy. On the one hand, there was the pastoral order of governance of the Church, supported by an economic ethic and a shifting theological and canonical knowledge-base and, on the other, the changing demands of a mercantile form of life experiencing radical transformation within the context of the Commercial Revolution. This tension was represented in the promulgation of the decretal Naviganti by Pope Gregory IX in 1236. A decretal is a pontifical letter which formulates decisions in ecclesiastical law. Through this decretal the Pope explicitly forbade the use of a kind of insurance, the *fœnus nauticum*, considering it usurious practice, as will be explained below. However, although the Church struggled to enforce its ruling, merchants developed two new instruments to bypass the prohibition. The *fœnus nauticum* or sea loan evolved into the *cambium nauticum* or maritime exchange and later into the ordinary cambium contract in the form of an insurance loan which involved a third party and the payment of a premium. By means of the last instrument, the third-party form of insurance, merchants had developed a licit mechanism through which they could make uncertainty tradable and exchangeable. Using the third-party form of insurance, traders could insure against a future unknown *event*. The third-party form of insurance was the mechanism that made uncertainty fungible and became the foundation for modern insurance instruments still in operation.

One of the central moral problems for the Church during the period of the medieval Renaissance, and indeed the key problematic around issues related to the making of uncertainty fungible as *periculum*, was that of 'usury'. The authoritative economic canonical definition of usury followed by medieval theologians came from Gratian's *Decretum*, the systematic compilation of Church law completed in AD 1140.[6] Usury is 'to demand, to receive or even to expect to receive more in a loan (*mutuum*) than the sum lent (the capital). This excess may be in money or in kind (e.g. in wheat, wine or oil) or in some other favour (e.g. a gift or merchandise from a merchant)'.[7] While 'establishing that usury violates divine and natural law, Gratian invoked a conciliar tradition reaching back to the Council of Nicaea and beyond, a tradition largely preoccupied with condemning and punishing as *'turpe lucrum'* (foul gain, filthy lucre) the clerical practice of usury'.[8] O'Donovan described how the earlier theological explanations of the canonical prohibition on usury were integrated 'through the leading themes of patristic economic ethics'.[9]

> Among the Greeks, Clement of Alexandria, Cyprian of Carthage, Basil the Great, Gregory of Nyssa and John Chrysostom charted the economic landscape within which usury was understood, and among the Latins, Ambrose, Jerome and Augustine. The main concern was over the exploitation through 'exorbitantly profitable loans' of persons in need of consumption goods or 'of the productive base for a livelihood.[10]

The very possibility of making uncertainty fungible, bypassing charges of usury, as will be analysed in this chapter, was not a simple matter. It involved a negotiation between forms of imagining and ruling God's world and the development of mechanisms to protect trade as a condition of possibility for a merchant form of life. Wealth created through trade was supported on an ethic which rivalled the Church's canon, hence the debate on usury. The process through which third-party insurance became morally and religiously accepted, documented by Pesce,[11] Bergfeld[12] and Spagnesi,[13] is a process whereby a form of life which does not arise from a pastoral or a sovereign form of power exercises a form of power that challenges and modifies a pastoral sovereign order. In the late twentieth century, Michel Foucault would refer to biopower as the form of power through which the life of populations, population understood as species-life, is made to live through the implementation of a political science. He would interrogate the emergence of this form of power in the late seventeenth and early eighteenth centuries in

Europe. However, what the emergence and subsequent use of third-party insurance indicates is a case of a thirteenth-century merchant form of life developing a security instrument to promote and protect its own way of being in the world. The form of power employed in the process, one that seeks to develop its own security instruments under conditions of radical uncertainty and which, for want of a better term, is called in this book 'entrepreneurial power', differs from Foucault's biopower in that merchants were not a population derived from sovereign decisions on how to understand subjects and objects of governance. The merchant way of life involved in the third-party form of insurance, although intimately linked with the order of governance of the Church, imagined and sought to govern a world in which merchant's security arose from their capacity to trade, as well as from alliances with sovereigns and the Church. In this respect, Gregory IX's decretal Naviganti was a form of resistance against an ethic that rivalled the Church's order of governance. This ethic of insurance had, of course, a long tradition.

It is commonplace to argue that Babylonian, Hindu,[14] Phoenician, Greek and Roman civilizations all developed insurance systems that 'corresponded in most essentials to written contracts used some 2,000 years later in marine ventures to the New World'.[15] Life insurance, for example, has, if controversially, been argued to have existed in one form or another since as early as 5000 BC. Benfield commented that at that time a rudimentary form of insurance existed in China by which boat owners found it advantageous to redistribute their cargoes into several boats as they approached treacherous river rapids or on long sea voyages. If one boat was lost, all the boat owners shared the loss and hence no one faced financial ruin.[16] According to Trenerry, writing in the 1920s, the ancient Egyptian and Chinese civilizations left evidence of burial societies and other insurance activities in their communities.[17] He described how, at the time of the first Babylonian Empire, about 2500–2250 BC, organized commerce had already devised risk-spreading systems by which losses derived from robbery or attack over property, perhaps even the life of slaves and of merchants themselves, could be compensated by forms of insurance that resembled *contracts of bottomry*. Contracts of bottomry operated in the form of a loan in which, effectively, a ship or its cargo was hypothecated as a security.[18] The loan would be paid, with an added premium, only if the voyage was completed. In Babylonian times these practices became codified by King Hammurabi (1792–1750 BC)[19] and, indeed, clauses 100–107 of the Code of Hammurabi legislatively regulated transactions between merchants, brokers and agents in relation to loans on interest to be repaid on the day of the settlement. It also established the requirement to issue and demand receipts for transfers of money and made legal provisions in the absence of mercantile arrangements. This ancient legislation clearly resembled, in elementary form at least, the later contracts for loans on bottomry in that,

> firstly, [...] the repayment of the loan was dependent on the safe arrival (as far as robbery was concerned) of the merchandise representing the advance, and secondly, that the rate of interest charged for such loans was very much higher than that charged in ordinary loans.[20]

There has, equally, been much speculation about the Greeks and Romans having developed and used forms of insurance. In 1945, Florence de Roover wrote that 'most authorities on the subject agree that marine insurance was unknown to Greek and Roman antiquity' and that the brevity and generality of the work of Trenerry does not contribute to a solid historical proof of the existence of such instruments.[21] However, there seems to be proof that these civilizations did in fact develop complex forms of insurance in direct relation to 'life'. Benfield made reference to the case of excavations in Milete (Asia Minor) which suggest that a form of annuity was in operation as early as the year 2052 BC, when

> citizens paid 3600 drachma into a common fund and in return received 30 drachma per month for life. On death, any balance remaining reverted to the fund except for 150 drachma which was paid to the next-of-kin to provide for funeral expenses.[22]

Benfield also provided another illustration of the Greek knowledge of the principles of life insurance.

> The Eianoi and The Thiasoi in ancient Athens were benevolent societies established and maintained by contributions from members. They later developed into societies providing for the payment of burial expenses and the immediate needs of deceased members' dependants.[23]

Trenerry suggested that there was direct evidence that proved the existence within the Roman Empire of a 'widely extended system of mutual insurance' carried out by the burial clubs (e.g. the Collegium Cultorum Dianae et Antinoi et Lanuvium) and possibly of societies for ordinary insurance. Indeed, as he argued, some terms of insurance were already incorporated in certain passages of Roman civil law.[24] However, not much is known about the systems through which they would have calculated risks. Trenerry suggested there might have been some form of imperfect system to measure mortality and that it might have been used as a means to allocate proportional premiums to the class of risk.[25] It is possible that Ulpianus's tables were such a system. Domitius Ulpianus, serving as Roman prefect and jurist around the first decade of the third century AD, perfected the compilation of information by which an estimate of the length of a person's life could be made.[26] His tables were to be used as the sole source of mortality rates in Europe up until the late seventeenth century, when Edmund Halley developed a new mathematical system.[27]

Regardless of the controversy about the existence of insurance instruments prior to the thirteenth century, it was at this time when the practices of insurance evolved into its third-party premium form. Between the end of the thirteenth century and the end of the fourteenth, insurance changed from being a clause included in contracts and became the main object of the agreement.[28] As Ceccarelli described it, following De Roover,[29] Perdikas[60] and Boiteaux:[31]

> this break was evident in the evolution of agreements in which security (particularly the safe arrival of the cargo of a ship) was simply an additional clause inserted into another contract (insurance loan), to pacts in which *security became the main object of the agreement itself.*[32]

Making security the main object of the agreement constituted insurance into a fundamental instrument to foster a way of life reliant on trade. The third-party form of insurance, which transformed uncertainty into fungible matter, became a fundamental condition to promote and protect the acquisitive spirit of the merchant people.

This instrument is central in the understanding of the history of liberalism in its forms of power, economic theories and doctrines, as well as the way liberal forms of life secure themselves. It has been important in theoretical debates in the context of the Reformation, particularly in Luther's thought in the sixteenth century.[33] As argued by Odd Langholm, contemporary understanding of economics and theories of value and money relate in one way or another to the development of these twelfth- and thirteenth-century debates.[34] The emergence of the third-party form of insurance and the decretal Naviganti around which it developed are the empirical space interrogated in this chapter to understand the relationship between insurance and security for historical and contemporary mercantile forms of life.

Commerce versus faith

The development of insurance instruments in the thirteenth and fourteenth centuries took place within a mercantile resistance to the pastoral power of the Church. Such power was exercised through the articulation of an economic ethic, a collection of principles and practices comprising moral arrangements in the form of codes of canon law and a theological doctrine inherited from the Fathers of the Church.[35] The Christian economic ethic explicitly opposed practices that made a profit out of lending money to needy people.[36] Central to the moral order developed around this ethic was an understanding that there was no uncertainty but only the mercy of God. Uncertainty was merely a human apprehension that contradicted faith.[37] Men should not attempt to anticipate God's will but rather commit to it. However, for the buoyant merchant people of the thirteenth and fourteenth centuries, uncertainty was becoming a complicated phenomenon. Uncertainty was not simply the mystery of God's will. Nor was it simply the instance of danger. It was also the opportunity to make profit. Fuelled by an acquisitive and entrepreneurial spirit, merchants were constantly seeking to expand the frontiers of trade in order to improve their material standing in the world.[38]

Instrumental for these purposes was the development of systems through which enterprises could be financed under the promise of an economic return. Making credit available entailed the practice of charging an interest on loans. This had been a controversial issue within canon law since at least the eleventh century.[39] The Church constantly denounced it not least because it challenged the very edifices of the Church's onto-theology but also because it could cause social distress. After all, Jesus himself had ordered men to look after the poor.[40] However, the practice of credit had been in use for centuries as a means by which enterprises that would generate a profit could be undertaken. A case in point was that of a merchant who had to meet the costs of fitting a ship and the costs of the voyage until reaching a port of destination. Arrangements made for these cases would cover not only such costs on a temporary basis but also some of the risks involved in the journey. These arrangements, as will be elaborated later in the chapter, were known as the *fœnus nauticum*, also known as the 'sea loan'. Sea loans were specifically prohibited by Pope Gregory IX in 1236 under the understanding that they constituted usurious practices which ran contrary to the Church's economic ethic. However, these early forms of insurance had been instrumental not only in making credit available for trading ventures but had also become important means for splitting the risks involved in the voyages. In light of the prohibition, but apparently not as its direct consequence,[41] merchants evolved the sea loan into alternative schemes that combined the provision of credit with added layers of complexity in the diversification of risks.[42]

The mercantile resistance to the pastoral power of the Church in this period was not a clash between sovereign and divine orders in the world. It was a conflict between different understandings of what should be accepted as the material conditions for existence. The Church sought to reconcile the doctrine of its fathers and the current canon laws with a changing commercial environment characterized by a voracious acquisitiveness. Concerned with fulfilling the primordial objective of salvation central to the Christian pastoral mission, the Church had developed what Michel Foucault has interpreted as an 'art of conducting, directing, leading, guiding, taking in hand, and manipulating men',[43] an art 'with the function of taking charge of men collectively and individually throughout their life and at each moment of their existence'.[44] This art, described by him as a pastoral form of power, was employed by the Church as a means to promote and protect its economic ethic, its material and spiritual imaginary of life.

By analysing the Epistles of Saint Cyprian, 'the crucial treatise by Saint Ambrose entitled, *De officiis ministrorum* (the responsibilities, the offices of ministers), and then the *Liber pastoralis*, which [was to be in use] until the end of the seventeenth century as the basic text of the Christian pastoral',[45] Foucault traced the origins of pastoral power in Christianity and sought to identify the unique features of this form of governance that distinguished it from ancient practices focused on the direction of the spirit.[46] Without going into the details of his analysis, Foucault portrayed pastoral power as connected to salvation, to the law and to truth. Each one of these aspects was composed of meticulous operations that sought to control the morality of individuals in the slightest detail, details that led Foucault to typify the crucial Christian characteristics of governing men as that of a shepherd looking after his flock. In Foucault's words:

> [t]he pastorate is connected to salvation, since its essential, fundamental objective is leading individuals, or at any rate, allowing individuals to advance and progress on the path of salvation. Second, the pastorate is connected to the law, since for individuals and communities to earn their salvation, it must make sure that they really submit to the order, command, or will of God. Finally, third, the pastorate is connected to the truth, since in Christianity, as in all scriptural religions, earning one's salvation and submission to the law are, of course, conditional upon acceptance, belief, and profession of a particular truth. So, there is a connection to salvation, the law, and to truth; the pastor guides to salvation, prescribes the law, and teaches the truth.[47]

Pastoral governance meant first, 'that the world was subject to an economy of salvation'.[48] Men were to earn their salvation; it was not granted – it had to be sought and fought for. However, God had created the world for men to be able to do so. It was a world 'made for man', and man was made to live in it, 'but only in order to pass into another world'.[49] Therefore, men had to abide by the law of God and not seek to 'make' their world.[50] Pastoral governance was a function of guiding men in their path to the other life through a world of final causes.[51] Second, it meant 'that the world was subject to a system of obedience' which meant that 'whenever God wished to intervene [...] for any particular reason, he did so.[52] However, men were expected to be agents of their own salvation which would be certified by their communion with God. A very powerful instrument in the economy of salvation was therefore the threat of excommunication, by which individuals could be deprived from passing into the other world under the grace of God. Finally, pastoral governance meant living in a world with an entire system of truth, truth that could be taught, but also hidden if required.[53] As described by Foucault:

> [t]he world was a book, an open book in which one could discover the truth, or rather in which truths taught themselves, and they taught themselves essentially in the form of their reciprocal cross-references, that is to say, in the form of resemblance and analogy. At the same time it was also a world in which it was necessary to decipher hidden truths that showed themselves by hiding and hid by showing themselves, that is to say, it was a world that was filled with ciphers to be decoded.[54]

These truth-telling practices characterized and institutionalized the pastoral power of the Church. By these means the Church sought to regulate the everyday lives of individuals. Pastoral power was, in effect, the order of power relations which articulated the prohibition of usury. In effect, pastoral power was the order of power relations which was contested by the exigencies and fiscal inventiveness of the mercantile class. In what follows, an analysis of this resistance will be developed by focusing on specific events and processes that were taking place during the time of the decretal Naviganti.

A quest for 'the uncertain'

The Commercial Revolution of the thirteenth century was the pre-modern condition of possibility for a form of life premised upon its capacity to accumulate wealth through trade. The period between the mid-tenth and mid-fourteenth centuries witnessed a process by which the idea of 'the uncertain' was to be slowly incorporated into a Christian world. Thinking 'the uncertain', however, was a major challenge to the pastoral power of the Church and the regime of knowledge that supported it. For the Church, the world was a creation of God, and He provided the source of certainty that men should seek. Nonetheless, 'the uncertain' began to be represented in this period through features which eventually generated the conditions for instruments of insurance to render it as fungible. Three interrelated processes were central to this phenomenon. First, a change in the way things were counted and accounted for began to take place after the adoption of the Hindu numerical system and the concept of zero. Second, a transformation in the knowledge-base supporting the Church resulted, amongst other issues, in the establishment of universities under the leadership of the newly established mendicant orders. These new centres for knowledge helped to develop the scholastic economic theory that was to allow the operation of third-party forms of insurance. And, third, a change in the conception of temporality made it possible for men to measure time and consequently design 'their' time in chronological ways. This last process was fundamental for designing instruments to secure a present in sight of a future and were also tightly linked with the organization of economic activity around urban centres.

The Commercial Revolution took place in the context of massive demographic changes in the Eurasian continent. It was framed by the catastrophic pestilence that swept these lands in 742–43, and the Black Death of the mid-fourteenth century.[55] During this period, population growth was characterized by its concentration around larger villages and towns apparently related to insecurity in the open country but also to the opportunities that trade and the pooling of basic services brought.[56] Demographic growth, partly as a result of the improvement of cultivation techniques and agricultural technology, and the urbanization that followed the demand for urban services and jobs, revolved around the creation of a surplus. As a result of the improvement of basic material conditions for life, communities were slowly led towards an economic reorientation from 'agrarian balance to commercial restlessness'.[57]

This period, as Florence de Roover described, 'saw the decline of the travelling or caravan [...] and the rise of a new type of business organization in which the "sedentary" or resident merchant was the central figure'.[58] The travelling merchant had little use for insurance.[59] When trading by land he usually travelled together with other merchants in armed caravans that could provide protection and 'banded together in hanses and universities for the protection of their rights in foreign lands'.[60] When travelling by sea, protection against pirates and privateers could be provided while sailing in convoys. Protection against the perils of the sea was likewise unnecessary as in the event of crashing against rocks or wrecking 'the travelling merchant often lost his life as well as his possessions'.[61] However, the fact that merchants in the twelfth and thirteenth centuries usually operated with borrowed capital which 'was often supplied in whole or in part by a partner who stayed ashore'[62] makes evident that the use of instruments of insurance was an absolute necessity for travelling merchants. Lenders and borrowers would not have cooperated had there not been a system in place by means of which the risks involved in the trade could be reduced.

The requirements of the sedentary urban trader, in contrast to his nomad predecessor who made a living whilst following trading 'events' such as the fairs in Champagne, slowly began to develop the mechanisms by which trading activities would improve profit. The resulting surplus constituted investment capital that could be used to fund new enterprises. Moreover, the sedentarization of trade saw the development of new trading roles. As noted by de Roover, 'the new type of businessman tried to direct all his affairs from the counting-house; he used partners, factors,[63] or correspondents to represent him in foreign parts'.[64] The new circumstances began to weave networks of international trade which demanded more complex and sophisticated forms of coping with uncertainty in trade and of circulating money. This is the context for the emergence of the third-party form of insurance. In what follows, three major changes that contributed towards making 'the uncertain' fungible will be explained.

First, and central to these changes, was the introduction of a new numerical system that opened up the possibility of a different kind of knowledge. Bernardelli argued that 'the beginning of modern economic theory in the Western world can be dated back with precision to the year 1202 A.D.',[65] the year in which Leonardo Fibonacci of Pisa published his book *Liber Abaci*, which introduced Hindu numerals to the West. However, the introduction of the Hindu–Arabic numerical system, having been available for centuries to Arab and Hindu traders, had to be encompassed into the imaginary of Christian Europe. Encompassing a new numerical system involved the acceptance of assumptions that were not necessarily correlated with those of the Church. For example, Rotman noted that the notion of 'zero' as one of the Hindu numerals involved a notion of nothing, and 'nothing' was not possible within a Christian cosmology. The Christian world was a world created by God and there was no possibility of nothingness. As he noted, 'medieval hostility to zero rested on a Christian antagonism to "nothing", since to talk about something being no-thing, to give credence to that which was not and could not be in God's world, was to risk blasphemy or heresy'.[66] However, there was a practical need for the new numbering system. The mercantile way of life in the form of what Rotman called 'mercantile capitalism' 'rode on the vector of trade, business, commerce, finance, money. And money required a system of writing, which included bookkeeping and calculation, to enable it to function as an international medium of exchange'.[67]

The introduction of Hindu numerals to the West also involved the introduction of a new metric, algebra. As Langholm noted, Fibonacci's book 'introduced oriental algebra to the Latin world and taught its merchants and bankers new principles of computing prices and profits'.[68] The translation of the *Liber Abaci* triggered the diffusion of a system of counting finitely and infinitesimally. Trade was no longer restricted to the units of Roman numerals. A direct application of this form of counting and measuring was the invention of double-entry bookkeeping and the concept of circulation in monetary theory.[69] This was to have a lasting effect in setting the basics for capitalism. As argued by Rotman:

> [t]he central role occupied by double-entry bookkeeping (principle of the zero-balance) and the calculational demands of capitalism broke down any remaining resistance to the 'infidel symbol' of zero, and ensured that by the early seventeenth-century Hindu numerals had completely replaced Roman ones as the dominant mode of recording and manipulating numbers throughout Europe.

The benefits of this numerical revolution for European merchants meant the possibility of counting in fractions and decimals. The calculation of profit and interest, the conversion of currencies, and the approximation of square roots, all applications of this new form of measuring, were to become very quickly indispensable instruments for the development of trade. Algebra became a tool of the merchant trade and way of life. However, and central to the argument of this book, the tools introduced by Fibonacci were fundamental to the merchant's resistance to the pastoral economic ethic of the Church. With this new form of measurement merchants could develop a cost structure with which to justify the price of interest in a transaction bypassing usury restrictions. Such was the practical and symbolic importance of Fibonacci's work that the Holy Roman Emperor Frederick II made him his guest and advisor. This was not a simple recognition or a celebration of the merchant's resistance to the pastoral governance of the Church. By then Frederick had already been excommunicated by Pope Gregory IX.[70]

A second significant element that contributed to the representation of uncertainty as something amenable to be traded and exchanged was a transformation in the knowledge-base for the pastoral governance of the Church. Until then centres of knowledge in Christian Europe had been the abbeys and monasteries. Knowledge was zealously kept within walls and was accessible only to those literates who were allowed to know. During this period, however, universities such as Paris and Oxford began to be established as new centres of intellectual life attracting some of the most active intelligences of the time.[71] The mission of these new institutions was to analyse in a systematic manner the bases of knowledge of the Church which stemmed out of the study of philosophy and theology together with the great law schools that focused on the study of Roman and canon law.[72]

Closely linked to the emergence of these institutions were members of the new mendicant orders of the Franciscans and Dominicans. In contrast to the Order of St Benedict, mendicants were expected to preach God's truth to the communities.[73] As noted by Sabine, friars 'played a large part in the development of the universities, setting up courses of study for the training of their members and providing an important part of the faculties'. Albert the Great and Thomas Aquinas, among the Dominicans, and Duns Scotus and Roger Bacon on the Franciscan side, were among the most original scholars that populated the membership of these universities in the thirteenth century.[74]

The new knowledge through which the Church intended to make sense of God's world was also influenced by the recovery of 'ancient works of science', amongst which the thought of Aristotle occupied a predominant role. Known in the Arab world, his books permeated Europe through Italy and Spain.[75] His understanding of value and economics was taken as a cornerstone for scholastic concern with the problem usury for the following four centuries.[76] Aristotle's work 'brought to the Middle Ages a new vision of the intellectual life of Greece and the belief that reason is the key which must unlock the door to a knowledge of the natural world'.[77] His thought, however, was not completely acceptable within the core of the Church. Aristotle 'bore the stigma of infidelity' and to reconcile it with the patristic truth an intense intellectual effort of adaptation and harmonization known as 'reconstruction' was required. This process intended to build a Christian system of belief, an 'all-embracing system of natural and theological knowledge'.[78]

Thirteenth-century theologians were therefore faced with the challenge of reconciling the patristic canonical inheritance with the pressure of the times related to the demographic expansion, the sedentarization of trade and the acquisitive character of a merchant population. An urgent analysis of economic affairs was required and tasked to the scholastics. Odd Langholm described this urgency as the problem of how to rectify the ills of humanity when satisfying its material needs.[79] Because the satisfaction of such needs was not an individual endeavour but took place within society, 'part of their spiritual guidance must relate to the means of their bodily sustenance'.[80] Since 'common material means are scarce, and men tend to be avaricious, anxious about the future, and adverse to Christian sharing', and since 'such weaknesses are not only sinful and distract man from his individual destiny' and disrupt human society, there was a need for the development of what he called a 'scholastic economic ethic'.[81]

The decretal Naviganti established as usury the practice of receiving from a debtor something in addition to the capital on loan and explicitly stated the prohibition even if it was the lender who had assumed the risk (*periculum*).[82] Playing a similar role to that of today's 'ethical committees', as described in Chapter 4, the duty of canonists and theologians was 'to evaluate the incidence of ["risk"] in any contract in which an investor finances a merchant's commercial venture'.[83] Canonists and theologians were the security experts of an order of governance reliant on the observance of the canon and the logic of God. When tasked with the job of analysing the liceity of the insurance instruments described below, canonists, however, already had some conceptual tools to work with. Evidence indicates that by the end of the twelfth century the concept of 'risk' was already understood as an element of credit (*periculum sortis*).[84] *Periculum sortis* had been a central issue in the scholastic debates over annuities (the *census* contract) in the twelfth century. Ceccarelli, who studied the role of *periculum* in the 'theological analysis of contracts in which credit is connected to commercial activity', has asserted that medieval thought already differentiated between 'profit in a partnership' and 'gains obtained by loans on the basis of the ownership of the goods invested'.[85] Canonists and theologians therefore had the logical instruments to decide in each case if the particular contract under scrutiny posed a threat to the economic ethic of the Church.

However, at the faculty of theology of the University of Paris, which Langholm described as the intellectual nucleus of these debates, studies concentrated on explaining the nature of God and His creation and the guidance of men towards Him.[86] Scholastics, Langholm argued, had but 'the vaguest notion of economics', which they understood as 'a set of separable social phenomena and relationships' hardly worth investigating. Aristotle's knowledge proved of use for this purpose. He had already understood economics as the management of households and this provided a point of departure.[87]

The scholastic economic ethic was therefore intended as 'a moral doctrine in the areas of property and wealth, exchange and value, money, usury, and related subjects'.[88] In order to rectify the ills of society it became necessary to develop knowledge around economic phenomena and the relationships involved.[89] The new economic ethic wanted to resolve a complex negotiation between different ways of understanding materiality in the world. In Langholm's words:

> [s]cholastic economic ethics, in the century and a half in which we are to trace its development, tells the story of such a conflict, and of a painful reorientation, worked out on the level of general principles. It was the conflict between the Christian deontology inherited from the patristic tradition, and the Christian utilitarianism forced upon the medieval scholastics by social and economic change. This reorientation is certainly reflected in legal and philosophical literature. But its justification was basically a theological matter, and it finds its purest expressions in the works of the theologians.[90]

Within the pastoral mission of the Church, the new economic ethic had to devise a way through which the individual as well as society could be advised on how to handle the economic transactions through which their material life could be improved. As Langholm put it:

> [t]he scholastics were mainly interested in economics because exchange situations involve their participants in a particular type of moral conflict. The market is either a place or an analytical construct. The moral reality is the individual person encountering his neighbour in the context of exchange, each possessing something which the other wants, each obliged, as a mere steward under God, to consider his neighbour's need. Focus on exchange, for our authors, meant focus on the individual, in order to advise him on proper terms of exchange with his neighbour.[91]

This is precisely where the mendicant orders sought to intervene. Franciscans and Dominicans were the result of an immanent critique of the Church's power. It is this critique that sought to negotiate between the worldview of the merchant and that of the canon. The Franciscans for example, emerged out of merchant families that knew the ways of trade and commerce quite well.[92] Traditionally, clergy and monks arose from the nobility and their economic practices differed from those who conducted trade.[93] In contrast, the venality of the world in which St Francis grew up as the son of a rich merchant family, and the spirit of acquisitiveness that characterized his people, led him to formulate the rules of his order based on utter poverty and stringent asceticism through which his brotherhood was to find the safe track towards God.[94] This radical position brought along a syncretism in the ways in which the Church was to approach the challenges of the commercial revolution. This was for example reflected in the economic thought developed by Franciscans such as Peter Olivi.[95]

The economic thought of Peter Olivi, educated at Paris, was an example of this process. As noted by Ceccarelli, 'the *Decretal Naviganti* compelled canonists and theologians to evaluate the incidence of risk in any contract in which an investor finances a merchant's commercial venture'.[96] Pressed by the decretal,

> Olivi formulated a general rule of risk-taking in commerce: canon law's prohibition is bypassed, he argue[d], only when the investor has the ownership and the use of the commodity which is risked; the use of the good can be either direct or indirect.[97]

It is worth noting in passing that this idea, which will appear again in eighteenth-century Britain in a modified form as the principle of insurable interest, as discussed in Chapter 2, and in the principle of evidence-based underwriting in the twentieth century, analysed in Chapter 3, has become a central element for differentiating between insurance and gambling. As a crucial concern for the morality of risk it has implications in contemporary debates on the liceity of trade on financial derivatives, as will be noted in Chapter 4.

The concept of just price that concerned Olivi remains at the core for understanding the moral aspects involved in transforming uncertainty into matter amenable to trade and exchange. Olivi's economic contribution 'reconstructs' Aristotelian economic thought, however wrong he found Aristotle's idea that 'wealth is an instrument of felicity'.[98] Olivi's problem was not about championing a commercial private life but trying to make Christian sense of the ideas of 'value' and 'just price' that made relations between merchants and the Church so tense. These concerns were as important to the Church and to the Franciscans as to the mercantile class since they constituted the basis for commercial order and commercial society. Although they also became central for ideas of political community later, in the Enlightenment period, the bases of value and just price stand at the centre of a relationship between ways of life, security, and community – either in state or religious form or any kind of collective enterprise. Olivi's economic ethic points towards the fundamental relation between security, economy and power in relation to forms of life. This relation cannot be identified through the public–private divide so common in modern political analysis but must be analysed in the 'securities' that emerge from it. Insurance instruments are an example of such securities.

The third major element of this analysis of how uncertainty was rendered fungible in insurance is related to a change in the understanding of temporality, from God's time, to merchant time. During the period of the Commercial Revolution merchants began to actively design 'their' time by challenging the precept that 'time' was God's will. As noted by Le Goff, '[a]mong the principal criticisms levelled against the merchant was the charge that their profit implied a mortgage in time, which was supposed to belong to God alone'.[99]

Although the theological argument that merchants sold time was analysed from the perspective of usury, what was really at stake, as Le Goff rightly pointed out, was the very possibility of credit. 'For the merchant, time is an opportunity for profit'.[100] The fact was that merchants already traded *in* time. They had turned time into the vehicle for *periculum* (risk) as will be illustrated in the last section of this chapter. This process has been described by Le Goff as a shift from an event-centred time dictated by the Church to a normalized and regularized concept of time.[101] While studying the transformation in the concepts of time that took place during this period he documented a struggle between what he called 'merchant's time' and 'Church's time'.[102] His analytical strategy was to adopt 'the bell' as the epistemic object from which to analyse changes in concepts of temporality. He found that

> what was clearly new in the contribution of the work of the bell or the city bell used for purposes of work was that instead of a time linked to *events*, which made itself felt only episodically and sporadically, there arose a regular, normal time. Rather than the *uncertain* clerical hours of the church bells, there were the *certain* hours [...] Time was no longer associated with the cataclysms or festivals but rather with daily life, a sort of chronological net in which urban life was caught.[103]

For Le Goff, this shift in the conception of time meant a profound transformation both for the merchant and for the scholar devoted to canon law and theology.[104] He argued that an essentialist conception of time was replaced by that of a 'conceptual form and mental tool'.[105] For scholastics, time was to be used according to specific needs. In this sense time was prone to be counted, divided and measured.[106] Time could then be seen as discontinuous, as a frame that suited the purposes of ways of life. Meanwhile, technical developments began to make possible a more or less accurate measurement of time. The bell, for example, was only the device through which the metrics of time could be made knowable in a massive scale.[107] Bells became a time alerting device, an output of the timekeeping machines that began to be developed in the period.[108]

Within the context of these three general transformations within the context of the Commercial Revolution, and alongside the development of the scholastic economic ethic, the mercantile spirit of acquisition continued to unfold the instruments through which trade could be enhanced and protected. Within a century, two novel forms of insurance instruments had been developed to bypass the Church's condemnation of the sea loan and to serve as instruments to enhance a mercantile way of life. Through the practices that led to the development of these instruments a form of entrepreneurial power was exercised to resist the patristic dogma of the Church. This form of power contributed to the development of an order of governance of which the renewed economic ethic of the Church was to play a significant role into modernity.

The birth of the third-party form of insurance

The history of insurance instruments in the thirteenth century can be characterized as a quest for making uncertainty fungible as security objects under the rubric of *periculum* (risk). Fungible or 'mercantile uncertainty', however, could be possible only when detached from the certainty of God. Scholastic debates around usury in the twelfth and thirteenth centuries revolved around this point. What happens when the certainty of God is doubted? What happens when uncertainty is not the obscurity of the mind of God but something fungible? Reason, through the introduction of revised versions of Aristotelian thought into Christianity, was rendered as an instrument of God through scholastic thought, a system of thought through which the world that God created could be revealed by the study of science. Uncertainty was, therefore, seen by the scholastic, paradoxically, as the confirmation of the certainty of God, as the epistemological arena through which one could learn and know about God and of how He created the world.

On the other hand, among the developing merchant class, uncertainty became the condition of possibility for resisting the institutionalized power of God on earth. Uncertainty unlocked the world and enabled the formulation of scenarios on the basis of which future events could be imagined and protection against them could be sought. As noted in the introduction to this chapter, the possibility of formulating strategies to compensate for adverse situations in a future was not a new phenomenon. What the period witnessed was the appearance and rapid development of specialized instruments through which future adversity could be accounted and compensated for. Through changes in the conception of temporality, linear time allowed for figuring the future as a continuum subject to human design and agency rather than a divine collection of events. Ultimately, *periculum* was not divine providence. This was the context under which the *fœnus nauticum* or sea loan, the *cambium nauticum* or maritime exchange, and the third-party premium insurance contract began to offer alternative forms of security to those provided by the divine power representative on earth. The redeeming politics and economics of the Church were not the precarious politics and economics of the merchant class. The soteriological economy of pastoral power, as analysed by Foucault,[109] began to give way to a political economy of uncertainty. The security of God began to be replaced by emerging securities in the form of insurance relations.

The sea loan was such an arrangement. It constituted the instrument 'by which an investor lent a given sum of money to a travelling merchant with the understanding that the loan would have to be repaid only if the ship returned safely to port (*sana eunte nave*)'.[110] They constituted, according to Hoover, 'one of the most ancient forms of contractual relationship between individuals for the purpose of providing the entrepreneur with the funds of the capitalist'.[111] There is evidence of the use of forms of sea loans in Greek and Roman times, the latter calling them *fœnus nauticum*, but little evidence seems to exist as to why and how they came back into use in the medieval Renaissance. Hoover speculated that given the references to its use in the *Basilica* (compiled between AD 867 and 880) would prove that these arrangements were in use by the Byzantines who traded with Genoa and Venice. This, he noted, could have been the medium through which, after the great revival of commerce following the Crusades, the sea loan came back to the western Mediterranean.[112] The fact was that they were widely used during the twelfth and thirteenth centuries, as de Roover confirmed by making reference to Genoese notarial records related to trade with the Levant.[113] What made them particularly relevant was that they were 'the sole type of contract for the loan of capital funds at interest which was not illegal'.[114] As such, they constituted an instrument by which the merchant class could further its way of life without raising the suspicion of the Church.

As a practice, the sea loan did not fall within the realm of usury. Usury was, of course, illegal under canon law. Its civil law status 'was uncertain at best'.[115] As a legal instrument, the sea loan protected both the lender and the borrower as the former would not trust his capital on the latter if the legal enforcement of the contract was not possible.[116] However, the sea loan was, for all practical purposes, a loan at interest, a *fœnus*. De Roover illustrated this fact by arguing that sea loans 'were not made *gratis et amore*, even when the contract so stipulated'; 'the lender received interest and a compensation for the risk, probably by withholding part of the sum named in the contract'.[117] Under canon law a 'loan contract which provided for the repayment of a loan together with a sum in addition to the principal is a *fœnus*, and according to canon law a *fœnus* was illegal'.[118] For this reason, a sea loan was frequently referred to in notarial records as a *mutuum*, which, according to Hoover, 'demonstrates the scrupulous care of the notaries lest the sea loan contract should come within the purvey of the anti-usury laws'.[119]

In legal technical terms a *mutuum* was 'the loan of a *consumptible* [...], with no provision for the payment of usury'.[120] As O'Brien argued, 'the essential thing to notice in this explanation is that the contract of *mutuum* is shown to be a sale'.[121] In that sense, what was being sold, that is the object of the contract, should be subject to the law of justice in exchange, the observance of a just price, rather than to canonical law.[122] The distinction between 'things that are consumed in use' and those which are not was known to civil lawyers, but it was Thomas Aquinas who identified the loan of a consumable thing as a sale through which ownership was transferred.[123] While adapting theological thought and relating it to canonical law, this way of understanding a loan opened a new legal dimension within the economic ethic of the Church. It presented a loan as a contract that rendered uncertainty as something fungible and that could therefore be sold. A sale of 'something' as opposed to trade in the certainty of God or 'His time' was not seen to constitute a usurious practice.

Hoover's historical analysis of notarial records in which such contracts were registered led him to distinguish between three different forms of sea loans: the *bona fide*, the *pignus* and the usury–evasion type.[124] In his work he argued that the *fœnus nauticum* 'seem[ed] to have been regarded as legal according to canon law, at least until the middle of the thirteenth century'.[125] The special uncertainty that the lender in a maritime loan necessarily underwent was generally considered enough justification for the payment of a premium.[126] However, after 1236 the sea loan fell under suspicion of usury and was officially condemned. As de Roover and Hoover coincided in arguing, whether or not this decretal produced a decline in the use of this instrument is a point of dispute. Evidence shows that it was replaced by a more complex instrument better suited to the purposes of contemporary trade.

Such was the context under which the *cambium nauticum* or maritime exchange made its appearance. The maritime exchange was a more refined version of the sea loan and it is still used today as an instrument for the transfer of sea risks to the lender. De Roover has argued that this contract was, however, not an unconditional instrument as the sea loan, but 'was contingent upon the safe arrival of goods pledged in security'.[127] Other sources do not mention this characteristic, and it is not at all clear what she meant by this conditionality of the contract.[128] However, the added value of this form of insurance over the sea loan was its instrumentality in avoiding the explicit prohibition over usury. As the monies that the lender transferred to the borrower were repaid at the port of final call in local currency, there was no doubt that the transaction constituted a sale. The exchange rate between currencies was usually inflated in order to compensate for the 'price' of the risks the lender incurred. As de Roover put it;

> the permutation [of monies] was made at a rate which included both interest and compensation for risk. Interest in the Middle Ages was always included in the price or rate of exchange, so that the lender or buyer of foreign exchange was bound to gain in most cases.[129]

Indeed, de Roover mentioned that '[i]n general, the terms of the contract placed such a low valuation on the foreign monies that the charges to the borrower were not infrequently greater than the profits which he could make from the sale of the goods pledged as security'.[130] For this very reason some authors argued that the sea loan remained in use under different forms throughout the Middle Ages and evolved into forms of bottomry contracts operating still in the early twentieth century.[131]

This mechanism, as useful as it was in bypassing the prohibitions of Gregory IX, and having been used widely after 1298 in the sea trade between Genoa and Sluys (the port of Bruges),[132] revealed new characteristics in the merchant way of life. A slight detour is here required to explain one of them as it helps to explain the transition onto the third-party form of insurance. In de Roover's analysis on the inconveniences of the *cambium nauticum* for small investors it is possible to observe that a set of logistical arrangements that the *fœnus nauticum* did not require was now in place.[133] The new instrument could operate only with an adequate commercial infrastructure *and a vehicle* for the transfer of monies. The payment of the loan in foreign lands required that the lender had an agent present at port that would at the same time operate as lender to other merchants wishing to finance their voyage.[134] The *cambium nauticum* required not only agents but also the development and refinement of communication systems so that instructions could be safely and effectively delivered to the recipient. For bigger lending families this was not a problem, but for smaller ones this proved a burden difficult to overcome. Complex trade networks and the expedient circulation of monies became the environment under which the maritime exchange had to operate. Furthermore, the new logistical demands denoted an emerging complexity in the form of security sought by the merchant class. The merchant class now depended on its capacity to foster networks of trade and to devise and operate a system for the circulation of money. The form of security demanded under these conditions required enough flexibility to adapt to the shifting circumstances of trade between different places and cultures.

The merchant way of life under the commercial revolution saw the establishment of complex trading networks that originally operated under family bonds.[135] The growing trading families extended the trading partnership also known as the company. As a company they established permanent agents in the principal towns with which the company was engaged in trade.[136] However, not only family links constituted the bond for the companies. There are traces going back as far as 1272 that make reference to non-family-related partners operating between Montpellier and Bologna, which made Usher assume that this situation was already common after the middle of the thirteenth century in northern Italy and southern France.[137] References to the existence of permanent branches among the larger trading families exist after 1290,[138] which seems to coincide with the period in which the *cambium nauticum* began its operation. These companies operated on the basis of unlimited liability under which all members could profit but could also lose it all.[139] Coping with uncertainty was therefore a prime concern, and the maritime exchange was then not only an effective way of bypassing the prohibitions of the Church but also a way of devising a form of security that would minimize losses when things went wrong. Operating outside the certainty of God, the merchant class depended on the security technologies it could devise. The development of adequate security technologies, such as the insurance schemes now under development, also meant the further development and promotion of a merchant class and a merchant way of life.

The development of the *cambium nauticum* is also linked to the development of the bill of exchange, another central element arising out of the Commercial Revolution. The establishment of companies holding several branches created the necessity for the development of money transfer facilities, which evolved into the bill of exchange. This system replaced transactions through itinerant agents who not only were vulnerable in their transit but also prevented the smooth circulation of money.[140] The notarial form required for the sea loan was no longer necessary. Usher noted that at this stage the 'simple letter of one member of the firm was sufficient to create an obligation on the other establishments'.[141] In this respect, 'the unlimited liability of the company furnished adequate security' and the simple mercantile paper began to play its role 'in the cosmopolitan credit system'.[142] This also meant, however, that the security of the merchant class depended on its capacity to devise schemes by which the possibilities of loss could be distributed and minimized. Wealth within merchant networks depended on their capacity to circulate goods and money. The security of the merchant way of life was therefore dependent not on specific assets or goods but on their capacity to *circulate*. Thus, circulation constituted the condition of possibility and operability of a mercantile form of life. Smooth circulation, however, relied on the building of trust. This is a recurrent feature of an entrepreneurial form of power explored in the following chapters.

The fact that these mercantile papers were not supported by notarial records is significant. The simplicity of these documents brought along an almost complete freedom from strict legal forms, forms influenced and in some cases controlled by the pastoral power of the Church. Merchants developed their own systems of authentication and control in which trust had to be proved in every transaction. As Usher noted, 'while a definite body of custom seems to have arisen by the beginning of the fourteenth century', the private nature of these papers, however, did not leave traces in the public archives.[143] This was a key characteristic of the merchant way of life in the medieval Renaissance, an active entrepreneurial spirit which developed highly innovative financial instruments through which trade could be promoted and protected. The role of the unlimited liability of companies as the prime security for transactions became a trust-building instrument for the operability of the system. Bypassing the prohibitions of the Church and the regulations of the temporal order of the territorial rulers, traders built in the security required to solidify and further a way of life that demanded flexibility and confidence.

The development of the bill of exchange in the early fourteenth century very quickly led to the ordinary *cambium* contract's becoming more popular than the *cambium nauticum*.[144] Access to credit now took place through the purchase of bills of exchange but this kind of operations required the services of already established banking houses. De Roover noted how these houses were, however, not yet specialized. They combined trade and banking and bought as well as sold bills of exchange for others on a commission basis. As clearly stated by this author '[t]o divide ["risk"] was the keynote of the business policy followed by the international merchant-bankers' of the time.[145] The decline of the fairs of Champagne in the late thirteenth century, with the consequent establishment of sedentary traders who sent instructions to their agents abroad, allowed them to accept payment in one office in local currency and arrange repayment at another office in the coin current there.[146] Profit was made by means of playing with the time between remittances and payments. As Kohn described it, '[r]emittance by bill of exchange involved a delay between the receipt of funds in one place and their repayment in another of from two weeks to three months, depending on the distance. This "float" provided trading companies with funds they could lend to others'.[147] Indeed, a fact that quickly became evident was that 'as early as the fourteenth century, most bills of exchange were related to finance rather than to trade'.[148] The financial use of bills of exchange not only made funds ready for trade but operated as an instrument to put monies in circulation and therefore allowed for the operation of more complex commercial networks. The circulation of monies was based on a whole new set of transactions which played upon future time as a means to create a profit.[149] Trade now operated in excess of the economic ethic of the Church.

In the fourteenth century the third-party form of premium insurance made its appearance. This form of insurance was and is still an instrument through which uncertainty, in the form of an event to be insured against, is transferred to a third party amongst the stakeholders in the insurance contract.[150] For example, in the following insurance policy of 1350, cited by de Roover, the role of the underwriter is already specifically separated from that of the merchant who is shipping its product to a foreign port and the agreed premium is stipulated as the price for covering the risks involved in the journey. The insurer assumes all risks in exchange for a premium. The insurer is no longer the lender of the money required by the merchant to get his shipment to safe port, as was common in the case of the sea loan.

> The first of the Palermo insurance policies is dated March 15, 1350. From its contents it appears that a Genoese merchant, Leonardo Cataneo, underwrote or insured (*assecuravit*) a shipload of wheat, belonging to one Benedict de Protonotaro of Messina, up to the amount of fl. 300 for a voyage from Sciacca, on the island of Sicily, to Tunis. Leonardo Cataneo declared that, from the time of the ship's sailing from Sicily until its safe arrival in Tunis, he would assume all risks arising from an act of God and of men and from the perils of the sea (*omni risucum, periculum et fortunam Dei, maris et gentium*). The sum of fl. 300 was due one month after receiving 'certain' news of the cargo's loss. If the loss was only partial, the insurer's responsibility would be commensurate with the extent of the damage. The premium was 54 florins or 18 per cent. It was clearly stated that the contract was concluded for purposes of insurance (*ex causa assicurationis*) and that the underwriter had received from the insured the 54 florins 'for that insurance' (*pro qua securitate*).[151]

This contract appeared already as a modern form of insurance through which the merchant diversifies the risks involved in his enterprise. In the event of a loss he could have made a claim from his insurer and in doing so he would have protected his capital. Having incurred a higher business cost, the merchant was able to improve his possibilities for profit by using a specialized financial service, that of insurance, a service that a third person in an underwriting capacity was willing to provide. The effects of this innovation over the merchant way of life were clear. Merchants could now trade at distance protected by an instrument that allowed them to render uncertainty fungible, as an event to be insured against. The exacerbation of trade through commercial networks was only possible through the risk-spreading strategies that this instrument allowed for. For the insurer, hedging risks became a way of making a profit. This 'making of money' went beyond the scholastic debates on usury since it could now be shown that risk was a tradable asset. The ethical issues arising now were related more with the 'just' pricing of risk, as noted in Olivi's work, than with the liceity of insurance.

2 Securing by capitalizing life

> The values of the possessions, and the reversions, of much of the greatest part of the real estates, in these kingdoms, will, one way or another, depend on the value of lives.[1]

In early eighteenth-century Britain, within the context of the agricultural/agrarian and financial revolutions, the emergence and rapid development of a growing landless gentlemen class fostered demand for a new type of security: life insurance. The law of large numbers, developed in the Low Countries in the second half of the seventeenth century, provided the basis for a new regime of calculation and a system for measuring uncertainty. This system found its first commercial application in the London life insurance market. The emergence of probabilistic life insurance in early eighteenth-century Britain highlights a remarkable relationship between insurance and security: *the security of the land became intrinsically related to the insurability of lives.*

The probabilistic form of insurance emerged initially as a way of securing landless English gentlemen's lives against death and accident. Central to life insurance was a problem of access to credit. In the absence of land as collateral for debt, gentlemen could acquire investment capital by allowing lenders to insure against their lives in relation to their future capacity to pay. Insurability depended on the insured's physical conditions, but most importantly, on the development of 'actuarial' techniques that enabled insurers to estimate, applying the law of large numbers,[2] the longevity of the productive life of a client. Life insurance also became instrumental in protecting lifestyles. Gentlemen could buy insurance to protect their families' welfare in case of their own premature death or accident. In doing so they could ensure a relatively stable standard of life for their widows and children. Related to this, life insurance also became instrumental in enabling marriage. As a condition for marriage and as a way of corresponding to the bride's dowry, gentlemen could be asked to provide a security to protect the family if he deceased. Such was the general use of life insurance by the mid-1700s that James Dodson (Master of the Royal Mathematical School and later head of the first life insurance company to employ actuarial methods) noted that the values of most real estates in the kingdom depended, in one way or another, on the value of lives.

The emergence of the probabilistic form of life insurance, or 'assurance' as it was known then, and the process of the insurability of lives was also closely related to the state's capacity to tax property and professional activities. The transformation in the nature of property that took place during the Augustan period was supported by capital produced by the activities and business of this gentlemen class. Gentlemen capital was invested into public loans and was also used to develop a market of securities. The government, badly in need of resources to support war efforts at a time of great European powers competition, benefited from a growing taxable base and fresh loans.

The emergence of probabilistic life insurance analysed in this chapter was made possible by a drastic change in the ways in which uncertainty was rendered fungible as risk. The third-party form of insurance of the medieval Renaissance now found a new way of mathematical reasoning that brought along the possibility of calculating probabilities. Probabilities provided the means by which uncertainty in relation to the duration of lives could be calculated mathematically.[3] This required, of course, a statistical base on which to apply the law of large numbers.[4] These numbers, central to a new political rationality closely linked to Foucault's analysis of governmentality and biopower, sought to identify the particularities of populations as an object of government.

The emergence of life assurance, however, is also related to a process that de Goede analysed as the emergence of speculation as a legitimate practice.[5] Whereas insurance over lives was considered illicit in most European countries, life assurance flourished in Britain closely linked to the rationality of government depicted by Petty and his followers as 'political arithmetick'. The role of life insurance in eighteenth-century Britain, however, quickly degenerated into gambling. Gentlemen were found to be insuring against their own fathers' lives and individuals betted on the lives of prominent figures, including the king, creating a moral problem. As a way of counteracting gentlemen's greed and recognizing the role of life insurance as a liberal security, the 1774 Gambling Act was passed demanding that an 'insurable interest' should be proved in any insurance contract. If an insurable interest could be proved, insurance was then a matter of tolerable speculation rather than gambling on people's lives.

The emergence of actuarial life insurance presented in this chapter is used to analyse an emerging relationship between life, property and security in eighteenth-century Britain. How the security of the land became intrinsically related to the security of lives, and how the security of lives became interlinked with the creation of capital, are, however, questions that escape current understandings of political theory in relation to political economy and security studies. Central to the answer to these questions is a form of entrepreneurial power, a creative kind of power which is not a function of sovereign or biopolitical political categories of governance, although it produces biopolitical effects. It is exercised in the Augustan period by a gentlemen population that negotiates its existence and activities with the landed aristocracy and the institutions of the sovereign state. Although it uses the statistical thinking developed by political arithmeticians, it employs probabilities to develop its own security instruments. These security instruments are to coexist with the sovereign form of security provided by the state in the form of rule of law. However, they are to remain a private activity with public consequences. The objective of these securities, explored in this chapter as life assurance, is to protect and further the way of life of what could be called an entrepreneurial middle class.

In what follows, this chapter is used to narrate a story that begins with presenting how and why life insurance became the object of legislation through the introduction of the principle of insurable interest. It then links this move of making interests explicit with the shift that Hirschman explored from a rationality of government premised on controlling passions to one devoted to the management of interests.[6] In this context 'political arithmetick' is explored as a strategy of government deployed to governmentalize the activities and businesses of gentlemen life. The section goes on to describe the particularities of political arithmetick and its reliance on collecting data. Finally, the chapter closes with showing how the gentlemen class exercised a form of power that employed the statistical knowledge developed through political arithmetick and encompassed it with probabilities to formulate the actuarial form of life insurance. The strategy to secure a gentlemen form of life was materialized in the establishment of the Equitable Life Assurance Society.

The insurable interest and the productive speculation on lives

Insurance on lives was not an invention of the seventeenth and eighteenth centuries. According to Clark, life insurance originated in the Mediterranean around the year 1400 'as an incidental circumstance when marine insurance policies happened to cover passengers or slaves on overseas voyages'.[7] There are, however, documental records that prove the operation of life insurance as early as the fourteenth century.[8] For example, Cleirac cited in 1661 a passage of an anonymous French treatise, *Le Guidon*, compiled for merchants travelling to the city of Rouen.[9] The treatise was allegedly written 300 years earlier and made reference to the use of life insurance for cases of kidnap and ransom. Life insurance was depicted as a compensatory system by which nations could insure the life of men who died during their voyage by paying certain sums to their heirs or creditors. Creditors were mentioned as being able to insure the life of their debtors if they were to travel abroad. Individuals could also insure their own rents and pensions so that in the event of death they would pass on to their heirs. However, at the time when Cleirac wrote, all of these forms of insurance practices, except against kidnap and ransom, were illegal in France.[10]

It is known that life insurance was a widely used instrument as a collateralizing device in the money-lending trade of the fifteenth century.[11] Clark noted, for example, the practice of taking large insurance policies on royalty as in the case of policies issued at Genoa in 1454 on the life of Pope Nicholas V and in 1457 on the King of Aragon.[12] As explained by Clark, these practices gave rise to purely speculative investment. For those who had a legitimate financial interest in the Pope's life, the instrument operated as a security. For others it was simply a wager on the length of his life.[13] Governmental bans on these practices followed. In 1419 the Venetian Senate reacted and explicitly forbade wagers on the pope's life.[14] In Spain insurance gambling was also suppressed together with all life insurance by the Ordinances of Barcelona in 1435.[15] These Ordinances became the 'first comprehensive code of insurance law and their prestige among merchant communities led to their adoption in places where no laws or customs relating to insurance yet existed'.[16] In this way, Clark described, 'the blanket prohibition over life insurance embodied in the Ordinances extended internationally.'[17]

In contrast, life insurance was not forbidden in England and was in fact a popular instrument for insuring the lives of both slaves and free men. It was a common practice for English merchants then to insure their slave cargoes en route to their American plantations.[18] Clark has argued that, owing to the great number of merchants in the African trade, 'it is safe to say that despite the precocious growth of the domestic life insurance market in eighteenth-century England, most insured lives remained African slaves in transit to the New World'.[19] In relation to the lives of free men, there were great abuses in the use of life policies. They became, as on the continent, an instrument for betting. Clark illustrated this fact by citing several renowned examples of the time which raised great moral concerns. Two of the cases are noted below to illustrate why cases of this kind contributed to the prohibition of such practices unless an 'insurable interest', as will be explained later, could be proven.

The first was the D'Eon case:

> In late 1770 rumours regarding the sex of the Chevalier D'Eon began to circulate round London, and by March of the next year books had been opened at Lloyd's and other places in the city on the truth of the reports. Offering premiums of fifteen to sixty guineas per cent, [...] underwriters issued policies reputedly totalling upwards of sixty thousand pounds upon proof that D'Eon was in fact a woman.[20]

The second was the Pigot case also in 1770.

> William Pigot and the son of Sir William Codrington each expected to inherit fortunes upon the deaths of their respective fathers, and they therefore agreed to 'run their fathers against each other', that is to bet on who lived longer. The idea was that the heir who first succeeded to his father's estate could afford to discharge the debts of his friend. Since Codrington's father was fifty years old and Pigot's over seventy, the bettors had Lord Ossory set odds to make the wager fair. When Ossory gave Codrington's father a better than three-to-one chance of surviving Pigot's, Codrington objected to the size of the handicap and withdrew from the wager. At this point another dinner guest, the Earl of March, offered to stand in Codrington's stead, and an agreement was therefore concluded between Pigot and March. Unbeknown to the parties at the time, however, Pigot's father had by a remarkable coincidence died earlier that same day 150 miles away in Shropshire. Upon learning of his

> father's death, Pigot refused to concede that he had lost the wager, claiming that because the bet was a contract *in futuro*, it was invalid since one of the lives had already terminated by the time the bet was made.[21]

In the first case, Chevalier D'Eon's sex was finally revealed in 1777, and those who had wagered on him being a woman brought suits against the underwriters to pay on the policies they had bought. Lord Mansfield held the contract legal and the jury determined the plaintiff to be the winner. However, on a similar case brought to Mansfield shortly after, as narrated by Clark, 'upon the jury's announcement of its verdict in favour of the plaintiff, Mansfield ordered an arrest of judgment and later overturned the verdict'.[22] The 'permissibility of the policies issued on the Chevalier's sex boiled down to a question of what limits could be placed on the creation of commercial property, and of how far the law could go to enforce speculative contracts made out of the fabric of other people's lives.[23] Mansfield ruled that 'all subjects of the Crown possessed a certain property in their private persons that others could not freely appropriate'.[24]

The second case was brought before the King's Bench by the Earl of March and was favoured by the jury. However, the case created a public outcry 'against two men wantonly betting on the lives of their fathers' and prepared the ground for an overall prohibition on gambling on human lives.[25]

Insurance until then had operated in Britain with minimum legal interference. As cited by Clark, in 1787 the Scottish jurist John Millar noted: 'It is pretty remarkable, that although the practice of insurance has been carried to a much greater extent in Britain than any other country in Europe, yet we have few statutory regulations on that subject'.[26] In 1774 the Act for Regulating Insurances on Lives (also known as the Gambling Act) was adopted as a strict regulation that sought to bring the wagering on life to an end and allow life insurance 'to serve the moral and ethical purposes for which it had been designed'. The Act stipulated:

> That from and after the passing of this Act, no Insurance or persons, or on any other Event or Events whatsoever, wherein the Person or Persons for whose Use, Benefit, or on whole Account such Policy or Policies shall be made, shall have no Interest, or by way of Gaming or Wagering; and that every Assurance made, contrary to the true Intent and Meaning hereof, shall be null and void, to all Intents and Purposes whatsoever.[27]

In fact, life insurance was seen as an instrument that enhanced family security and stimulated proper trade and economic development. The premises upon which insurance had developed during this period were seen as fundamental towards the nation's moral, social and economic improvement. By legislating against betting over lives without being able to prove an insurable interest, parliament sought to ensure that life was not to be corrupted as gambling stock but rather capitalised as productive property. However, as noted by Clark, the passing of the Act did not signal the end of life insurance's 'gambling phase' and the beginning of its 'prudential phase'. Rather, 'it represented the first thoroughgoing attempt to sunder activities that had previously been carried out side by side within a common domain and to consign them to different moral and political spheres'.[28] It is important to note in passing that legislation over the insurability of lives went in line with a central characteristic of the financial revolution in England, described by Dickson as the adoption of merchant practices into common law.[29] This is part of what will be later shown, following Foucault, as the governmentalization of the activities of the gentlemen class.

The concerns that led to regulation on the use of life insurance, however, were not solely a legal issue but one that had been present within the insurance community for some years. Gambling was seen as an existential threat for the correct operation of insurance schemes in the Augustan period. At a time when it was not yet possible to ascertain with probabilities the levels of risks represented by individuals, betting represented an irresponsible practice that threatened the functionality of an instrument deemed necessary for fostering commerce and trade and for supporting a gentlemen middle class. In Wright and Fayle's *A History of Lloyd's* it is argued, for example, that as early as 1711 'it was thought necessary to prohibit by law, the setting up of offices for insurances on marriages, births, christenings, or service'.[30] In 1734, an Act of Parliament was passed prohibiting the making of insurances on the course of public funds'.[31] The Act, however, seems to have been a dead letter.[32]

Political arithmetick and the quest to governmentalize gentlemen life

The principle of insurable interest of the 1774 Gambling Act was the manifestation of a Kuhnian paradigmatic shift in the imaginary of governance in the Enlightenment. The very idea of considering 'interests' as the foundational element for governance was not only radically different from the preceding moral discourse of governing passions but was also an incredibly useful feature for the governance of individuals and collectivities. Hirschman has classically described how 'the belief that interest could be considered a dominant motive of human behaviour' caused considerable intellectual excitement in the eighteenth century. 'At last a realistic basis for a social order had been discovered'.[33] Such an excitement was understandable. A world characterized by interest brought with it the possibility of predicting human behaviour. If only such interests could be interpreted systematically, as Kant endeavoured, there would be a possibility of reaching a state of perpetual peace and human happiness.[34] Such was the world of the Enlightenment that fought to replace the repressive and harnessing solutions that had been tried upon restless, passion-driven men without effect.[35] The moralists of the seventeenth century had tried a detailed description and investigation of the passions that drove men with the intention of discriminating amongst them and countervailing a dangerous and destructive set with 'a set of comparatively innocuous passions'.[36] The 'fighting fire with fire' solution that Spinoza, Bacon and Hume promoted was followed by an idea of engineering social progress 'by cleverly setting up one passion to fight another'.[37] As noted by Hirschman, this was one of the intellectual pastimes of the eighteenth century.[38]

The shift towards an interest-based analysis of behaviour in relation to government makes a lot of sense when studied in relation to the emergence and development of the gentlemen middle class and the transformation in the nature of property in that period. Many eighteenth-century writers, from Hume to Adam Smith and Fergusson, tried to make sense of the process. Fergusson's *An Essay on the History of Civil Society* illustrated, for example, how a highly specialized commercial society began to constitute itself into an agent of change within shifting relations in the nature of property and power.[39] If the activities of this class were to be governmentalized, that is transformed into tactics of government that would make possible the continual definition and redefinition of what was within the competence of the state and what was not,[40] it was necessary to be able to understand what was to be taxed and what not. The task was not simple in as much as the property base was being affected by the ongoing financial and agricultural/agrarian revolutions. The governmentalization effort sought to take stock of these transformations to support the public purse.

The financial revolution, as analysed by Dickson, was mainly characterized by the development of long- and short-term borrowing, the development of relations between the government and the City of London, the development of an emerging market of securities and the investment of private capital into public loans.[41] All these processes were closely linked to the development of the gentlemen way of life as well as other population issues. The agricultural revolution, on the other hand, changed outputs of production and also tenancy conditions by incorporating new planting techniques and agricultural machinery. The traditional open-field system of crop rotation that had been used in Europe for centuries had started to become an obstacle for increasing agricultural productivity. Pressure to change it led to an enclosure movement backed by parliament in 1710.[42] These transformations led to migration of agricultural workers to towns and cities, where economic activities such as cottage industries and domestic services were in growing demand. Taking the two processes together, the basis for taxation changed significantly. As Hacking put it whilst making sense of the emergence of probability during this period, '[w]hen land and its tillage are the basis of taxation, one need not care exactly how many people there are'.[43] New property was now mainly of mobile kind and depended more and more on lives than on traditional landed assets. The problem of taxation was now directly related to understanding the details of the transformations in forms of life throughout this period.

The rationality deployed to this purpose was known as 'political arithmetick' and had as one of its objectives the governmentalization of the activities through which value was being created. In a wider sense, this governmentalization process proceeded through the idea that learning about who people were and what people did allowed for an understanding of their interests and provided a knowledge-base for effective economic government. The process had begun in the seventeenth century. The term 'political arithmetick' was coined by Sir William Petty, who had gone to Ireland in 1652 as physician-general to the Cromwellian army, which had recently reconquered the country.[44] One of the new administration's most pressing tasks was to transfer vast amounts of Catholic-owned 'rebel' land to the soldiers who had accomplished the conquest and to the London investors who had underwritten it.[45] As a response to the problem, Petty proposed the 'Down Survey', a novel project that would allow the English government to make possible a real union between the English and the Irish.[46] The project was not so much a technique for counting people and differentiating between them but of rendering their differences politically irrelevant.[47] The details of Petty's political arithmetick are particularly useful to understand the political complexities involved in making sense of the transition from the government of passions to the government of interests and the political science that emerged from it. They help understand the biopolitical aspects of this rationality of government, some of which, as will be shown in the next section, were also central for the gentlemen class to develop its private form of security: actuarial life insurance. For this reason Petty's project will be explained below in some detail.

It was in the context of the English Restoration when the new establishment decided to modify the Irish settlement. In 1672, Petty presented the full scope of his political technology depicted as a matter of what he called 'political medicine'. The way to mend Ireland was to combine 'political arithmetick' with 'political anatomy'.[48] The medicine was simple: he identified the anatomy of the Irish lands as composed of a vast majority of poor Irish Catholics outnumbering by more than two and half the British Protestants. He then 'envisioned the basic problem of government in Ireland as that of rendering the first group [as posing] no threat to the second'.[49] His diagnosis was reported to the English government in the following way:

> That Ireland being a Conquered Country, and containing not the tenth part as many Irish Natives, as there are English in both Kingdoms, *That natural and firm Union is not made, between the two Peoples, by Transplantations, and proportionable mixture,* so as there may be but a tenth part, of the Irish in Ireland, and the same proportion in England; whereby the necessity of maintaining an Army in Ireland, at the expence of a quarter of all the Rents of that Kingdom may be taken away.[50]

Petty's concrete suggestion was to shift a sufficient number of Irish into England and to bring to Ireland an adequate amount of English women to constitute mixed families that would be brought up to the English morals and standards of life. As he put it in *The Political Anatomy of Ireland*:

> Whereas there are now 300,000 British, and 800,000 Papists, whereof 600,000 live in [wretched poverty]: If an Exchange was made of but about 200,000 Irish, and the like number of British brought over in their rooms, then the natural strength of the British would be equal to that of the Irish.[51]

Petty's plan was never carried out. However, at the end of the century Charles

Davenant isolated Petty's method from his politics and famously described political arithmetick as 'the art of reasoning by figures upon matters relating to government'.[52] Such matters were 'the revenues, number of people, extent and value of land, taxes, trade, &c. in any nation'.[53] Political arithmetick was thought of as a form of government with a remit not confined to estimating national income and population. It was extended 'to exploring public finances, economic performance, poor relief, military matters, religious affiliation, social order' among others.[54] Methodologically speaking it was a revolutionary way of accounting for things. As Petty put it:

> The Method I take to do this, is not yet very usual; for instead of using only comparative and superlative Words, and intellectual Arguments, I have taken the course (as a Specimen of the Political arithmetick I have long aimed at) to express my self in Terms of *Number, Weight, or Measure*; to use only Arguments of Sense, and to consider only such Causes, as have visible Foundations in Nature; leaving those that depend upon the mutable Minds, Opinions, Appetites, and Passions of particular Men, to the Consideration of others.[55]

Political arithmetick lacked at the beginning a precise statistical method on which to proceed. However, as noted by Hoppit, Petty's Down Survey of 1656, the Irish census of 1659, and a sort of census done in England in 1694, together with the bills of mortality began in Glasgow in 1670 and in Edinburgh in 1695, started to provide the critical mass of data that was to become instrumental in developing more refined statistical techniques.[56] Political arithmetick soon became an instrument for policy. Petty, King and Davenant, the three main supporters of this rationality of government, were all very close to the government.[57] This methodology came also at a time when the tax and debt dimensions of the financial revolution in government 'required departments and ministers to collect and think about quantitative materials.'[58] According to Hoppit, by 1696 the Inspector Generalship of Customs, the General Register of Shipping and the Board of Trade were all established as offices operating under the principles of political arithmetick.[59]

The advantages that political arithmetick brought to statecraft, as Petty noted, were based on its potential to render the world in terms of *number, weight or measure*. Through this rationality the government could now learn about the specificities of life in the realm and the characteristics of the forms of life of individuals and collectivities. This was the basis for the setting up of the technology of anatomical and biological individualization noted by Foucault in *The History of Sexuality*.[60] Making the particularities of the self measurable through the production of vital statistics, as well as measuring the commercial and economic transactions of individuals and groups, was to become a central function of government. These measures were to provide the senses for the exercise of government in the form of power that Foucault amply described as biopower.

The consequences of this rationality of government should not be taken lightly.

Making decisions on what to count, how to do it, when to do so and how to record data was and is central to practices of classification. Classification, as a basic biopolitical function, is a process of discrimination, of allocation of particularities by identifying differences. Bowker and Star have defined this process as '*a spatial, temporal, or spatio-temporal segmentation of the world*'.[61] A system of classification exposes '*consistent, unique classificatory principles in operation*' with 'multiple exclusive categories'.[62] It intends to depict a complete system that seeks to cover the world it describes.[63] The object of classification is to devise a system by which items enclosed within a category would receive a shared treatment. In this sense, classificatory practices are the basis for an economic form of government. They provide the conditions of operability for the multiplication of governmental effects. The process of identifying populations, or of 'making up peoples', as Ian Hacking labelled it,[64] is an active act of statecraft with political consequences.

Two studies were central to the establishment of a tradition on learning about the specificities of life within the political arithmetick tradition: John Graunt's observations on bills of mortality, and Edmund Halley's mortality tables. John Graunt's contribution, commissioned by Charles II, sought to provide a detailed analysis of the number of deaths, and especially of their causes, particularly in relation to the effects of the bubonic plague. Graunt's *Natural and Political Observations upon the Bills of Mortality* was based on an analysis of burials between the plague of 1592 and the year 1662 in London.[65] He observed, for example, that within a 20-year period, whereas 44,487 persons died of 'consumption and cough', 16,384 died of 'plague' and only 18 died of 'mother'.[66] Many other classifications, such as 'killed by several accidents', 'overlaid and starved at nurse', 'suddenly' and 'sciatica', were used by Graunt to depict morbidity at a time when systematic classification was beginning to solidify.[67] Graunt's work was to become instrumental in the calculation of life annuities both for public and private purposes. His objective was to use his observations on the London mortality tables to know, specifically:

> 1. The number of the People? 2. How many Males, and Females? 3. How many Married, and single? 4. How many Teeming Women? 5. How Many of every Septenary, or Decad of years in age? 6. How many Fighting Men? 7. How much London is, and by what steps it hath increased? 8. In what time the housing is replenished after a Plague? 9. What proportion die of each general and perticular Casualties? 10. What years are Fruitfull, and Mortal, and in what Space, and Intervals, they follow each other? 11. In what proportion Men neglect the Orders of the Church, and Sects have increased? 12. The disproportion of Parishes? 13. Why the Burials in London exceed the Christenings, when the contrary is visible in the Country?[68]

The second study, Halley's mortality tables of 1693, featured an analysis of deaths in relation to age taken from the records of Breslau, a Polish-German town which kept rigorous track of births and deaths. The application of a general knowledge on vital statistics was intended as an aid to the existing practice of selling annuities, a practice through which governments sought fresh and immediate resources for their operations, and mainly for their war efforts. Halley's *An Estimate of the Degrees of the Mortality of Mankind* was explicitly intended 'to give a more just idea of the state and condition of Mankind' by showing 'the Chances of Mortality at all Ages, and likewise how to make an Estimate for the value of Annuities for Lives'.[69] It was also intended as an aid to estimating the chance of a person of any age living to another given age.[70] Halley was explicit in wanting to show 'differing degrees of Mortality, or rather Vitality in all Ages, for if the number of Persons of any *Age* remaining after one year, be divided by the difference between that and the number of the Age proposed, the *odds* that there is, that a Person of that Age does not die in a *Year* [could be calculated]'.[71]

The work of Halley and Graunt provided the base for the implementation of a more ambitious governmental strategy to collect information on people, the conditions and particularities of life and death, and their relationship with property in Britain. However, the practice of such way of learning about the circulation of people proved to be somewhat difficult. The idea of a national census, as a plan submitted to parliament in 1753 revealed, sparked a firm reaction from the gentlemen middle class. The proposal was interpreted as a government strategy that sought to link lives to property, and this was seen as a clear erosion of civil liberties.[72] It was understood that the process of forcing every individual to expose his property to government authority would give rise to a new governmental force aimed at controlling the activities of the gentlemen middle class.[73] As analysed by Buck, the crux of the struggle was an opposition of country to court power. There was concern, or at the very least concern was mobilized, around the idea that the government would be trying to 'give the country a police, or a local administration of civil government upon certain and known principles'.[74] This was seen 'as symptomatic of broader "mischief" already 'arising from the union of the executive and legislative power in [the] country', a union that defenders of local prerogatives against encroaching court and administrative influence viewed as an unqualified threat to the 'delegation of power'.[75] The struggle to governmentalize the property and activities of this emergent middle class opened up a debate on the role that this emerging class should play in governmental affairs. The idea of a census was not viable and a greater degree of political creativity was required for the process.

Such was the struggle between the state, which sought to governmentalize its people and their circulations, and an emergent landless gentlemen middle class resisting the incorporation of their way of life into the government's economy. In the meantime, the entrepreneurial character of the gentlemen class was employed in developing the use of the statistical logic of political arithmetick and encompassed it with the mathematical logic of probabilities to develop actuarial life assurance.

Entrepreneurial power, security and life assurance

Under the rationality operated through political arithmetick specific populations were sought to be produced and shaped. However, not all populations result from governmental decisions and practices. In fact, the eighteenth century witnessed the resistance of a specific population to the implementation of political arithmetical practices and its effects. The Commonwealthmen, English Protestant religious reformers such as Richard Price, opposed the growth of the government as a threat to their republican interests. If until the 1750s political arithmetick had been an instrument for the state to constitute populations, after this period statistics became an instrument by which individuals constituted the populations out of which the state was to be performed. The unfolding of actuarial life insurance in the 1770s is evidence of this process. Peter Buck's analysis in this regard is illustrative.

> Until the 1750s it was taken for granted that populations were political creations, dependent on assertions of sovereign authority for their existence as aggregates open to statistical study. The connection was as clear to partisans of political arithmetick – who accepted that it was 'with the strictest propriety that his Majesty calls us a great People' – as it was to critics who accused statisticians of treating Englishmen as if they were 'the numbered vassals of indiscriminating power'. But by 1800 the logic underlying such exchanges had been reversed: F.M. Eden's *Estimate of the Number of Inhabitants in Great Britain and Ireland* carried the epigraph 'These constitute a State'.[76]

Commonwealthmen statisticians such as Richard Price sought to affect ideas about politics and property by fashioning a new conception of populations as 'assemblages of citizens rather than subjects.'[77] This conception was enabled by the Aristotelian idea that citizenship was possible only through autonomous participation in politics, participation made possible through the independence 'that property gave to its owners'.[78] Within the context of the agricultural and financial revolutions the development of specialized professions and services described by Fergusson in his essay on civil society led to the development of mobile forms of property. These mobile forms of property were based on a new reality. Property depended more and more on lives than on traditional landed assets.

James Dodson, Master of the Royal Mathematical School, was quick in identifying this trend. In 1748 he stated the epigraph heading this chapter. Alter and Riley explained this situation in the following way:

> Many of the assets commonly held by wealthy and some not-so-wealthy individuals in Britain and on the Continent depended, in one fashion or another, upon the survival of a designated person. Thus the women who brought to her marriage a dowry and who arranged for the dowry to revert to a third party if she predeceased her husband made the use of her dowry contingent upon her own life. Similarly, the owner of any life interest (e.g., an office, a leasehold,

> or a pension) held an asset whose value was contingent upon one or perhaps several lives. Parents who wished to provide an income for their children and husbands who wanted to provide for their wives also chose life contingent investments. In an age when the risk of the death of one or more parties was a persistent concern in any contract, contracts of this nature provided in advance for the contingency of death. As a consequence the valuation of life contingencies was a matter of concern to a wide range of officials and private interests, from the king of France whose treasury sold *rentes viagères* to the artisan who participated in a burial fund.[79]

This relationship between life and property was in fact being proved by the operation, if rudimentary, of life annuities issued by the government and by the life assurance societies that operated during the period. The intrinsic relationship between life and property, however, was not gratuitous. It resulted from implementing instruments such as annuities and life assurance. Annuities were meant to generate revenue to the government and future cash flow for annuitants. The assurance provided by life societies was intended to grant access to credit and a minimum form of financial protection to the emergent middle class. In the process of providing these securities, both annuities and life assurance effected a translation of lives into capital. The life being capitalized was in fact life *in potentia*. When individuals bought annuities or assurance policies they advanced money to provide themselves and their heirs with an income in case of survival or death. The capital came in the form of future reparation that could be used as collateral for debt, or a lump sum that could foster a lifestyle for the annuitant or his dependants.

Insurance societies calculated rates of mortality in a population based more on observation than on statistics, largely because of the 'uncertainty attached to all demographic data in the formative years of political arithmetick' rather than ignorance or 'gambling fever'.[80] Life insurance societies were provident associations created for the benefit of their members. By analogy with schemes of mutual help, life assurance were arrangements 'whereby the premiums contributed by the whole group [could] be shared among the dependants of those who die'. In the first decade of the eighteenth century a step forward was taken to establish mutual societies 'which would pay, in respect of each member's death, a sum dependent on the actual number of deaths and calculated so as to divide the aggregate amount of contributions equally between the claims of those who had died'.[81] The Amicable Society for a Perpetual Assurance Office was one of these companies; it received its charter in 1706 and it endured until 1806, when it was taken over by the Norwich Union Life Insurance Society.[82] Its purpose was 'to secure 2,000 subscribers of £6 4s each per annum on the understanding that £10,000 (i.e. £5 per subscriber) would be shared each year between the nominees of those subscribers who had died during the year'.[83] Based on their rudimentary systems to account for mortality and understand morbidity, insurance societies employed a similar mechanic when admitting members. According to Clark, '[p]rospective members were not quantitatively rated according to their susceptibility to a given hazard, as modern insurance practice does: rather they were simply included or excluded on the basis of whether they met a standard level of risk'.[84] Uniform fees and benefits were assessed on the 'approximately equal chance of death's striking each member'.[85] This meant that persons from 'high-risk groups', such as 'soldiers or seamen, drunkards, or those who were much distempered, or distracted, or under cure', were rejected.[86] Many societies also excluded from their cover overseas travellers and people whose residence was in the 'marshy and unhealthy parts of England', as well as people who had not contracted smallpox.[87] The profound changes in beliefs that would be required for life underwriters of the time to implement the emerging demographic and quantitative statistical techniques derived from practices of 'political arithmetick' were yet to happen.

During the first half of the eighteenth century, major transformations were to quickly affect the insurantial imaginary of life assurance societies. The greater availability of food as a result of the agricultural revolution, the great advances in medicine based on better understandings of the causes of infection, the establishment of many of the London hospitals between 1720 and 1745, and the expansion of commercial activity with its various specializations, were to radically transform the forms of life to be assured.[88] The establishment and expansion of mercantile, industrial and professional families in 'the new wealthier England' as the emerging civil society about which Fergusson theorized brought with it new forms of circulation. Circulation of people, goods and services was also enhanced by the great transportation projects of the time, such as turnpike roads and canal networks as well as improvements in port design and administration.[89] This, added to a relatively stable economy during the period, resulting from the changes effected by the financial revolution of the end of the previous century, led to a greater capitalization of English society.[90]

Against this background life assurance became instrumental for furthering a form of life that was increasingly characterized by the mobility of property and capital. Life assurance, in particular, became a mechanism through which individuals could capitalize their own life and make it circulate within the early financial markets. When an individual acquired a life policy of any kind, for example an annuity, this policy became a fungible security that could be cashed and traded. As described by Clark, 'insurance societies often granted their policyholders to sell their policies', and 'change[s] in ownership had to be registered with the society'. In fact, it was in the interest of insurance societies to permit and encourage the traffic of policies. 'If subscribers retained the options of selecting a new life to insure in an existing policy, or of selling their policies outright' they would be able to realize their invested assets 'should their finances take a downwards turn'.[91] By allowing this practice, insurance societies contributed to the liquidity of their products, which would ensure their desirability in the markets and allow for their financial survival.

The transformation of an individual's life into an asset, the making fungible of life, transformed life policies into a collateralizing instrument 'on the lives of people to whom they loaned money'.[92] A debtor no longer required immobile property or physical assets to guarantee a loan as his own life could be used to capitalize the potential repayment of debts. The 'flexibility of a full assignable asset' became a practical feature for a growing financial market.[93] According to Clark:

> [s]ince a loan might be assumed by another creditor before its complete repayment, the power to sell the appending collateralising device was crucial. Alternatively, once a loan had been repaid, the creditor would need to be able to switch the insured life to another of his or her debtors.[94]

'Some policies were in fact transferred many times, tracing out a labyrinthine social and commercial network as they were successively assigned or bequeathed'.[95] Proof of the liquidity of a life policy is given by the example of an order made by the Amicable Society directors in 1713, by which they 'reissue[d] one of their policies that had previously been reassigned no fewer than four times':

> That policy No. 1180 on the life of William Chaplain be cancelled and a new policy on the same life be made out payable to Matthias Cocksedge or his assigns, assignee of Henry Short who married Bridgett late wife and administratrix of Thomas Tarver deceased late nominee of the said William Chaplain.[96]

Regardless of the clear benefits that life assurance as a transferable commodity represented for the emerging populations of merchants and professionals, the need to register each transfer 'frustrated their free circulation in the marketplace'.[97] The need to register modified policies with the issuing companies highlighted a key characteristic of insurance. For policies to be valid they had to be issued in the form of contracts enforceable by law. Insurance societies operated under a charter from the government in order to be able to issue policies enforceable in court. Any modified policy was *de facto* a new policy which required a registry for its enforcement. Hence, insurance policies revealed a relationship between insurance as an expression of entrepreneurial power with biopolitical effects, and law as an expression of the sovereign power of the state.

At this stage it becomes evident that there was an urgent necessity to develop means by which lives could be accounted for in more accurate ways. If a life was to be capitalized and used as a collateralizing instrument, if a capitalized life was to be tradable in the market, if a life was to be insured for longer periods of time than those allowed for through a visual 'un-certain' inspection and interrogation, then new metrics had to be adopted for the reckoning of lives. The advances in political arithmetick with regards to vital statistics were to be slowly incorporated into the technology of assuring lives and gave rise to the modern life insurance companies. The first of them was to be The Equitable Life Assurance Society.

Central to the foundation of the Equitable, as it was popularly known until its bankruptcy in 2002, was James Dodson and his novel scheme to discriminate levels of risk represented by lives. As noted by Maurice Ogborn:

> [t]he study of life contingencies for the purpose of valuing annuities and reversionary interests evidently turned Dodson's thoughts toward life assurance. In the preface to the third volume of *The Mathematical Repository* he noted that 'little need be said concerning insurances on lives; as it is a subject not before handled and will shew on its own use'.[98]

Dodson then proceeded to provide the calculations on the Bills of Mortality of London that were the basis on which the new company would calculate its premiums.

The establishment of the company under the ideas of Dodson faced opposition from the very beginning. The promoters of the Equitable presented the company for incorporation under royal charter but the petition was rejected on grounds that the scheme had not been tested and represented too high a risk for the parties involved.[99] The ideas, however, under which the company was conceived were the following. Premiums for the Equitable were to be proportional to the sum assured and depended on the specific particularities of the applicants. The contracts issued were to be mutual assurances on the lives of those participating in the scheme, whose main purpose was to protect dependants against the premature death of the breadwinner. The life assurance fund was to be designed as free and open, that is to say life assurances were to be freely granted to all who were considered to be assurable. The incorporation of the company by royal charter was thought necessary for the effectual carrying out of the scheme. After the rejection of the royal charter in 1761 the company had then to be established by a deed of settlement by way of a voluntary partnership.[100]

Assurance societies had previously received their royal charter under a scheme designed for 'discreet and provident men, unable otherwise to provide sufficiently for their families or relations'.[101] They were reported to Queen Anne as 'an easy way of providing for the widows, children, or friends of those who would be subscribers to the project invented by Mr Hartley'.[102] The Equitable was thought of as a more extensive plan than that of Mr Hartley, and it aimed at providing expanded support for those assured and their families after they died.[103] In practice, the Equitable's insurance scheme was an advance on previous assurance societies in five ways.

First, the scheme built on a mainly landless emerging middle class, who could now use their own life, in a future capacity, as collateral for debts. On the other hand, the scheme was thought of as a system by which

> those who depend on widows or jointures, or on others who have pensions or salaries, may, by making assurance on the lives of the persons entitled to such incomes, be in some measure provided for after the decease of those on whom so depend.[104]

The provision of financial security based on the death of the employer or benefactor became a mechanism for building resilience within the emergent classes. It was presented as a way to reduce indigence, which represented a cost for society and the Crown. The same situation applied for those 'entitled to annuities determinable upon the lives of others, or to annuities during the joint lives of themselves and others'[105] so that, if such a life ended, the annuity could be protected. The scheme was therefore instrumental in enabling the transfer of securities, a process through which securities were enabled to circulate for the protection of the form of life of emergent classes.

Second, the Equitable promoted itself as a mechanism by which the financial conditions for marriage could be met.

> Those who, in consequence of a moderate fortune to be received on marriage, may be required, or for other reasons may desire, to settle a sum of money upon their intended wives, or upon their children, payable at their own decease, and are not in capacity to do it, cannot give security for it, or spare it out of trade.[106]

This particular feature illustrated a more complex security assemblage at work. Men could be required by the bride's family to ensure some form of financial protection for their wife and children in case of death. The life of the groom could, by means of this scheme, now be used to enable marriage, with the known positive effects that this brought in terms of social cohesion. At the same time, men who experienced difficulties in paying debts could secure the payment to their creditors in case of death without their families inheriting their obligations. It also became a mechanism by which people could advance cash over their entitlement to future benefits. For example, when someone was entitled to the reversion of an estate, it could make an assurance on his own life during the life of the person in possession.[107] In that way life insurance became a tool by which future incomes could be cashed in present time.

Third, the Equitable's scheme provided a specific kind of security to families dependent on a salary. The families of clergymen, counsellors, physicians, surgeons, attorneys, public and private office-holders, amongst others, could now secure a lump sum in case of a premature death of a husband, father or friend.[108] In a society with no public social security provision, the possibility of falling into poverty in the absence of the breadwinner could now be avoided by capitalizing on the future productive capacity of lives. This was, however, a possibility for gentlemen who were considered as such by their education and profession. The protection of 'artificers, manufacturers, and others who supported themselves through their labour' would depend not on the security that the Equitable promised, but on the 'friendly societies which operated in different parts of the kingdom'.[109]

Fourth, the Equitable provided insurance explicitly related to survivorships. In the situation in which the benefit of an estate, annuity or legacy depended on the survivorship of the named person upon another, a life policy could provide a security for the family in case of death of the assured.[110] It was also applicable for people who expected to inherit an office or future position. For example:

> Those who, upon the continuance of their own life beyond the life of another, will become possessed of any office, place, or preferment either ecclesiastical or civil, may in like manner by making a suitable assurance provide against an unfavourable event of such a contingency. And this kind of assurance seems to be in a peculiar manner adapted to the clergy, amongst whom expectations of this sort must be most frequent.[111]

Finally, the scheme could be used to provide security for widows with no family who survived their husbands. Indigence of widows was a problem for the society and the Crown. The Equitable now offered life policies that could be used to repair a situation that otherwise would have meant a radical change in the widow's lifestyle.

In sum, the Equitable's scheme could provide for the kind of contingencies that previous projects and companies had not been able to do. The key enabling element for this technology was the possibility of calculating individual risks through probabilities. The method was that which James Dodson had introduced by collecting the experiences on annuities and political arithmetick and developed further by the agency of Richard Price. Other schemes, such as the ones utilized by life assurance societies, could underwrite their clients/members only for a maximum of a year. They were also exposed to unaccounted risks that resulted from inadequate assessment of clients/members.[112] This excessive exposure compromised the security sought by the members of such societies, as evidenced in recurrent bankruptcies. In contrast, the kind of long-term underwriting that the Equitable implemented allowed for the creation of risk pools that were financially sound. These pools were, in fact, too sound as towards the end of the directorship of William Morgan, second director of the Equitable, it was discovered that the actuarial premises upon which premiums had been calculated were above mathematical requirements.[113]

The novelty of the Equitable's scheme for providing life insurance was evidenced in the invention of the word, the concept, and the role of the 'actuary'. Ogborn registered this novelty.

> The word 'actuary' is derived from the Latin *actuaries*, which was used for a shorthand writer in the specialised sense of the official who was responsible for the official record of the proceedings of the Senate under the Roman Empire. The *Encyclopedia Brittanica* (3rd. edn, 1797, which might reflect the ideas current in Mores's time) stated that, in the Eastern Empire, *actuarii* were, properly, officers who kept the military accounts, received the maize from the store-keepers and delivered it to the soldiers.[114]

He then added:

> It seems that the reasons for the choice of the curious title of 'actuary' lie in the character and interests of Edward Rowe Mores [an early director of the Equitable]. He was over-fond of the use of Latin and would have been

> familiar with the use of that title for the official who recorded the decision of court, a rare survival from the Tudor usage. It was used in the courts which met in Doctors Commons. He may have felt that some special title was required for the chief official of the new organization and that 'actuary' would be appropriate, since the principal duties of the new official would be to register the contracts made by the Society. More probably, however, he was merely indulging in an antiquarian whimsy, adopting an archaism to describe an official who was intended to be the Secretary in all but name.[115]

With an actuary on board, the Equitable began business in 1762 and operated until the beginning of the twenty-first century. The promoters of the scheme prided themselves in advertising the company as supported by three principles: that the assured were mutually assurers one to the other; that the premiums of assurance were proportionate to the chance of death attending the age of the life to be assured; and that the actuarial technology upon which premiums were calculated allowed for the calculation of premiums proportionate to the hazard of the age at which life began to be assured.[116] These principles, mainly the principle of mutuality (inherited from the early third-party form of insurance of the medieval Renaissance) and the principle of proportionality, were precisely the cornerstones of a biopolitical security technology that is currently providing an everyday kind of security to millions of people around the world.

The provision of insurance based on a capacity to render life fungible became a technology whereby the state was itself securitized in the very process by which 'assemblages of citizens' were made secure. The security of the state became the security of its citizens. The security of citizens was premised on the capacity of individuals to translate their own lives into property, property which was the condition of possibility in the early liberal life for the exercise of political rights. Individuals constituted themselves as populations through a technology that measured their specificities and calculated the value of their future existence. Life rendered as capital enabled a technology of protection that promised to repair a form of life in the event of death. Such protection was materialized in the possibility of compensating dependants and creditors for a loss of life. The financial and social security of the state came to depend in great measure on the social cohesion and economic well-being that resulted from the development of actuarial life assurance.

3 The quest for insurability in the molecular age

In October 2000 *The Economist* celebrated what was presented as an unprecedented decision by a committee set up by the British government to allow life insurers access to the results of consumers' genetic tests.[1] The decision was heralded as the beginning of 'a new era for the industry'. Arguing that 'Britain had done the right thing' and that 'access to the results of more tests would undoubtedly follow', the article stated that life insurers should be allowed to operate under sound liberal principles and that every effort towards legislation against insurers' use of genetic testing should be resisted.[2] The article finally argued that the problem of 'how to deal with the unlucky owners of harmful genes' was a government issue and insurers should not be expected to behave as another social service.[3]

The genetic test in reference was approved by the first Genetics and Insurance Committee (GAIC), a committee that arose from an acute politicization process developed around the use of genetic information for insurance purposes in the mid to late 1990s in the UK.[4] The decision to approve a test for the prediction of Huntington's disease was taken by many to be the first victory for the insurance industry in the quest to exclude 'harmful genes' from their risk pools.[5] Such was the hype surrounding genetic determinism preceding the completion of a working draft reference DNA sequence of the human genome published in 2000. From this perspective, insurance was considered to be a malignant technology that sought to discriminate amongst members of society in terms of levels of risk.[6] Individuals considered as being at low risk of falling ill within a given period were to be privileged with access to insurance cover at preferential rates (preferred lives), those considered normal risk would be charged at standard rates, and high-risk individuals would be excluded from cover altogether or charged extra. Many aspects would intervene in the kind of risk assessments conducted by insurance companies – some traditionally used since the eighteenth century, such as age, sex and occupation, and others more current, such as the results of specific predictive genetic tests. The malignant technology of insurance would use data derived from such tests to create a 'genetic underclass', a cohort of individuals not worthy of protection, the kind of people whom the state, rather than the private sector, should look after.[7] As naive and caricaturesque as this description might appear, the prospects of the insurance industry being allowed to use genetic information in their underwriting practices raised all sorts of ethical issues which were addressed at the highest institutional levels.

In the UK, patient groups argued that persons 'genetically at risk' should not be subject to exclusions imposed by insurers using genetic information. Patient groups recognized the social benefit of insurance but opposed the exclusions to which they were being subjected. For example, as a brochure by the Multiple Sclerosis Society stated:

> [t]he whole purpose of insurance is to protect us from the financial consequences of the unpredictable. Whether it's a car accident, a holiday cancellation, home contents destroyed by fire or the early death of a loved one – most people would expect to have no trouble getting insurance to fully cover such eventualities. But for people with MS [multiple sclerosis], that security is often either unavailable, prohibitively expensive, or inadequate for their needs.[8]

In a presentation to the Manchester Statistical Society in 1997, Onora O'Neill, then Chair of the Human Genetics Advisory Committee, a government advisory body, highlighted some of the forms of discrimination that could result from the use of predictive genetic testing for the pooling of risks in life, health, critical illness and income protection insurance.[9] In her opinion, insurance policies should be *demonstrably fair*, 'as between customers with like known risks', and *demonstrably reasonable*, 'as between proposers in ensuring there was no extra loading where no extra risk had been established'.[10] The primordial point of the ethical debate was to prevent forms of unfair, unreasonable and legal discrimination that would exclude individuals from insurance cover and also deter applicants from undertaking predictive genetic tests that could be used to promote their own health. The claim was made from 'the ancillary ethos of evidence-based policy'.[11]

The public debate, however, had began earlier and became politicized in 1995 with the publication of the House of Commons Select Committee on Science and Technology (HCSTC) report *Human Genetics: The Science and its Consequences*.[12] The document stated that even if it was not clear yet if the use of genetic testing was relevant for commercial underwriting, the insurance industry should develop an unambiguous policy on how unfair discrimination of the public would be prevented. The committee suggested that insurers be given a year to propose an acceptable position to this problem and did not rule out the possibility of legislation on the matter.[13] It also recommended the creation of a statutory Human Genetics Commission to monitor advances in clinical genetics and provide evidence-based advice to the government.[14]

As a response to this report the Association of British Insurers (ABI) stated in 1996 that its members' 'right to underwrite' should be preserved, as underwriting practices were not arbitrary but operated under sound actuarial bases.[15] That same year the government issued its reply to the committee's report, arguing that legislation was not the appropriate course of action, especially as the industry could be expected to develop its own code of practice making evident what its policies on the use of genetic information would be.[16] The government, however, followed the committee's advice and established the Advisory Committee on Genetic Testing (ACGT) and the Human Genetics Advisory Commission (HGAC) as non-statutory bodies charged with offering 'timely and independent views' to the government on how to deal with these matters in the future.[17]

In December 1997 the insurance industry announced its position by publishing the report *Life Insurance and Genetics: A Policy Statement*.[18] The ABI cautioned that being denied access to results on predictive genetic tests would lead to what is known as 'adverse selection' with potential catastrophic consequences for the industry.[19] As described by Mittra, 'adverse selection arises under conditions of knowledge asymmetry between insurer and insured regarding the latter's risk status.'[20] 'High risk applicants may consequently acquire excessive insurance at standard rates, leaving the insurer to bear the costs associated with the uncalculated risk'.[21] If underwriting were to take place under conditions of asymmetric information, the financial stability of the industry would be compromised. The HGAC replied to this statement with the report *The Implications of Genetic Testing for Insurance*, in which it was argued that any additional costs resulting from adverse selection could be absorbed by the industry as only in rare cases would genetic information alter current actuarial calculations.[22] At this stage actuarial evidence that substantiated the HGAC's position began to emerge.[23] As a means of creating some breathing space for the debate, the HGAC also recommended a two-year statutory moratorium on the required disclosure of genetic test results and called for the creation of an independent authority responsible for deciding the actuarial relevance of new predictive genetic tests.[24] The principle of evidence-based underwriting became the cornerstone for the discussion of the insurer's right to underwrite.

At the height of the debate, the ABI announced a strategy to deal with the public and parliamentary concerns.[25] First, it appointed a clinical geneticist as its permanent genetics advisor. Second, it announced the introduction of a code of practice to which all its members would abide as a condition of membership. The code, later amended in 1999, banned any form of genetic testing for life policies connected to mortgages of up to £100,000, and allowed companies to use results that applicants had already obtained only after clinical and actuarial validation by the Association's genetics advisor. It also forbade the offering of lower than standard premiums to individuals with favourable genetic test results. As its third tactic, the association announced a list of eight, later seven, single-gene disorders regarded as significant for insurance for which the industry would seek actuarial and clinical validation to be used in future underwriting. Fourth, the UK Forum for Genetics and Insurance (UKFGI) was created as a space for the analysis of the implications of advances in genetic knowledge for insurance in all its forms and to serve the public interest by reporting on its findings. Finally, the ABI decided to provide funding to the Genetics and Insurance Research Centre (GIRC) at Heriot-Watt University in Edinburgh to develop mathematical and actuarial models to estimate the costs of genetic knowledge to individuals, insurers and service providers.[26]

Following the ABI's initiative, the government replied to the HCSTC's report in December 1997, stating that the recommendation for a moratorium was no longer required in light of the insurers' newly established code of practice.[27] It argued that the industry had taken steps to ensure that 'genetic test results should only be taken into account by insurers in making underwriting decisions where the relevance of the test results to the risk assessment had been demonstrated'.[28] It also suggested that 'an effective mechanism should be established to evaluate the reliability and actuarial evidence relating to the use of specific test by insurers'.[29] The Genetics and Insurance Committee (GAIC) was created for this purpose and was commissioned to draw up criteria and guidance for insurance providers to submit information on genetic tests and their proposed use for insurance purposes for approval by the committee.[30] The approval of a predictive genetic test for Huntington's disease that *The Economist* heralded was its first public deed.

However, concerns about violation of the principle of evidence-based underwriting were not unsubstantiated. Consultation leading to the HCSTC's fifth report, *Genetics and Insurance*, in April 2001 highlighted concerns from user groups, insurance companies and advisory committees in this regard. The Wellcome Trust's response to the consultation, for example, questioned the correlation of gene changes with mortality experience and the procedures that led to GAIC's acceptance of the Huntington's test, and warned about the effect on public confidence of the lack of provisions for individuals whose applications were rejected on genetic grounds.[31] Research conducted in 1996 by the Wellcome Trust found that there was a lack of consistency among insurers' policies regarding the issues of assessing genetic information and acting on risks brought to their attention.[32] In a study on public perceptions on the collection of human biological samples, the Wellcome Trust also found that issues such as informed consent and anonymity were crucial for the public's confidence in genetic research and that confidence could be seriously affected by underwriting practices.[33] Based on the consultation process, the HCST called for a *voluntary moratorium* on the use of genetic testing for at least the following two years to allow time for more research on how to reconcile the parts with the principle of evidence-based underwriting.[34] It called on the UK government to enforce the moratorium through legislation if the industry rejected the scheme.[35] It also called for a reform in the membership and procedures of the GAIC, which was found to be operating under dubious ethical standards, and recommended a re-examination of its decision to approve the Huntington's genetic test to be used by insurers.[36]

This claim for a moratorium was supported in May 2001 by the Human Genetics Commission (HGC) – the institution that replaced the ACGT and the HGAC in 1999.[37] The HGC argued for 'a clear and defensible regulatory system which not only balances the interests of insurers, insured persons, and the broader community but also enjoys the confidence of the public'.[38] In October, the government responded to the report by announcing an agreement with the insurance industry on a new and stronger moratorium for five years which would be reviewed after the third year.[39] The threshold for non-disclosure of genetic information was raised to £500,000. The ABI agreed to continue to monitor its member companies' compliance with the code of practice and agreed to review the membership and procedures of GAIC.

Throughout the process the public remained opposed to the idea of insurers using predictive genetic testing for underwriting purposes. A study commissioned by Swiss Re Life & Health in 1998 found that only 8 per cent of the public believed that they should be obliged to share the results of genetic tests with their insurance companies.[40] Patient groups and other organizations, such as Breakthrough Breast Cancer, Cancer BACUP, the Alzheimer Society, the Cancer Research Campaign, the Wellcome Trust, the Genetic Interest Group and the Huntington's Disease Association, argued for a solution to what they perceived would result in a 'genetic underclass'. However, the legislative option lobbied for by many was constantly rejected by the Wellcome Trust because it would contribute to exacerbate a crisis of confidence on genetic science and negate the benefits it could bring to the promotion of human health.[41]

In March 2005, a further agreement was reached between the government and the ABI to extend the moratorium until 2011 and to adopt a policy framework for cooperation, a concordat.[42] The concordat, subject to renewal in 2008, stated the official position of the industry in the use of genetic information as 'transparent, fair and subject to independent oversight, building on existing voluntary codes of practice'.[43] It also sought to preserve 'the principle that unless otherwise agreed, insurance companies should have access to all relevant information to enable them to assess and price risk fairly in the interest of all their customers'.[44] The industry's position continues to be one of preserving the right to underwrite under a framework of evidence-based underwriting.

Genealogy, not genetics

Resistance to the use of predictive genetic testing for life underwriting in the UK resulted in a quasi-regulatory framework whereby insurers voluntarily accepted to restrict and police their use of genetic information. Such a regime, however, has been the result not of one position prevailing over the other but rather the confirmation of two facts. The first is that the science that would support decisions on the use of genetic information is far from stable. Second, the insurance industry privileges vital genealogy over genetic determinism. These two features have significant implications in the ways in which the uncertainty of vital function is rendered fungible in the form of life insurance, as will be examined in the third part of this chapter.

The move towards evidence-based underwriting has demanded that insurers demonstrate the validity of their methods and the validation/accuracy of their metrics. Society, through the government, the House of Commons SCST and GAIC, has increasingly demanded such an evidence base on the grounds that insurance fulfils a social role and should therefore be held publicly accountable.[45] If insurance is to be allowed to exclude individuals from cover on genetic grounds, such exclusions constitute serious biopolitical decisions that would have to be substantiated through a solid scientific base. However, the last 10 years of the moratorium have witnessed at least three major changes in the science called upon to support genetically informed actuarial practice. The changes explained below help to explain why insurers have decided to privilege family histories over predictive genetic information.

In *Genes in Development: Re-Reading the Molecular Paradigm*, Neumann-Held and Rehmann-Sutter have argued for a change in the understanding of the 'gene-centric' perspective that characterized the deterministic way in which the decoding of the human genome was announced in the year 2000.[46] They argued, together with 14 contributors to the volume, that there is a need to deconstruct the molecular paradigm and the human genome. Consequently, they proposed a discussion of the molecular paradigm in terms of the 'developmental systems approach', methodical culturalism, the molecular process concept of the gene, the hermeneutic theory of description and process structuralist biology.[47] Each one of these aspects, elaborated in the book, constitutes a critique of the social and cultural biases surrounding the Human Genome Project. More than a critique, however, the contributors argued that the molecular paradigm under a deterministic perspective did not fulfil the promises made in the 1980s and 1990s to secure public and private funding on the grounds of medical benefits.[48]

Their main point, however, was that the decoding of the genome has shown the need to further the study of *developmental processes* through the analysis and manipulation of molecular interactions at the level of gene regulation.[49] Their argument was based on the idea that DNA contains information that is pertinent for informing developmental steps but is not anchored in a deterministic paradigm.[50] The ontogeny of the genome, understood as the developmental history of an organism, is assumed to be only temporally and locally present. In this sense, the idea of structures appears as causal for further developmental steps and not as a signal of its limits.[51]

Genes, according to this perspective, are therefore not ontological categories but pluripotential features of life. According to Rehmann-Sutter, each step in the developing sequence can have a double or multiple significance.[52] Following the argument, genes are a necessary intermediate for the success of the sequence.[53] Genes have therefore a performative function and matter in each one of the steps of the constitution of life rather than remaining an essential moment in the process.[54] According to such critique, the possibilities for genetic essentialism were unsubstantiated and presented as based on false premises in the explanation of life. A developmental approach has been offered as an alternative explanation to open up the possibility for an understanding of life in its multiple potentialities. For example, it has enabled the possibility of approaching life as reparable and regenerative and as such prone to reparative and regenerative technologies. The work of Melinda Cooper is illustrative of this fact. Tissue engineering, she argues, operates techniques of reproducible morphogenesis that are possible only when the biomedical paradigm of organ transplantation and prosthetics is overcome.[55] Regenerative medicine can operate only on the basis of 'capturing life in a state of perpetual *self-transformation*', emergence and unfinished morphogenesis.[56] Tissue engineering is made possible if life is taken to be prone to regeneration.

Technologies of vital enhancement would not have been possible under genetic determinism.

A second transformation in the field of molecular science has been suggested to be a shift towards 'informational bioscience'. In November 2006, Eric Davidson published in *Science* a brief analysis of the sea urchin genome.[57] Having digitized the first genome of a non-chordate deuterostome, he argued that the embryo of this organism was the first for which a 'global network analysis will become available, in which every input into every regulatory gene in the network comes from some other gene in the network'.[58] His promise was that in the future 'we will be able to account for the course, and hence the outcomes, of development – the body plan of each species'.[59] Davidson argued that:

> [i]mmortalised and arrayed in many thousands of small wells, the library of the sea urchin genome 'contains all the genes and all the hardwired regulatory instructions required for construction of this sea urchin's body and for his physiological performance in confronting the natural environment, as well as the millions of sequence differences distinguishing his maternal and paternal genomes'.[60] This finding would therefore directly contribute to solving the principles of design of gene regulatory networks for embryonic development.[61]

The promise went further:

> The genome will not only provide the 'code' for development but will also contribute to linkage between gene regulatory networks and the actual realisation of developmental events. For example, the genomics of gastrulation, epithelium–mesenchyme transition, and species-specific patterning functions are now accessible. It remains to connect the genes that execute these functions to the control circuitry that specifies their occurrence.[62]

This example from molecular biology is just an illustration of what can be termed 'post-genomic' research. The most appropriate metaphor for the genome is no longer the 'book of life', used by Lily Kay in her genealogy of the genetic code,[63] but rather 'an electronic circuit'.[64] On the poster of the sea urchin genome published in *Science* together with Davidson's article, it was announced that 'all complex animals, no matter how different they look, operate their cells the same way and use many of the same genes for transcriptional control and intercellular communication'.[65] The poster indicates an apparent trend for molecular biology to centre on understanding the regulatory network of genomes, seeking to shed light on the network architecture and system design of organisms rather than on their deterministic structure. This approach was sloganized by Davidson when he stated that '[t]he sea urchin genome sequence did not open the door to a new pathway to knowledge; it opened the door to a nexus of pathways'.[66] While heralding the emergence of what he called 'informational bioscience', Davidson argued that the time had come to reorganize a large area of bioscience as a scientific continuum 'over what used to be the distinct disciplines of regulation molecular biology, evolution, developmental biology, and genomics, together with their mathematical and computational support and more traditional descriptive knowledge'.[67]

Molecular biology, if Davidson's narrative is accurate, no longer thinks in terms of genetic programmes, at least not in a consistent manner. The metaphor of the network has replaced that of the system and even though there are still noticeable remains of a genetic ontogeny the assumptions are now radically different. Programme genomics understood DNA as having an ontological principle and gave it the status of an organizing molecule. Genetic information was seen as the nucleotide sequence of the genome.

The work of Neumann-Held and Rehmann-Sutter and Davidson's proposal for an informational bioscience have not been isolated efforts in a critique of the molecular paradigm. A third aspect confirms the fallibility of genetic determinism as a scientific approach. Since the year 2000, a shift of emphasis from genomics to proteomics has began to take place. The concept of genomics was coined in the mid-1980s to define 'the study of all the nucleotide sequences, including structural genes, regulatory sequences, and non-coding DNA segments, in the chromosomes of an organism'.[68] However, as the systematic study of sequences, genomics was soon challenged by a new approach that privileged the study of molecular interaction. As described by Tyers and Mann, proteomics 'evokes not only all the proteins in any given cell, but also the set of all protein isoforms and modifications, the interactions between them, the structural description of proteins and their higher-order complexes'.[69] In this sense, proteomics refers to the study of 'almost everything post-genomics' which has become the preferred term for the non-deterministic study of the 'blueprint' of life.[70] Away from the quest to map and sequence the human genome that characterized the second half of the twentieth century, which Peter Glasner described as a process of 'black-boxing' to ensure stabilization of life and of science,[71] the proteomic movement has sought to understand life in circulation. From this perspective new positions have arisen. For example, Marc Van Regenmortel has argued for a paradigm shift in proteomics from 'structure determines function' to 'binding determines function'.[72] The move emphasizes connectivity as a condition of possibility for vital function.

These changes in the understanding of molecular biology denoted a highly unstable knowledge-base for the constitution of regimes of truth upon which technologies such as insurance can operate. A preliminary assumption in the writing of this chapter was that, if the molecular revolution was indeed presenting insurers with a new kind of information, they would surely be seeking to unfold stochastic models to encompass the changes. The idea was premised on the understanding that changes in the truth-base used to explain vital function would bring changes in the kind and quality of information for stochastic modelling. However, as Angus Macdonald noted in an interview conducted for this purpose, genetic information has not acquired sufficient actuarial relevance to affect current models and practices.[73] Macdonald is a recognized leading academic working on the relationship between actuarial science and genetics. His work in recent years has shown that the use-value of genetic information for insurers is still to be determined.[74] This position has been reinforced by the fact that underwriting practices are concerned more with vital genealogies than with genetic information, as will be elaborated below.

In 1997, the ABI code of practice created a new role, the nominated genetic underwriter (NGU), charged with responsibility for ensuring that companies abide by agreements between the UK government and the ABI. In 1997, the code established that insurers should nominate 'an underwriter with sufficient seniority in the company (or each subsidiary) to whom an application containing a genetic test result must be passed'.[75] The NGU has since become the official expected to discuss applications containing genetic information with the company's chief medical officer and to make the final decision on the insurability of clients with a genetic record. An analysis of the role of the NGU in its tenth year of operation shows that the apparent opportunity to shift from an 'ex-post' to an 'ex-ante' regime of life underwriting has not taken place. The insurers' struggle to preserve their right to underwrite has been premised more on the interpretation of historical records in the form of family history.

The 1997 ABI code of practice dictated criteria on how genetic information should be treated by the industry and established procedures on how to deal with complaints. It has been part of the overall strategy of the agreement between the government and the industry to guarantee underwriting practices founded on clinical and actuarial evidence.[76] By creating the role of the NGU, the industry sought to ensure that cases involving genetic information would be dealt with at the highest levels of expertise and responsibility.[77] This has been confirmed by research conducted for this study, with all NGUs interviewed declaring underwriting experience of not less than 15 years and all of them having taken over the job from more experienced colleagues.

Since the inception of the scheme the role has acquired a high standing within the industry. When asked about the real importance given to the role of the NGU in different companies, a member of GAIC stated that 'NGU practice will differ slightly in different companies but I can guarantee that they will all have somebody extremely responsible looking after that, they will all have an NGU if they are members of the ABI'.[78]

The training of NGUs is generally the same as that of any other insurance underwriter. Typically they have not been educated as genetic physicians but have been chosen based on their capacity to interact with the expertise of chief medical officers and other clinical advisers. As one of the interviewees stated, 'my knowledge of genetics is on a need-to-know basis', 'an NGU is simply someone with relevant experience, perhaps with a special interest in genetics, and obviously with the other things that go without saying: trustworthy, reliable, hardworking'.[79] An NGU of a market-leading company expressed the view that the role 'is actually in some extent only an extension of what we do for other things. In fact, what the NGU does is not much different from other roles we perform, only that the person needs to be able to understand how the science relates to the practice'.[80] Another interviewee noted that the role of the NGU is that of 'a gate-holder if you like, a watch-keeper of what we do, a person that makes sure we comply with the code and on individual cases makes sure we do the right thing'.[81] All NGUs agreed that the main function they perform is to facilitate the process by which genetic information is dealt with through the mechanisms established by the code of practice.

NGUs have been key figures in genetically informed life underwriting. Life underwriting begins when the client approaches a broker or completes an online application. The form usually collects information related to the cover required (number of persons and type of cover), amount and length of cover and general details of the applicant (postcode, sex, residence, smoking status and some family history). An online quote is usually subjected to confirmation, with underwriting official reviewing the information. Because all insurance companies have limits below which they are prepared to accept clients without further underwriting, small amounts usually do not trigger any further investigation. Over a certain sum assured, or in the case of particular disclosures, applicants will be subjected to more complex underwriting. This has been the case, for example, for family history. Detailed application forms enquire about the existence of certain medical conditions amongst first-degree relatives. If the answer to any of these questions reveals a potential genetically related condition, for example 'mother age 40, breast cancer, and sister, breast cancer', the underwriting officer is instructed to transfer the case to the NGU of the company, who is usually located in the company's headquarters. As a member of the central underwriting team of a major life company stated, 'all underwriters in our offices across the country have been instructed that if they come across a reference to a piece of genetic information or genetic test result they should refer that information to the NGU at the central underwriting team'.[82]

When a certain sum or apparent medical condition triggers the need to explore further the medical condition of a client, the insurance company either requests a general practitioner's report (GPR) or commissions a medical examination. The second option is usually reserved for special cases as it incurs higher underwriting costs. The former is commonly used but because of the ethical issues it raises has been subjected to constant review and has led to agreements between insurers and the medical profession. GPRs resulted from an agreement between the ABI and the British Medical Association (BMA) in 2002 when criteria for the disclosure of medical information for insurance purposes and the medical fees for providing this service were agreed.[83] Both the ABI and the BMA provided guidance to GPs on how to complete these reports.[84] The agreement was based on the 'recognition that life assurance is a "social good" that is of benefit to patients especially at significant points in their lives' and it was recommended that reports be completed 'to appropriate professional standards'. Requests from insurance companies to GPs include a covering letter stating that the report should be based on existing information and should not necessitate further examination of the patient. The letter states that answers should be provided only in relation to the insurance product that the patient has applied for. Information collected is covered by the insurance companies' confidentiality policies and should not be used for any other purposes. By submitting the initial application form, the client has already given consent to the company to approach his or her GP. In principle, then, it is the duty of the medical practitioner to provide accurate and timely information with regards to his or her patient's medical condition which could have relevance to the product requested.

The current moratorium and concordat explicitly asks GPs not to disclose the results of any predictive genetic tests. The statement reads as follows:

> We do not need predictive genetic test results in this report as the insurance includes a temporary suspension on genetic test results. You must not include any predictive genetic test results that show that the patient has an increased risk of disease. You may include in the answer to question 5 any genetic tests results that show that the patient has a normal or reduced risk of disease. Some companies use this information in underwriting.[85]

However, my interviews with NGUs have revealed that insurers are concerned about the continued inclusion of predictive genetic test results, not only of their clients but in some cases of their relatives, in GPs' reports. The code of practice, moratorium and concordat do not allow insurers to consider this information in their rating. According to the code of practice, should any such information be revealed, the client's case should be reported to the NGU and rated without taking this information into consideration. Furthermore, a log should be created and included in the annual report to the ABI.

The filtering of results on predictive genetic tests into insurance files is seen as one of the contentious aspects of life underwriting. However, underwriters have constantly argued that genetic information lacks the underwriting value that has been credited to it by the public. Illustrative of this fact is the following remark by one interviewee:

> We can't use genetic test results as you know. It is frankly limited to certain situations in which the predictive genetic test is negative. So when we, when you know – because of that situation when we obtain a report from the doctor, – I mean the ABI moratorium and also, you know, what doctors can and can't, and should and shouldn't tell us, it's made clear to the GPs. So we don't ask for genetic test results, um, we do make the point that a negative test result, you know, if you want to tell us, can be, you know, will be looked at favourably, it's in the client's best interest. So in other words we will rate, you know, we will give a decision based upon a family history which at the end of the day may be inappropriate. So you know we... any reference to genetic information on a GPR is usually disclosed by the doctor, um... I wouldn't say an error but um, you know, of their own free will. We don't specifically say, you know, we are not entitled to genetic information and what have you.[86]

NGUs interviewed for this study declared that this involuntary disclosure of results added to the burden of their job and had the potential to become increasingly politically problematic for their professional practice. They were asked why they thought GPs continue to include this kind of information on their reports. The general answer was that they thought many GPs simply copied and pasted information into the report from their files. Some of the NGUs went further, asserting that it would not surprise them if reports were being completed by assistant staff under the GP's supervision, although this was attributed not to a lack of goodwill on the part of GPs but to time constraints. However, the fee for a GPR in April 2007 was £79.20 (£94.30 in May 2010) and this and the fact that it can take up to 20 working days to produce a report has led some companies to contemplate alternative ways to improve life underwriting while reducing reliance on GPRs. This is in line with the general belief that clients' family history, that is, their clinical genealogy, is more relevant to underwriting than are the results of predictive genetic tests. As one interviewee categorically put it, 'genetics have very limited use to us', 'the amount of hassle it causes isn't proportional to the benefit even if we were to be allowed to use the data anyway'. That same NGU added, 'we are looking for other ways of getting the information… um, you know, getting information that's drilled down from the clients, so you get the level of detail that you wouldn't probably get from the doctor'.[87]

> I think we should give a lot more credibility nowadays to client disclosure. So a lot of companies familiar to us have the application form now, you look to drill down the answers to a level where you can actually start to underwrite or make a decision based upon client disclosure. And therefore reduce reliance on doctors' reports, which, you know, they delay things which added to the fees we have to pay add to the expenses of the policy. And very often you, you know, if you asked the right questions you could have a better level of disclosure of somebody's illness than you might from the doctor's report. Especially in this day and age where unfortunately a number of doctors will just press a button and print off a record to come off, which – it might contain everything but there is no detail, there's no colour around the disclosure, very often it raises more questions than answers.[88]

This privileging of genealogical information over genetics has begun to permeate the role of the NGU. As an interviewee mentioned, in his company the role of the NGU has been expanded to include 'complex family histories' involving disclosure of medical conditions of relatives other than first-degree relatives. The example given was that of breast cancer, where wider family history is often relevant.

> So you have maternal aunts, maternal grandmothers, and when this kind of information reaches the conventional underwriter it does not fit the company's rating manuals and rating guidelines. So these cases have been sent to the NGU who has decided if a conversation with the chief medical officer was needed or if there was sound actuarial and clinical evidence for loaded rates based on wider family history.[89]

Genetics-related life underwriting is not, however, restricted to insurance companies but also forms the basis of the underwriting manuals and guiding practices of reinsurance companies.[90] As the head of life of a major reinsurance corporation stated in an interview, 'reinsurers have been created to spread the risks of insurance companies. We have written manuals which we use to underwrite our own risks which are brought along by the companies that we underwrite'.[91] This logic has resulted in a tight interaction between conventional insurers and reinsurers in the form of an audit performed by the latter on the former. This is known as 'operational risk transfer'.[92] Under contemporary reinsurance treaties, which is how these contracts are known, reinsurers avoid the risks and claims that arise when underwriting has not followed the prescribed standards. As reinsurers are usually multinational organizations and dictate the procedures and practices for genetics-based life underwriting, life underwriting is a massive international activity that is often overlooked. Decisions made by reinsurers in Munich, Zurich, London or New York affect the rates given by life companies operating in the UK. The knowledge that underlies reinsurance manuals permeates down to the local underwriter, who will have to base decisions on what the underwriting manual says. The NGUs of conventional insurance companies have acquired a special role in this relationship. Vested with the responsibility for handling genetically informed cases, they have to determine the actuarial and clinical relevance of cases not only in dialogue with the chief medical officer, but also in the light of reinsurance treaties. In this way NGUs have exercised a pivotal role in the wider complex of genetically informed underwriting. Reinsurance companies operating in the UK have also been obliged to have a NGU, who in practice has become a 'gatekeeper, a watchkeeper' of the code of practice.

A document published by Swiss Re provides strong evidence that the pressure felt within the UK for evidence-based underwriting is also present at international level. The report stated that:

> [o]ver the past three decades, the private life and health insurance industry has come under increasing pressure from regulators and government to demonstrate that its risk selection process is fair, and to prove that the price charged to the consumer of insurance products is actuarially sound.[93]

The report has been part of a wider international effort of the industry to ensure their 'right to underwrite' by means of providing accurate, ethical and demonstrable methods to obtain and process relevant data for insurance rating purposes. These efforts have permeated the British life industry and been reflected in the underwriting manuals that conventional insurers use.

Finally, another contentious issue that has emerged in relation to the role of the NGU has had to do with the nature of the information compiled and reported to the ABI. Under the code of practice, NGUs are expected to assist the company's chief underwriter in preparing the annual compliance report on the code of practice and the moratorium. If a client discloses the result of any kind of predictive genetic test, or if any form of genetic information is disclosed by a GPR, the underwriting official is expected to report the case to the NGU. Each case involving genetic information must be logged in a file with restricted access and the file will then be used for the compilation of the report. Decisions on what is to be logged have been the responsibility of the nominated genetic underwriter. This was described by one of the interviewees:

> We never ask for a genetic testing to be done. And we don't ask for results. But um, you know over a period of time we will – we will get results with medical evidence or even the client may disclose it on the application form. But if we have results of a genetic test given to us, we keep that information securely, it's not recorded on our normal underwriting system, which is computer-based. It's not handwritten on any paper file or anything. On the computer record there will be a reference to a log number, and that's an electronic log which I maintained and, as I say every case, well not every case is referred to me, only the ones with actual genetic test results or where councillors have taken place that I then log. And then each year, companies have to do the annual return to the ABI which is an anonymous return, um, to which gives the numbers, types of genetic tests and things like that.[94]

After 10 years of systematic data collection on genetic disclosures and after three years of ABI surveys on compliance with the code of practice on genetic testing (compliance reports began to be collected in 2002), a body of data has began to be accumulated which could potentially be used to reassess the value of genetic information for underwriting purposes. When NGUs were asked about how they saw this possibility, their reply was that they would not know how to use it. The body of data is insufficient to enable for the identification of solid, statistically proven, trends. On the other hand, the information has been collected with the purpose of demonstrating compliance with the code although it is not intended to constitute an actuarial database. The report *Temporal Trends in ABI Genetic Testing Data 2002–2005* did precisely that. It identified an 'annual increase in the number of test results disclosed, with a similar increase in the number of conditions for which genetic tests are being used, mainly for diagnostic purposes'. It found that, in the case of the tests which the ABI is expected to monitor (Huntington's disease, BRCA1/2, familial polyposis coli, muscular dystrophy, multiple endocrine neoplasia and hereditary motor and sensory neuropathy), the majority of tests have continued to be predictive and have reported 'normal' (favourable) test results. However, in the case of other conditions, the results of predictive and diagnostic tests have been increasingly disclosed, and the proportion of adverse results has also increased. In general, there has been an increase in the proportion of applications being accepted at standard rates or at a slightly higher rate, whereas the proportion of applications accepted with exclusion or at revised terms has fallen slightly. Although there has been an increase in the number of applications declined, the proportion has remained at less than 1 in 10.[95]

This data have proved that the use of genetic information for underwriting practice has brought more difficulties than opportunities. There is no evidence of the use-value of genetic information for a shift to an ex-ante regime of life underwriting or indication that the role of the NGU could have been used to explore such possibility. The actual value of genetic information for insurers, at least for the time being, has been genealogical and not genetic.

The 'right to underwrite'

> Liberalism is to be analysed as a principle and a method of rationalising the exercise of government, a rationalisation that obeys – and this is its specificity – the internal rule of maximum economy.[96]

The obsession with the evidence base is an obsession with measurement. How can the fairness of the system be measured? How can it be proved that an insurance technology is being scientific enough? Is insurance rendering itself to political and social accountability? A key problem results, however, from the process that precedes measurement. For measures to exist, concepts need to be defined and categories constructed.[97] Decisions on what is to be counted, and how, are part of the process by which calculation takes place. Likewise, the process through which risk is constructed as fungible uncertainty requires a process of objectification. The very process of objectifying what is to be measured provides the parameters through which its existence can be verified. When a nail is manufactured, the parameters to decide if the final product is indeed a nail rely on its 'nailness', which can be compared with the concept of nail employed in its production. If there is a correspondence between the salient features of the product and the concept upon which it was made there would then be enough evidence to assert that the item is certainly a nail. When a whole advisory/quasi-regulatory apparatus is put in place to determine if insurers in fact constitute risks out of the uncertainty surrounding genetic information, the effort is in verifying if the product they are offering, expressed in each unique insurance quote, is based on relevant and substantiated evidence. In this sense, it cannot be overstressed that the campaign for evidence-based underwriting involved in debates on the use of predictive genetic testing and insurance is centred on a demand that insurers make the procedures through which they render uncertainty fungible as transparent as possible. Calculation is, then, central to the decision-making process that leads to underwriting insurance policies and also to verify that such underwriting is supported by relevant evidence. As Theodore Porter has argued, 'the key purpose of calculation is to expound and justify choices, rather than to make them'.[98]

The problem of quantification as a means for verification highlights the complexity of systems of measurement. Quantification requires a subject matter, as has been proved once and again, notoriously for example in the work on the history of probability of Gigerenzer and others.[99] The subject matter, which is precisely what insurers constitute in the process of rendering uncertainty as risk, can, however, be objectified in various ways. In the seventeenth century, when probabilities had not yet been determined, risks were expressed in terms of aleatory contracts of the kind that Daston and others refer to.[100] Quantification was thus a juridical and rhetorical debate. When risks became a function of a system of measurement that weighed the probabilities of events occurring against the consequential events that such materialization would represent, risks became a mathematical issue. This is not to say, however, that insurance ceased to be a contractual problem, only that a new layer of information was added to the verification process. Then not only did insurance have to be contractually proved, but the validity of insurance depended on the insurer's capacity to prove that what was being sold was in fact evidence-based fungible uncertainty.

This introduces a more complex debate that needs to be mentioned here in passing but requires a more refined and detailed elaboration that escapes the purpose and space of this book. If the problem depicted as a campaign for evidence-based underwriting around genetic information is a metrical problem, a problem that depends on the capacity of insurers to prove scientifically that what they are rendering as risk is indeed the result of an accurate quantification, then this problem is related to the old problem of 'just price', mentioned in Chapter 1, and so prominently promoted by the advocates of insurance in the medieval Renaissance.[101] The arguments of Thomas Aquinas and his followers with regards to the liceity of insurance in the face of charges of usury were premised on the fact that if a premium corresponded to the risk incurred there was no exploitation of the other party and, therefore, no grounds for accusations of usury. If, on the other hand, the price did not correspond to what was being sold, then there was justification for the charge of the sinful practice of usury. The problem, thus put, becomes a matter of regulating speculation: speculation that would lead to gambling on lives, as noted in Chapter 2, but also to unfair profits, which, it could be argued, from a modern liberal economic perspective, would lead to market inequalities.

Central to this problem then is the need to make accountable the process of translating uncertainty into risk. Accountability, however, is enmeshed within a wider problematic of government that is not concerned only with the policing of just prices. Accountability has become the characteristic feature of an ethos of governance, within neoliberal models,[102] premised on its own capacity to invigilate responsible risk management. Responsible risk management is expected to bring market stability and growth with its thought consequences of economic opportunities for all and social and political cohesion leading to peace. Under this Kantian-inspired liberalism, risk management has slowly evolved into a science that supports itself on the also recent profession of risk analysis. The process is scarcely older than 40 years. Ian Hacking began to trace the emergence of risk analysis by observing the emergence of new institutions and professionals of risk in 1969. In his opinion the process was a reaction to 'the fears played upon by militant activists' in that decade.[103] However, even if, as argued by Hacking, 1969 is 'a good enough date to mark the establishment of the profession as profession, with numerous specialised journals, organisations, meetings, and all the usual paraphernalia of establishment coming in train', what is relevant is that it helps to show the importance of this activity for society.[104] With risk analysis as a solidified practice, the management of risk evolved into a profession on its own right.

Michael Power and Ian Hacking have argued for 1995 as the year when a wave of institutions, journals and in-house corporate structuring took place giving rise to a new professional, 'the risk manager'.[105]

Although the date is important, it becomes evident that the scrutiny of responsible risk management is a recent phenomenon that has, however, become an all-encompassing technology of control. Pat O'Malley has described, for example, how different understandings of risk have become enshrined within governmental discourses of all kinds (health, education, security, business, defence). When government 'is always an *attempt* to create subjects of a certain kind, or achieve results of a certain form', risk management becomes the all-encompassing profession of governance within all sectors of liberal life.[106] Michael Power pushed this idea further while characterizing what he called 'the risk management of everything' as the 'centre-stage of public service delivery' and as a model of organization in its own right.[107] Risk management is becoming a mechanism through which decision makers, at the public as well as the private level, can be held accountable and their judgements, as well as those of experts and scientists, made publicly transparent.[108] Audit, as the practice of public accountancy, is, however, based on the auditee's capacity to render itself fit for inspection. As Power argued, auditability is the capacity to be inspected, but this capacity gets constructed at the organizational level.[109] Auditability in this regards becomes one of the microstructures through which governmental organizations and quasi-regulatory regimes influence the conduct of individuals and collectivities. If risks are fungible uncertainty, as argued in Chapter 1, risks are now sought to be made auditable and governable to the point in which Power argues that the 'growth of risk management strategies [...] displaces valuable – but vulnerable – professional judgement in favour of defendable process.'[110] Such has been the case within the moratorium on the use of predictive genetic testing for life underwriting in the UK as the previous section on the role of the NGU describes. The adoption of responsible risk management discourses in the liberal political imaginary calls for an open and continuous disclosure of the methodologies and knowledge implemented in decision-making.

Demands for evidence-based risk management highlight a deeper transformation in governance techniques not restricted to the public sector but also, and mostly deriving from, practices in the private corporate sector. Michael Power tracks three critical aspects in this process: the emergence of risk-based internal control, where internal control becomes the very activity of risk management; the invention of 'operational risk', which becomes the security portfolio that redefines organizational governance and regulation;[111] and the emergence of the category of reputational risk, which embeds a whole culture of corporate responsibility representing the stakes to be protected and promoted when handling risks.[112] These three characteristics, allied to the definition of the Nobel Prize winners Bodie and Merton of risk as 'uncertainty that matters',[113] are reflected in the ancillary ethos of evidence-based risk management prominent within governmental discourses since the mid-1990s.

Beyond the bareness of life

The rationality of governance central to the debates surrounding the moratorium analysed in this chapter operated at the intersection of two distinctive forms of power, both with biopolitical effects. On the one hand, a sovereign form of power was employed in governmentalizing the practices of insurance in light of the potential implications of the production of a genetic underclass but keeping in sight the importance of insurance as a security technology for a liberal capitalist system. On the other hand, an entrepreneurial form of power was employed by insurers to resist the governmentalizing efforts of the British state, preserve the private character of their business and ensure their right to underwrite under market conditions. The biopolitical effect of the simultaneous exercise of these forms of power was the speciation of life as 'evental' and the capitalization of life in the form of biovalue, as will be explained below.

The governance of uncertainty through practices of risk assessment and risk management central to the moratorium is related to the problem of establishing the *event* to be insured against. Whereas the insurable interest in the debates surrounding the 1774 Gambling Act discussed in Chapter 2 revolved around the requirement to demonstrate a rational stake in the insurable 'object', the insurable interest at the beginning of the twenty-first century in Britain revolved around the very process through which the fungibility of uncertainty is transformed into an insurable event through sanctioned practices of risk assessment and risk management. These practices exceed the traditional scope of state governance and relate to assemblages of power that include traditional actors such as the state, individuals, and the corporate sector, but also interactions amongst them, self-organizing networks, specialist knowledge and authority assemblages, and the emergence of new expertise (sometimes evolving into new roles such as the NGU).[114] The obsession with measurement, as reflected in the voracious appetite for forms of evidence-based governance characterized by the hype of risk management of the mid-1990s, is part of defining the event that is to be insured against when using any form of life insurance. The HCSTC report of 1995 reflects this tendency and brings it to the fore.

The definition of the event to be insured against lies at the core of the contestation of the most fundamental ontological levels of speciation that insurance technologies have utilized when classifying the lives of individuals into risk pools. The resistance of members of the public to being interpreted in terms of levels of risk which result from statistical allocations of people into already encoded pools has been deeply embedded in the claims for evidence-based underwriting. The insurer's struggle against insurantial determinism, anchored on a genetically determined understanding of life, has been a campaign against reducing the speciation process to a technological rationality that fails to respond to what has elsewhere been analysed as the biopolitical imaginary of species being.[115] Mitchell Dean, in *Putting the Technological into Government*, noted that reducing the analysis of technologies of government to the merely technological could lead to a technocratic or instrumental reason.[116] He warned about missing the particularity of certain forms of governance as they become technological.[117] If the analysis of the moratorium were to be reduced to the dangers of insurers using genetic information to create an underclass and the need for the state to intervene and legislate against this possibility, then the debate would be reduced to the technological level. In contrast, the debate invites reflections on the biopolitical effects of insurance as a security technology in relation to the definition of events to insure life against, and the capitalization of life that results in the process.

As noted in Chapter 2, and when applied to the case of contemporary advanced liberal economies, life insurance in its various forms translates biological functions into levels of risk as a way of constituting collaterals that provide access to credit and other forms of financial protection. Insurance operates then on its capacity to make life live, to promote and protect the conditions of possibility for a form of life. When the Multiple Sclerosis Society claims that the security of insurance is 'often either unavailable, prohibitively expensive, or inadequate for their needs',[118] it makes a claim for the insurability of patients' lives against events that still fall within the scope of contemporary insurance practice. It calls for the use of an actuarial rationality to challenge genetic certainty and offer to patients with multiple sclerosis affordable insurance against accidents, premature death and fortuitous events. The event to be insured against is not the genetic understanding of their lives but the 'life events' to which their life is exposed.

In other words, popular resistance towards the use of genetic information by insurers is resistance towards the violence that gets enacted through the very process of selecting lives 'worthy of insurance'. It is a resistance towards the speciation process that threatens to translate lives into risk pools therefore rendering life in raw terms, as 'bare life' as theorized by Agamben.[119] It is a call for a biopolitical understanding of insurance not as the instrument to discriminate insurable from uninsurable life in genetic terms, but as a technology that if properly employed can make any kind of life flourish. It is therefore a call for insurers to employ their entrepreneurial power to develop products that speciate life not on genetic terms, but in terms of the events to which lives such as those with multiple sclerosis are exposed. Speciation is therefore the process whereby the claim for entrepreneurial novelty is made. Speciation involves an active process of identification and classification of life, but, as will be noted below, such reading of life is anchored no longer on a depository of past facts, but on the potentiality of future life events. This can be traced in Foucault's history of ideas.

In *The Order of Things* Foucault spoke of coherence as the process of 'liking consequences', of grouping and isolating, of analysing, 'of matching and pigeonholing concrete contents'.[120] Coherence, however, displays a changing character of the ways in which classification and ordering of life has sought to transform vital signs into governable matter as events. When Foucault analysed this process he also described how the coherence of the Classical Age, comprising a theory of representation and language, the natural orders, and theories of wealth and value, acquired a new form from the nineteenth century onwards. The theory of representation, as 'the universal foundation of all possible orders', disappeared; language lost its position as 'the primary grid of things' and became a historical form articulated with the destiny of its past. Historicity now became the penetrating factor of existence which isolated and defined things in their coherence while imposing 'the forms of order implied by the continuity of time'.[121] The emphasis on taxonomic characteristics typical of the previous age was replaced by an emphasis on 'the organism'.[122] The theory of representation of the Classical Age constituted a political imaginary that began to be replaced by one centred on the idea of organic life which could be explored in the continuity of histories, the analysis of labour and a language that derived its coherence from the density of its own past.[123] Life as organic matter appeared now to be anchored on a deep problematic of temporality that understood a present as a result of a past.[124] Organic life, labour as the condition for production, and language as an instantiation of the past into the present, became the transcendental features of a political imaginary that promised to scientifically interpret the present and anticipate the future under complex forms of scientific endeavours. Biopolitics under those markers became a matter of scientifically modifying the species in such ways that 'making live' and 'letting die' were the natural outcome of rationalized and measured biopolitical action. Eugenics is perhaps the best example of this biopolitical practice. However, at the beginning of the twenty-first century, and with the history of the Human Genome Project, this biopolitical function meets the challenge of genetic determinism offered in this chapter. Organic life is not only the site where Agamben and others have interrogated the biopolitical logic of a sovereign form of power that led to the human catastrophe of fascist and communist regimes in the twentieth century. Organic life is also the site for regenerative and prosthetic medicine as a means to enable decreased biological function.[125] It is the site where Fries has described the phenomenon of compression of morbidity, with patients now surviving disease and conditions that would have killed them a generation ago.[126] Consequently, the biopolitical character of this kind of organic life is expressed not solely as a technological interpretation of statistical trends but as an entrepreneurial promotion of the capacity for life events. Organic life as evental life is expressed in the form of potentiality. Such potential is not restricted to a finitude but remains open to creative entrepreneurial possibilities. The potential life of individuals with multiple sclerosis is not limited at the moment of the medical diagnosis but becomes a biopolitical function of the capacity of sovereign and entrepreneurial forms of power to formulate it as evental life. Life rendered as evental is interpreted in relation to the event to be insured against (a car accident, a holiday cancellation, home contents destroyed by fire, the early death of a loved one).

Speciation in the twenty-first century is, then, not only a matter of the governmentalization function of sovereign power or the technological actuarial logic of the entrepreneurial power of insurers, but the biopolitical effect of a rationality of risk management that combines both forms of power. As a result of the speciation of life as evental life, the employment of a rationality of risk management results on the translation of life into biovalue and the constitution of what Rose has begun to call economies of vitality.[127]

Waldby used the term 'biovalue' to refer to the production of a surplus out of vitality itself.[128] Rose referred to economies of vitality as those that result from 'novel links formed between truth and capitalisation'.[129] Value is ascribed to different organs and tissues of the body for which an exchange value is actively sought. However, value is also created in the process of capitalizing one's own life through life insurance, as described in Chapter 2. The resulting commodification of life through the use of life insurance is therefore not only restricted to creating markets for biological parts as those sought to emerge out of stem cells or tissue engineering. Biovalue today results, as it did in the early actuarial life insurance forms of the eighteenth century, from translating evental life into capital by means of life insurance.

When a client approaches an insurer seeking life, health, critical illness or income protection cover and a policy is issued, what has taken place is a translation of the client's 'life' into a form of security expressed as a financial product: a commodification of life. Underwriters, as described above, assess the actual conditions of the client's 'life' in terms of its present health and lifestyle and family history. The underwriting role, concentrated in assessing the client's capacity to endure the event against which an insurance policy is being written, effects a translation of evental life into risk. Evental life as risky life is life rendered actuarial, life transformed into fungible matter in the language of risks. However, the biovalue features of life insurance go further. It has become common commercial practice amongst insurance companies to trade in their life portfolios. The totality or parts of life portfolios are sold to other companies or 'securitized' in financial markets as a means for insurers to increase their underwriting capacity.[130] In fact, securitization is defined as 'a financial technique that pools assets together and, in effect, turns them into tradable securities'.[131] It is a relatively new technique first employed in the life insurance business in the early 1990s and is sought as a way to improve return on equity through capital efficiency.[132] While selling risks to investors, insurers reduce their need to hold capital and thereby increase their capacity to write new business.[133] When the life policy of client A, underwritten by company B, gets sold as part of a package to company or investor C, the capitalization on the life of A is no longer simply the result of insurantial technologies. It is now also the result of an active market of circulating securities that simply complicates the matter even further. A molecularized-evental life is then prone to be promoted and protected by a complex ensemble of actuarial technologies speciating life combined with financial strategies that seek to exacerbate the circulation of risky lives. This is a process yet in need of theorization and it requires a separate study which escapes the object of this book.

The capitalization of life, however, understood as a biopolitical effect of rendering life as evental through speciation processes that operate an actuarial logic, represents the infinite frontier for making life insurable. When an entrepreneurial form of power is deployed to resist the governmentalizing action of the state, as described in this chapter, the outcome is purely biopolitical. No such thing as the bareness of life in contrast to political life has ever been at stake. Efforts to characterize the metaphor of the 'book of life' as raw life that would have inevitably led to the collapse of the actuarial logic of insurance have demonstrated only that understandings of life are the result of processes of power/knowledge. When the knowledge base changes, so do the paradigms through which life is read and later acted upon. This leads to an evident conclusion contra Agamben. The process of insuring the security of lives never renders life bare.

4 Securitizing catastrophic environments, insuring uninsurable lives

In 2006 the government of Ethiopia together with the World Food Programme and the World Bank ran a pilot to provide insurance cover for farmers at risk of severe drought. That same year, the government of Mexico subscribed to the first sovereign parametric insurance scheme designed to generate insurance cover for populations affected by earthquake risk.[1] The two cases offer an illustration of how sovereign states have resorted to global insurance schemes as a means to enable their role as sovereign security providers. Because of the difficulty in calculating probabilities of occurrence and the magnitude of environmental hazards, environmental risks had escaped the logic of insurance at a global level and had traditionally been rendered as 'catastrophic'.[2] However, creative financial and insurantial schemes developed since the early 1990s have led to innovative moves that enable the functioning of insurantial technologies in relation to these risks. Strategies deployed for this purpose have articulated two manoeuvres: first, the conception of 'parametric insurance', a shift from the traditional indemnity insurance that required that an agent verified a loss once it had occurred; and, second, a financial manoeuvre involving the securitization of catastrophic risks in the global markets by means of financial derivatives.

The significance of these insurantial and financial schemes is that, if effective, they could represent a credible alternative for issues such as international humanitarian aid for developing countries. Their inception in the 1990s, manifested by the development of the parametric weather insurance for parts of the United States, was followed by pilots in developing countries in the 2000s, and by 2008 more than 26 projects were in place in emerging economies and the developing world.[3] Based on their potential, pressure was exercised to include forms of micro-insurance and environmental insurance in the final agreement of the United Nations 2009 Climate Change Conference in Copenhagen. The remarkable aspect of these schemes, however, for the purpose of this chapter and book, are the forms of power involved in their production and their effect in transforming sovereign understandings of security. Moreover, the interaction of these forms of power, as explained below, has a significant biopolitical effect in fostering the development and protection of uninsured and insured populations.

Parametric insurance with its allied financial securitization manoeuvres is inscribed within complex private–public partnerships between sovereign states, (re)insurance companies and in some cases international organizations. The traditional sovereign form of power of modern states is employed in seeking to provide populations with a form of security that will allow them to get back in circulation once environmental catastrophic events have taken place. However, an entrepreneurial form of power exercised by the global (re)insurance industry plays a fundamental role in enabling this sovereign provision of security. Whereas Chapters 2 and 3 of this book focused on analysing different strategies through which sovereign power was employed in governmentalizing the activities and lifestyles of gentlemen and business groups such as insurers, the strategies explored in this chapter can be described, in want of a better term, as the 'entrepreneurialization' of a sovereign form of power. This entrepreneurialization of sovereign power is, however, more of a productive tension than an accomplished process. Where sovereign power ceases and entrepreneurial power begins is not clear-cut. The parametric schemes analysed in this chapter and the processes that led to them indicate a constant cohabitation of these two forms of power in the production of two specific biopolitical effects. The aim of productive interaction between the global (re)insurance industry and sovereign states, in some cases through the mediation of international organizations, is to transform developing countries' governments into responsible risk managers. Second, through responsible risk management, enabled through private–public insurance partnerships, states seek to effect a transformation of populations' livelihoods into insurable lifestyles. In so doing the key objective is to provide populations with the technologies of financial reparation required to bounce back after catastrophic events and to protect the capital required for further liberal–capitalist development.

The chapter proceeds in four parts. First, parametric insurance is explained in relation to the way it modifies the provision of traditional forms of sovereign security. Second, the process of insuring through private–public partnerships is explained through the interaction of international organizations and the global (re)insurance industry. Third, forms of insuring through parametric insurance are explained with regards to the cases of Ethiopia but mainly Mexico. Finally, some reflections are offered in the form of a conclusion in relation to the two biopolitical effects of these sovereign parametric forms of insurance mentioned previously.

Parametric insurance and the provision of sovereign security

Parametric insurance is a form of cover whose contingent payout is based on the outcome of an underlying variable.[4] Rather than seeking to compensate for losses deriving from accidents on specific assets, as traditional forms of insurance do, the scheme fixes parameters that when breached give rise to claims. For example, as will be detailed in the third section of this chapter, rather than insuring Ethiopian crops for the year 2006, the government and its international partners insured against a parameter of minimum rain within a given time and territory. A similar logic operated in the case of Mexico, where the insurable event was centred not on the destruction of assets but on parameters measuring the magnitude of earthquakes. In this form, earthquakes surpassing an agreed level within an agreed territory and period of time would trigger claims.

It is important to note in passing that traditional insurance schemes operate in tandem with parametric schemes. For example, private insurance covering properties, contents and mortgages operate together with federal forms of insurance.[5] Parametric insurance schemes have been developed not to replace traditional risk management insurance products but to cater for the traditional uninsurability of environmental hazards. What is particularly novel in the use of parametric insurance is that insuring against a parameter modifies the insurable event and by doing so renders uncertainty prone to insurance management. This is not a simple move and will be analysed throughout the chapter.

The provision of security by governments has traditionally been understood as a legal responsibility to protect the lives, property and culture of individuals and collectivities. Seen in a biopolitical fashion, this responsibility is related to the promotion and protection of the life and lifestyles of populations. Central to this biopolitical security function is the development of schemes that allow governments to protect populations from environmental hazards. The use-value of parametric insurance for the provision of sovereign forms of security derives from the fact that governments will always have limited resources with which to cope with environmental emergencies. Emergency relief efforts as well as post-crisis reconstruction usually exceed national financial capacity. In 2006, for example, more than 31,000 lives were lost as a result of man-made and natural disasters worldwide.[6] Such disasters demanded immediate emergency relief efforts followed by expensive reconstruction projects aimed at restoring the regions to their pre-disaster conditions and enabling their populations to continue with their ways of life. Governments have traditionally resorted to self-insurance schemes whereby funds are created for the alleviation of such catastrophic events. This was the case in Mexico when, after the 1985 earthquake, a federal fund, FONDEN, was established. However, as stated by a Mexican official, governments will always find more urgent matters on which to spend their money rather than capitalizing a fund.[7] When environmental hazards become a pressing political matter within a context of what appears to be enhanced environmental risks, governments are compelled to explore alternative financial mechanisms.

The development and implementation of parametric insurance schemes for environmental risks is circumscribed within the wider problematic of neoliberal governance. O'Malley analysed this problematic as one in which governments are increasingly moved towards responsible risk-taking and responsible risk management.[8] Under a rationality of risk management, states are called to assume responsibility for the provision of security in a prudent manner. As described by Ericson, state entities are called to learn to choose between 'appropriate risk management techniques that will yield security and prosperity'.[9] This leads to what is being called a new prudentialism that operates as much on a principle of prudence as on one of active risk-embracing.[10] Neoliberalism, as analysed by Ericson, Barry and Doyle, operates a regime of responsible risk-taking based on a political economy of 'self-informed, self-sufficient, consumer labour markets'.[11]

Governments are called to embrace risk rationalities that enable them to problematize environmental hazard as 'risk' through the aide of regimes of risk knowledge.

The use of insurance, as a technology of risk employed as an instrument for government, is however not a new invention. It was been used in the modern period by liberal governments in various ways. O'Malley analysed, for example, different forms in which classical liberalism, social liberalism, and neoliberalism rendered uncertainty manageable through different forms of insurance.[12] As shown in Chapters 2 and 3 of this book, different forms of life have unfolded forms of insurance that have in one way or another interacted with sovereign forms of power. What is novel in the sovereign parametric insurance schemes appearing in the 2000s is that they are enabled through financial securitization strategies. Bougen has described this process as the 'crossbreeding of insurance and the capital markets'.[13]

The manoeuvre enabling the securitization of catastrophic risks is one in which risks are distributed within the capital markets through a financial derivative known as catastrophe bonds (cat bonds). Risks which would otherwise be considered to exceed insurable cover are transferred to the capital markets through this form of derivative.[14] Financial derivatives apply the option-pricing theory developed by Black, Scholes and Merton in 1973.[15] Understood away from the orthodox neoclassical tradition of finance theory,[16] derivatives have been presented by Pryke and Allen as 'high yielding liquid investment instruments'.[17] They have arisen out a need to make securities traded as futures financial instruments liquid in the capital markets. As such they have been designed as 'a means to take deliberate (optimal) positions on future asset price movements and to sell off or take on the risks of price movements in a calculated way'.[18] Bryan and Rafferty have described them as convenient and cheap instruments by which futures can circulate. According to them they offer the added convenience of being 'products which give exposure to risk (price or index changes) but without having to own any of the underlying assets from which the risk derives'.[19] In this way financial derivatives are conveniently designed to circulate in the global capital markets and have been instrumental in risk distribution schemes such as the ones employed in the parametric insurance strategies explained below. Bryan and Rafferty have gone as far as arguing, if controversially, that derivatives are commodified risk and as such can be theorized as a new form of money.[20]

Derivatives must be understood in relation to the changing demands of trade characteristic of liberal capitalism. They are not natural instruments but have been invented responding to a requirement of what can be understood as a neoliberal form of life. MacKenzie has argued that they did not simply 'evolve' but were 'invented' as the result of 'conscious deliberate processes of design'.[21] It is in this context in which it is possible to understand cat bonds as derivative instruments resulting from processes designed to distribute catastrophic risks. The 'crossbreeding of insurance and capital markets' in relation to environmental risk is a strategy designed for making uncertainty governable through vehicles of risk management (e.g. insurance) and risk distribution (e.g. financial derivatives). The strategy is, however, related to a wider process of governing through assemblages of risk. For Bougen, risk networks arising from the process that enables securitization illustrate 'the remarkable capacity of assemblages of government to combine different elements in diverse and productive ways'.[22]

> Reinsurers, capital market participants, catastrophe information systems, catastrophe-modelling agencies, investment-rating agencies, financial underwriters and existing financial products have all become imaginatively assembled. From a liberal government perspective, the very emergence of such risk networks capable of supporting securitization as an alternative method of catastrophe financing can itself be considered as illustrative of the moving and creative possibilities of government.[23]

This 'moving and creative possibilities of government' are a defining characteristic of Foucault's description of the active governmentalization of the state.[24] Understood as a tactic of government 'that make[s] possible the continual definition and redefinition of what is within the competence of the state',[25] the securitization of catastrophe risk is the result of a problematization of uninsurable risk under a rationality of risk management. The political economy problem that results from the demand for a provision of sovereign security in light of environmental hazard is then met with a strategy of risk management, enabled and fuelled by the private global (re)insurance industry, that makes the, until then, uninsurable insurable.

Through a novel strategy of rendering uncertainty fungible by means of changing the insurable event from the protection of assets to parameters and indexes, and by using cat bonds as a way of distributing risk and making reinsurance practice possible, sovereign parametric insurance has been deployed as a governmental response to environmental risk. In the process of rendering catastrophe risk governable, the state performs itself through the provision of sovereign protection to populations 'at risk'. This sovereign form of security is aimed at transforming livelihoods exposed to the changing circumstances of the elements (such as small-scale uninsured farmers) into lifestyles that can be promoted and protected through insurance, or repairing the possibility of populations at risk to carry on with their lifestyles after catastrophic events. In the first case, uninsured populations are offered a mechanism that makes them resilient to adverse environmental circumstances and renders them insurable. In the second, insured populations are provided with the financial means to repair their way of life when things go wrong. In sum, by means of sovereign parametric insurance schemes, states perform their role of security providers by getting populations back in circulation, that is, enabling them to continue to embrace risk. The sovereign function of security, as it will be evident by now, is enabled through the entrepreneurial form of power exercised by the global (re)insurance industry.

Insuring through private–public partnerships

Sovereign parametric environmental insurance solutions are the result of private–public partnerships that are global in nature. They are the result not of international charity or good international citizenship but of profitable global enterprises that involve sovereign states, the global (re)insurance industry and, in many cases, the mediation of international organizations. If governments are increasingly concerned with devising strategies with which to foster the lifestyles of their populations by coping with environmental hazards, insurers are seriously concerned with the effects of climate change and environmental risk in the process of maximizing profit for their stakeholders. For governments the concern is, as mentioned before, a political economy problem. For insurers the worries are financial and market driven as evident in the next example. Whereas the terrorist attacks of 9/11 incurred insured losses of $US21.3 billion, those of Hurricane Katrina and its consequent floods, burst dams and damage to oil rigs resulted in claims of $US66.3 billion.[26] Three times as expensive as the events of 9/11, Katrina alone has alerted the world to the serious consequences that environmental losses can bring to the insurance industry. This has led insurers to reposition themselves with regards to how climate change is being understood and to develop novel strategies to compensate for its consequences. However, contrary to Ulrich Beck's risk society thesis,[27] the industry still believes that it is precisely through these challenges that markets can be made to grow, margins for profit gained and novel forms of protection extended to vulnerable populations and clients.[28]

For instance, in 2006, Lloyd's of London launched its forum '360 Risk Project', intended to generate discussion 'on how best to manage risk in today's business environment'.[29] During one of its first events, 'Climate Change: adapt or bust', it was claimed that the frequency and magnitude of natural catastrophes affecting the insurance industry will be significantly increased as a result of climate change. It was noted in the forum that it is expected that by the year 2050 mega-catastrophes, such as Hurricane Katrina, which used to occur every 100 years, will now happen every 25 years.[30]

The position of the industry has been to continue to adopt a strategy of risk-embracing whilst doing its best to shape circumstances to reduce its exposure to economic losses. As global players, insurers are conscious of their entrepreneurial power. They understand the position they play as economic actors in a global market and they are willing to put it to their benefit. The forum concluded that insurers would do their best 'to use their influence as investors, in order to encourage responsible and climate-proof behaviour from the boards of corporations in which they invest, and with which they do business.'[31] Rather than assuming a conservative approach of risk prevention, the industry has announced its willingness to embrace risks deriving from climate change. Attendees stated that even if they 'don't know exactly what impact climate change will have' they 'do know that it presents society and the economy with an increasing level of uncertainty as it seeks to manage its risk' and this demands immediate strategic action.[32] For insurers, climate change has become a priority that can no longer be treated as peripheral, or as an issue of compliance, but that needs to be translated into a strategic imperative.[33] In the industry's words, acting on climate remains 'business as usual', and failing to do so 'will put companies at risk from future legal actions from their own shareholders, their investors and clients'.[34] Climate change, as a business priority, must therefore 'inform underwriting strategy, from the pricing of risk to the wording of policies'.[35] It must 'guide and counsel business strategy – including business development and planning'.[36] Climate change 'must lie at the heart of a new impetus to engage with the wider world through meaningful, tangible partnerships to mitigate risk – bringing corporate and social responsibility plans to life.'[37]

Other global players in the industry share this idea and are exercising their entrepreneurial power to support it. In the 2007 luncheon speech to the Large Cities Climate Summit, New York City, the chairman of Swiss Re America, Roger Ferguson, announced that 'Swiss Re believes that global warming and the resulting climatic changes may be the greatest challenge facing society'.[38] Swiss Re, as the largest and most diversified reinsurance company in the world, is seen to be able to operate an industrial shift in aligning climate change priorities with its business plans.[39] Environmental hazard, after all, means business opportunities. Of the total loss incurred through natural and man-made disasters (life and non-life) in 2006, only one-third was covered by insurance.[40] This gap presents insurers with opportunities and challenges to extend the limits of insurability.

The traditional claim of insurers to operate independently from the regulation of state or, in other words, to resist the governmentalizing agency of sovereign power, is central to their enterprising role in rendering environmental risks insurable. In the case of Lloyd's, the traditional global marketplace for special risks underwriting, the vast majority of natural perils are seen as insurable within existing actuarial technologies as long as insurance markets are left to operate under market forces.[41] Rather than see their insurantial role governmentalized, insurers seek to operate in partnership with governments to 'securitize' the environment. According to the Risk 360 project of Lloyd's, the best way of providing solutions to what appear to be uninsurable risks is through 'meaningful partnership with government and business, supported by a series of practical actions'.[42] A primal concern for the industry is, then, to develop the ability and the capacity to achieve working public–private partnerships to permeate markets that would otherwise be unreachable in market, political and operational terms.

A curious professional figure has arisen in the process of developing this ability and capacity to achieve public–private insurance partnerships and is worthy of comment at this point, albeit tangentially. Swiss Re has proposed the creation of a new role, that of 'chief risk officer' (CRO) for cities and governments.[43] The new role would be the means for transplanting 'the role and functions of a private sector executive into a public sector environment'. This role can be thought of as enabling an integrated long-term partnership between the private and public sectors.[44] The CRO would act as an interface for

> joint initiatives to identify and assess emerging risks; evaluate the risk landscape based on the best scientific knowledge; communicate the risk responsibly to policy makers and the general public; help steer mitigation efforts towards the biggest risks; and manage a pool of so-called mega risks which cannot be carried by the insurance community alone.[45]

The CRO would also act as the pivot around which international organizations such as the United Nations and its agencies, NGOs with significant ground influence, national, regional and local governments, and other global service providers would function.[46] The CRO would, in other words, operate a liaison service seeking to transform reality into problematics of governance through technologies of risk. If there was further need for evidence of the entrepreneurial power of the global (re)insurance industry, Swiss Re's investment portfolio of over $US130 billion provides an example of the capacity of the industry to engage in fruitful partnerships.[47] Thus, it is not difficult to imagine, although research on this area is required, the effects that a CRO figure embedded in a particular government will have in modifying the traditional sovereign provision of security – hence, the idea portrayed in this chapter of the entrepreneurialization of sovereign power.

An example of the kind of public–private partnerships in operation at the time of writing this book is the Insurance Working Group (IWG) of the United Nations Environment Programme Finance Initiative (UNEPFI). Formally established in 2006, it has been charged with the responsibility to undertake and promote research, further education and development products and methodologies on sustainable insurance. The group operates under the wider remit of the United Nations Environment Programme (UNEP) and has been set up with the objective of 'promot[ing] sustainability on a wide range of issues by demonstrating its materiality in enhancing company value, seeking to embed sustainability in the financial sector's strategies and processes'.[48] Since 1995 UNEP has sought to promote a global partnership with the insurance sector, first through the Insurance Industry Initiative and the organization of the Statement of Environmental Commitment by the Insurance Industry. As described by the head of the UNEPFI, the insurance industry has been identified as performing a vital role that 'helps understand the future' and 'provides the thorough risk analysis and early warning system that allow informed choices to be made, businesses to prosper, and sustainable livelihoods to be built and flourish.'[49] 'The global insurance industry sits in a pivotal intersection that helps individuals, communities and businesses understand, manage and mitigate risk, and protect their assets'.[50]

The IWG is an alliance of 16 leading insurers, reinsurers and brokers from Australia, Bermuda, France, Germany, Greece, Japan, Norway, Spain, Sweden, Switzerland, the Netherlands, the United Kingdom and the United States. It integrates companies such as Achmea, Allianz, AIG, Axa, Folksam, HSBC, IAG, Interamerican, Mapfre, Munich Re, Norwich Union (now Aviva), Storebrand, Swiss Re, Tokio Marine & Nichido Fire Insurance and XL Insurance, as well as the Lloyd's market of London.[51] As a public–private partnership, the IWG seeks to identify and capitalize the benefits of engaging in sustainability issues. To this end the strategic approach of the group has been defined as one of sustainable insurance, a concept supported by what is being termed as the 'triple bottom line' of people, planet and profit.[52] This bottom line understands sustainability as 'making the business viable in the environmental, social and financial dimensions over the long-term'.[53] This is supported by the industry's self-appraisal as an indispensable technology for the world's economic viability. In the words of the IWG:

> [i]nsurance is essential for a viable economy. Without it, businesses and individuals would be unable to take risks and protect their assets. The availability of insurance encourages individuals to acquire assets and invest for the future. Insurance allows the victims of accidental losses to recover financially and helps households manage their finances in the face of death and disability. Annuities reduce the likelihood that a retiree will run out of money. By providing these services, insurers reduce the pressure on public sector resources. Insurers and intermediaries provide risk management advice and through the pricing of risk, they can signal danger to other parties. Finally, with the premiums they receive for providing protection, insurers are also major contributors to the economy through their substantial investments.[54]

The insurance industry has identified as major concerns, in addition to climate change and environmental risks, sustainability issues such as insurance for the poor, protection of natural resources, emerging risks from nanotechnology, and health and lifelong income.[55] All these aspects have been encompassed as part of a wider strategy based on the principle of sustainable insurance.[56] Sustainable insurance has been presented as the basis on which insurers seek to manage sustainable development and exercise influence over the corporate governance and social corporate responsibility of companies worldwide. Under the umbrella of sustainable insurance new strategies that enable insurance technologies beyond traditional actuarial techniques have begun to emerge. Pushing the boundaries of insurability, or 'innovating to insure the uninsurable', as the title of a major reinsurance industry report presented it, sustainable insurance has been presented as the objective for the operation of a sustainable worldwide insurance–reinsurance practice.[57]

Against this background, the IWG has asked 'How can insurance assist developing countries grow more sustainably?' The answer is, arguably, to follow the eight key sustainability challenges in developing countries proposed by the 2001 UN Millennium Development Goals.[58] Following this line, it has been suggested that an appropriate strategy would be to use micro-insurance schemes as a means for delivering products 'such as weather derivatives for farmers and health insurance for families'.[59] Specifically, the IWG has suggested that 'the solvency of such schemes could be underpinned by natural catastrophe bonds, public–private partnerships and alternative risk transfer products such as catastrophe bonds'.[60] Mobilized through global public–private partnerships, new insurance schemes have begun to emerge based on the logic of parametric insurance.

Parametric insurance is a form of insurance contract that operates when a threshold is breached rather than when damage results from an accident. In technical jargon, it is a form of insurance whose contingent payout is based on the outcome of an underlying variable.[61] The underlying variable is not necessarily the yield itself, but instead serves as a proxy. For example, rainfall, extreme temperatures in relation to a micro-climate, winds, vegetative indices, solar minimum requirements, hurricane trajectories and earthquake magnitude can be used as events for index insurance. The main difference between parametric insurance and conventional forms of insurance, including peril policies, is that the former is settled based on the outcome of the underlying variable rather than on the real loss.[62] A peril policy is one that insures against exposure to injury, damage or loss. It is a policy that insures the negative consequences of an event. Parametric policies are concerned not with the losses deriving from an insured event but rather with the parameters through which an insurable event is defined. In this sense, the underlying variable becomes the trigger for claims even if no damage has occurred.

The shift from peril policies to parametric insurance is related to a shift in the insurable event. Under traditional policies, accidents were taken to be the insured event. Within the new parametric schemes, specific parameters are identified as the benchmark to define the event to be insured against. In doing so, parametric forms of insurance reduce the space for disagreement with regards to what constitutes a legitimate claim. This shift has wider biopolitical consequences, as will be noted in the conclusions to this chapter. For the moment, it suffices to say that because accidents are events prone to moral agency they allow for the allocation of fault. The behaviour of insurable subjects is therefore to be assessed during the claims adjustment process that follows an insurance claim. In contrast, the insurance of parameters is sought as a strategy to objectify judgement always in relation to a prearranged evidence base, as will be shown in the cases below.

Parametric insurance products rely on the design of variables that ideally meet the following criteria: observable and easily measurable, objective, transparent, independently verifiable, reportable in a timely manner and stable and sustainable over time.[63] All of these variables are features required to objectify uncertainty in terms of risk or, in insurantial terms, used to match 'the right premium' with the 'right level of risk',[64] which, as noted in Chapters 1 and 2, is a central condition for the liceity of insurance. When insurance premiums correspond to the real costs incurred in compensating for such levels of risk, insurance is said to be supported by a sound evidence base. It follows, then, that claims originating from such policies would be easily justified. In the case of parametric insurance, fungibility is achieved by means of employing expert knowledge and technological instruments capable of verifying when insured parameters have been reached. They facilitate the indexing of hazards such as drought, flood, hurricanes and earthquakes, as well as others.

Because it is relatively simple to measure their thresholds, index products are presented as offering some critical advantages with regards to other conventional forms of insurance.[65] For example, they reduce moral hazard as they do not depend on human agency.[66] There is also low adverse selection as the insured parameters are built on objective and observable indicators. Administrative costs also tend to be low owing to the possibility of employing established underwriting procedures in verifying triggers. They also offer a standardized and transparent structure that can be replicated in various contexts if appropriate communication strategies are in place. Based on the market size, they are also likely to be widely available and prices can be flexible in adapting to various markets. Reinsurance for this kind of product is presented as usually also readily available because of the presumed facility in forecasting occurrence based on historical trends which at the same time are easily recordable through the use of technological instruments.[67] Finally, these kinds of products are depicted as highly versatile in allowing adaptation to various micro-climates. These features have been used to privilege the use of parametric schemes to meet environmental insurantial challenges in the developing world. Where uncertainty in regards to moral hazard and high risks of adverse selection prevail, parametric insurance has been taken to be a more viable option.[68] As described by Ibarra and Mechler, parametric insurance trades transaction costs for basis risk.[69]

The operational difference between parametric insurance schemes and traditional ones is that risks are layered in such a way that they 'facilitate clear delineations of public–private roles and the transfer of low-probability, high impact indexed risks from developing countries to the international markets'.[70] Based on these comparative advantages, parametric insurance has been identified as a privileged instrument for helping governments to tackle the consequences of environmental hazard such as drought and earthquakes. Owing to the costs of crisis management and post-crisis reconstruction, governments are challenged with developing strategies to provide proactive disaster recovery in anticipation of catastrophic events. The challenge of migrating a post-disaster assistance paradigm into an ex-ante management investment strategy[71] demands governmental tactics capable of generating a multiplier effect in the response capacity of the state. Under a rationality of risk management, as noted before, governments are expected to assume a prudential attitude towards the management of risks. Parametric insurance schemes are beginning to be acknowledged and developed as meeting these economic government expectations. Sovereign parametric insurance schemes, enabled through the entrepreneurial agency of insurers, are constituted into governmental risk management strategies aimed at enabling the provision of sovereign security in relation to environmental hazard.

Insuring through parametric insurance

An example of a parametric insurance operating under a public–private partnership is that of the 'rain insurance' scheme for Ethiopia. The case has been used by UNEPFI to demonstrate the benefits of this form of cooperation. The World Food Programme (WFP), together with the World Bank Commodity Risk Management Group (CRMG), implements a pilot scheme to cover farmers against severe drought during the 2006 agricultural season in Ethiopia. Claims would be triggered if rainfall turned out to be significantly below historical averages with consequent widespread crop failure. The contract was awarded to Axa Re. However, rainfall in 2006 turned out to be above average, so no payment was made. In the event that the contract had been triggered, Axa Re would have transferred funds to the WFP, which would then have paid the claims to the Ethiopian government. The government would then have distributed cash assistance to individual households through its Productive Safety Net Programme.[72]

The scheme was intended to prove that insurance technologies could indeed be employed as an instrument for emergency and humanitarian relief in regions where national states and private individuals lack the capacity to provide for their own financial risk management mechanisms. The value of the scheme was celebrated in press headlines as the 'World's first humanitarian insurance policy'.[73] The WFP's executive director was quoted as saying '[t]he humanitarian emergency insurance contract might, in the future, offer us a way of insuring against these massive losses before they spell destitution for millions of families'.[74] At a major United Nations conference in Kenya in November 2006 Jeffrey Sachs, architect of the UN Millennium Development Goals for easing world poverty, 'urged countries plagued by natural disasters to take out insurance policies rather than hope for humanitarian aid.'[75] According to Armin Sandhoevel of Dresdner Bank, who headed a UNEPFI climate change working group, the underwriting of weather becomes a safety net, a viable option for coping with environmental disasters.[76]

A UNEPFI report issued in November 2006 warned that losses from extreme weather events linked to climate change are doubling every 12 years.[77] It has been reported that potential losses from droughts, hurricanes, storm surges and floods could reach $US1 trillion a year during the next three to four decades.[78] The emphasis of the report, and indeed of the agency, was that it is an imperative for public–private partnerships to introduce financial cover in developing countries, where the impact of climate change is felt the most.[79] Matching seed money from public sources with the private skills of the private sector and the insurantial technology and know-how of major reinsurance companies, the UNEPFI argued that it is possible to provide a form of security for developing countries that have traditionally relied on international charity when disasters occur.

Mexico provides a second case in which the principle of 'sustainable insurance' has been implemented for developing a public–private risk management alternative to environmental risk. However, in contrast to the Ethiopian case, the Mexican government operated autonomously under a rationality of risk management, that is, it had in place mechanisms through which to assess environmental hazard in terms of risk and treat it as such. The novelty of the Mexican case arose from the role that the government assumed as the insurer of first resort through its 'treaty' relationship with Swiss Re. The reinsurance treaty was in turn enabled through a third-layer risk management strategy that securitized earthquake risk as a derivative in the capital markets.

The Mexican government resorted to the use of parametric insurance as an alternative to the political economic problem of providing sovereign security after catastrophic earthquake events. In doing so Mexico became in May 2006 the first sovereign state to conclude a reinsurance arrangement (curiously called 'a treaty') with a major reinsurance company to provide parametric earthquake insurance cover.[80] Having experienced catastrophic losses of $US1.8 billion caused by Hurricane Wilma in 2005, the Mexican government concluded that existing 'risk warehousing' financial arrangements to cope with disasters were insufficient. These arrangements were in the form of a natural catastrophe fund called FONDEN, which was the governmental self-insurance response to the 1985 Mexico City earthquake.[81]

Mexico is highly exposed to natural catastrophes. The penetration of insurance in the country, compared with the global average, 'means that most economic losses are not insured'.[82] Non-insured costs are met by individuals and governments, a situation that places a large burden on national finances. The traditional approach to post-crisis reconstruction and humanitarian relief after natural catastrophes was based on government funds, soft emergency loans and self-insurance. The last constituted Mexico's strategy, with the FONDEN being the first self-insurance scheme of its kind in Latin America.[83] From 1996 until 2001 regular transfers to the fund were made and emergency expenditures could be met in general terms.

After Hurricane Wilma, however, the FONDEN was found to be an insufficient instrument to compensate for non-insured losses caused by natural catastrophes. As stated by the Ministry of Finance and Public Credit of Mexico, resourcing the fund posed a difficult political economic question as there was always a good reason not to 'save for a rainy day'.[84] In years of low fiscal revenue the government had to reduce its contributions to the fund. Meanwhile, natural catastrophes continued to generate expenses that were difficult to cover.[85] By 2006 the fund was almost empty and an urgent solution had to be found by implementing innovative financial instruments. Under a liberal democratic regime, the government would be held accountable for the effectiveness of its preparations for environmental catastrophe. This was the context in which the sovereign parametric insurance scheme was found to be the risk management solution of choice.

Parametric earthquake insurance in Mexico was modelled on a similar pattern used for other special risks. First, it incorporated actuarial risk modelling premised upon the metrics of probabilities and expected impacts. Second, it involved professionalized expert knowledge specifically to be used for the technical assessment of risks. And, third, it employed specialized strategic risk management for the design and implementation of tailor-made risk management strategies.[86] Having rendered natural catastrophes as a risk management issue and having explored the alternative of self-insurance, the Mexican government and its team of advisers hired Applied Insurance Research Worldwide Corporation (AIR), a leading private risk modelling agency in the financial and insurance sector.[87]

AIR was asked to model the Mexican earthquake risk using the knowledge and expertise of the Engineering Institute of the Mexican National University. Companies such as AIR apply probabilistic modelling techniques 'to estimate the magnitude of potential losses' that clients can experience as a result of extreme events.[88] Based on technical expert knowledge that in many cases needs to be supplemented by working together with research institutes, as in the Mexican case, consultants seek to estimate the client's potential catastrophe losses, the optimum amount of insurance cover required to compensate for such losses, and the desirable amount of deductible that the client should assume.[89] The role of modelling agencies of this kind is to conduct as technical a measurement as possible to try and identify insurance requirements for a given problem. Of course, such measurements can take place only once a situation has been problematized in terms of a risk management problematic that calls for insurance expertise to come into play.[90]

AIR undertook a survey of the geographical and geological features within Mexico that could be used to map the seismic regions within the country. This information was then incorporated into a detailed hazard database to identify critical locations for potential losses.[91] The result of this assessment was plotted on a map and led AIR to concentrate its analysis on three major geographical zones identified as the main sources of earthquakes: zones A, B and C. This exercise provided the basis for an earthquake risk model for Mexico.

AIR's model comprised three phases. The first phase was seismic hazard evaluation, for which historical records in existence in the consultant's databases as well as information from the Mexican government, the Engineering Institute of the Mexican National University and the United States Geological Survey were used.[92] The objective in this phase was to identify the sources of 'event generation', which involved answering questions such as 'Where will an event be generated?', 'How big is such an event likely to be?' and 'How frequently has the event taken place in the past?' Taking this information into consideration, ground motion calculations and detailed information about the assets and resources affected in the event of an earthquake were used for the second phase, called engineering evaluation.[93]

The second phase sought to compile as much information as possible to estimate the degree of damage that would result from an event. Details on the construction characteristics of assets and infrastructure as well as the possible correlation of earthquakes with other phenomena such as flooding were analysed. Results were used as inputs for the third phase, loss estimation. This final phase was specifically designed to calculate the total loss derived from an earthquake contemplated in the model. The technical term used in this case was 'ground-up loss', which is 'the total amount of loss sustained by an insurer before deductions are applied for reinsurance and any applicable deductible'.[94] The loss estimation phase also included the monies required for the initial governmental response to the event, emergency loss calculation.

Once the phases of the earthquake risk model were completed, the risk-transferring mechanisms of the Mexican Earthquake Insurance were designed considering three levels of losses.[95] Each level was covered by three different entities. The government, through the FONDEN, played the role of insurer of first resort. If an earthquake covered by the scheme took place, it would be the responsibility of the government to provide immediate recovery efforts and finance reconstruction projects.[96] Losses by the government deriving from these activities would be indemnified by the Swiss Reinsurance Company. If such losses exceeded the capacity agreed in the reinsurance treaty, the remaining loss would be transferred to the next level, that of cat bonds.[97] Under the Mexican scheme, CAT-Mex Ltd. (a Cayman Islands-based special-purpose company) has been in charge of issuing 'floating rate notes (catastrophe bonds) to capital market investors to hedge its obligations to Swiss Reinsurance Company'.[98] Capital raised by CAT Mex would then be used to compensate the loss excess up to a certain limit defined in the contract. Finally, an event payment account was established with the Bank of New York providing FONDEN with the capacity to receive loss payments directly from CAT-Mex Ltd.[99]

The scheme was set to operate based on the geographical risk classification resulting from AIR's earthquake risk model. Three geographical zones were identified as especially vulnerable and subject to insurance cover. Zone A (northwest Cocos) offered 0.63 per cent loss probabilities, zone B (central Cocos) 0.96 per cent and zone C (outer Mexico City) 0.30 per cent. These figures became the foundation for the pricing model that would seek to match the right premium with the right level of risk (premium expected = cost expected).[100] The total amount of cover agreed in the contract between Swiss Re and FONDEN was $US450 million. Of this sum, $US160 million was securitized in the capital markets as a collateral trust. Establishing the triggering conditions was the next step.[101]

AIR recommended a binary system that would consider the magnitude of the earthquake and its maximum focal depth. The binary parametric trigger was established as the index for 100 per cent loss recovery if conditions were met. However, an independent body had to be appointed as an event verification agent, and this role was awarded to AIR, which would have to base its judgement on reports by the United States Geological Survey.[102] The trigger event conditions were established as threefold.[103] First, the Mexican government would have to declare a state of emergency through its Ministry of the Interior and publish it in the *Mexican Official Gazette*. Second, the epicentre of the earthquake would have to be located inside or on the boundary of one of the three zones mentioned before. And, third, the earthquake would have to be of a magnitude of 8.0 Mw and 200 km of depth in zones A and B, and 7.5 Mw and 150 km in zone C. If the above criteria were met, an immediate claim could be made by FONDEN to Swiss Re and onwards.[104]

One of the innovations of this scheme has been its resort to capital markets as a means to provide a second layer of reinsurance to the scheme, thereby making what would otherwise be catastrophic risks insurable. Reinsurance capacity is limited to the amount a reinsurer can commit to insure a particular book of business. If claims exceed this capacity, losses would, in principle, escape the logic of insurance.[105] Cat bonds, however, operate as an alternative source of capacity, in this case not for the reinsurer but for the original insurer (e.g. FONDEN).[106] In practice, then, the use of financial securitization strategies within the environmental risk management complex enables the operation of an instrument of economic government which multiplies the governmental capacity to provide a sovereign security in case of earthquake risk. Whereas FONDEN's budget for 2006 was around $US100 million,[107] the parametric earthquake insurance scheme enables the government to provide three times as much money after a catastrophe without having to deplete its resources.[108]

Biopolitical security effects of parametric insurance

This chapter has offered an analysis of the ways in which the global (re)insurance industry, exercising its entrepreneurial form of power, has sought to affect the traditional sovereign provision of security. By means of shifting the insurable event from the accident/catastrophe to the parameter, parametric insurance has evolved into an instrument with the potential to support the reconstruction of affected areas after devastating environmental events. Parametric insurance has been supported by the establishment of public–private insurantial partnerships which have been financially enabled by the use of financial derivatives in the form of catastrophe bonds.

Parametric insurance is the result of combining the exercise of sovereign power with entrepreneurial power. Sovereign power has been required for the provision of legal security in the form of a stable rule of law, the regulatory frameworks and arrangements to enable the interaction of state agencies with private (re)insurance partners, and for the provision of knowledge and information on populations, territory and property required for the design and operation of the schemes. Entrepreneurial power has been exercised by insurers to provide the risk management know-how and expertise for the design and operation of the insurance and reinsurance strategies, the liaison with governments to create the risk distribution schemes in the form of securitization in the financial markets and, overall, to produce value for their stakeholders through the responsible embracing of risk. The two forms of power have, however, cooperated in generating two specific biopolitical effects that will be analysed below.

First, they have cooperated in seeking to transform the state's traditional sovereign responsibility to protect into a responsible risk management enterprise. Whereas governments are accountable to their constituencies and insurers to their stakeholders, both sovereign and entrepreneurial powers have combined to instil a rationality of risk management in the sovereign provision of security. This has involved the adoption of discourses and practices of risk in governmental strategies aimed at protecting populations from environmental hazards. It has involved the creation of new professionals to operate a liaison between the private understandings of risk-embracing with the public provision of risk management. Swiss Re's suggestion of creating the role of chief risk officer in the government of Mexico City is illustrative of this fact. It has also involved the services of experts in different technical aspects of risk assessment, risk management and risk distribution to support the role of the partnerships in operating the parametric insurance schemes. This form of private expertise, for example in the role that AIR has played in the Mexican case, is supported by other forms of technical knowledge provided by third-party sovereign states, as the role of the US Geological Survey in the Mexican scheme also illustrates. It also involves the good offices and technical work of international organizations in the form of different UN agencies and dependencies of the World Bank and the International Monetary Fund to support schemes such as the one used for Ethiopia and currently in Malawi and the Caribbean, as noted below. The sovereign provision of security through parametric insurance schemes therefore breaks the traditional public–private divide in the state's responsibility to protect and adopts a process that has been depicted in this chapter as the entrepreneurialization of sovereign security.

The second biopolitical effect of these partnerships is the intended outcome of transforming the uninsured livelihoods of people into insured lifestyles of populations. Livelihoods are characterized by traditional structures of self-help and support provided by family and communities. The capacity of uninsured individuals to bounce back after catastrophic events depends on the availability of personal and family savings and the cooperation of neighbours and peers with the very limited support of states and in some cases non-governmental organizations and churches. The state is called to give aid to uninsured individuals and families, but such support will never be enough in light of the need to provide for emergency medical services, the reconstruction of vital infrastructure and getting basic services back in place. The capacity of the state to support uninsured populations, very likely supported by donations and help from the international community, will by necessity be limited to emergency response. Responsibility for restoring livelihoods will most likely be left to individuals' own devices supplemented by charitable aid to endure the trauma and economic loss resulting from the environmental catastrophe.

Lifestyles, in contrast, are developed as a result of the accumulation of knowledge resources and capital, and at least a basic level of financial protection, that enable populations to repair the economic damage after catastrophic events. Lifestyles will be able to sustain a degree of loss while retaining the capacity to recover even when state support is limited and the help of international agencies is prioritized to the poorest populations. Lifestyles will be able to afford some level of insurance, be it over the life and capacity to work of breadwinners, or over property and capital. The reparational security provided by insurance after an insured event has materialized will provide some means for self-recovery. What is repaired, of course, is not the loss of life, but the loss of capital and income that supports a particular lifestyle. Lifestyles are the forms of life of resilient populations capable of bouncing back after catastrophic events.

As noted in Chapters 2 and 3, insurance over lives is directly related to the security of property and capital and has become a condition of possibility for liberal lifestyles in the modern period. The capacity to repair capital in light of catastrophic events is related to the capacity of populations to provide themselves with the means to recover and develop their way of life. Enabling the insurability of lives, property and capital is therefore at the core of the rationale to develop parametric insurance schemes, particularly to support emerging and developing economies in the face of catastrophic environmental events. However, there is still a long way to go to achieve any of these biopolitical effects, as the following example illustrates.

At the time of finishing this book, the effects of an earthquake measuring 7.0 on the Richter scale that took place in Haiti on 12 January 2010 are starting to emerge. Private insurance coverage in the country is practically non-existent, and although the country is part of the Caribbean Catastrophe Risk Insurance

Facility (CCRIF), which since 2007 has operated a parametric form of insurance, the country will receive less than $US8 million dollars, which is approximately 20 times the premium for coverage for this kind of event. All this money is in fact part of a wider scheme of development aid. The fee for access to the scheme, as well as the premiums for the first three years, were paid on Haiti's behalf through an International Development Association Grant from the World Bank. The cost of rebuilding the country will run into the hundreds of millions of US dollars, and much of the recovery will have to continue to come from international aid. With more than 78 per cent of its population living in poverty, according to the World Bank's threshold of poverty of $US2 per day, the lump sum received from the CCRIF will make no difference in repairing the capital represented in lives, infrastructure and capital lost in the earthquake. The livelihood of Haitians will remain mainly unaided.

As illustrated by this last example, the biopolitical outcome of creating entrepreneurial governments responsible for managing risks and fostering the creation of insured lifestyles is far from a reality. The biopolitical effects of the scheme will, of course, be different in Mexico, Ethiopia and Haiti because of the difference in levels of development. Whereas Mexico is one of the top 15 economies of the world and has developed significant expertise in biopolitical government, less developed countries will need to undergo significant processes of capacity building to achieve these biopolitical results. However, what remains clear in the cases and analysis offered in this chapter is that insurance is already a central technology of risk in enabling the provision of sovereign security in the twenty-first century. The analysis of such a form of security can no longer remain separated from the analysis of the political economic processes that make it possible. The potential biopolitical effects of public–private insurantial partnerships constitute a moving horizon for the interaction between sovereign and entrepreneurial forms of power.

5 Kidnap and ransom insurance[1]

Eight o'clock in the evening and Mrs Smith is anxiously waiting in her London house for her husband, who should be back from a business trip in a South American country. In half an hour they should be leaving to attend a concert at which their 12-year-old daughter will be giving her first orchestra performance. The telephone rings; it's the CEO of the mining company for which Mr Smith works as chief exploration officer. He tells Mrs Smith that there has been an unfortunate security incident and her husband has been abducted on his way to the airport in this South American country. He then adds, 'but you must not worry, the crisis management plan has been activated and the leader of our crisis management team is on its way to your house'. Minutes later, Mr Phillips, a hardened security consultant in his mid-40s and former SAS officer, arrives together with Mr Harris, the security manager of her husband's employer. The briefing begins by stating that Mr Smith is covered by a kidnap and ransom (K&R) insurance policy which forms part of the company's risk management strategy. The fees and costs of Mr Phillips and his team, at the service of a London-based 'priority crisis response' company which works in tandem with the insurer, are covered and their expert advice will be provided throughout the negotiation. Mr Phillips explains that from intelligence reports provided by his people on the ground this appears to be a 'conventional' case and that every measure will be taken to recover the victim unharmed. While shaking hands prior to departure he says, 'you're in good hands, our company has the best record in the safe retrieval of hostages in the business'.

Mrs Smith fears for her husband's economic and psychological welfare as well as that of herself and her family. She knows that a quick resolution of the crisis must be reached for them to continue their 'normal' life, and gains reassurance from the fact that her husband is covered by the K&R policy. This was news to her. She later learns that had her husband disclosed the existence of the policy it would have been rendered invalid by the insurer. There is also the legal aspect. Since her husband's company works in association with a state-owned corporation and under local laws purchasing and holding K&R policies is a crime, disclosure of the policy's existence could jeopardize the association. The government of this country considers that payment of ransom supports what they consider terrorist organizations. Any form of 'cooperation' from a state partner company would terminate the association contract and result in criminal proceedings. Mrs Smith is later also told that all communications with the press will be handled by the consultants for 'security purposes' and that all reimbursement of monies surrendered, all consequential expenses (recall expenses, lost earnings, legal and medical expenses), as well as all additional related costs (such as rewards, travel and accommodation, her husband's salary, the salaries of those who replace him, any personal financial losses resulting from his absence and the fees for the security guards that will look after her and the family while he returns) will be covered by the policy. However, her fears remain. How will her husband be physically and psychologically affected? Will he be traumatized for life? How is their daughter going to react? Will this be the end of a happy family life? The consultant team tells her there is nothing to fear; after all her husband is an *asset* that must be returned in good condition for the ransom to be paid. Post-traumatic counselling is also included in his policy.

Four days later Mrs Smith is presented with an international news brief stating that a British mining executive has been released from his abduction by a South American guerrilla organization in remarkably good health. The next morning Mr Smith lands at Heathrow Airport and while hugging his wife and daughter says: 'I'm back, *life goes on.*'

The story of Mr Smith and his abduction is based upon interviews conducted with families who underwent real kidnapping experiences in Colombia between 1998 and 2003. As a means for setting the problem, the story contains the central elements to present a form of insurance used to facilitate the operations of national and multinational corporations in hostile criminal environments around the world. Companies and groups of individuals use K&R insurance to 'let things happen' while they conduct their commercial enterprises. This instrument depicts a rather complex security apparatus involving the constitution of a K&R market, the deployment of expert knowledge in the form both of designing and operating the product and the provision of allied services. The apparatus, however, involves a very special biopolitical economy of values that results from the intersection between two distinctive forms of life: the life of kidnappable prospects and the life of kidnappers as organized criminals. These forms of life exercise two different kinds of entrepreneurial power which at the same time interact with the sovereign form of power of the states where the kidnapping events take place. At the centre of this security apparatus is the biopolitical effect of promoting and protecting a form of life whose value depends on its capacity to circulate, that is, in its capacity to generate a revenue for the employing company. However, as noted in the last section of this chapter, the security of this circulation is more complicated.

The chapter is organized in three sections. It begins by analysing the security apparatus of K&R insurance. It then moves on to interrogate the process through which K&R transforms uncertainty into an insurable risk and the biopolitics of value constituted in the process. Third, a reflection on the interaction between the forms of power interacting in the process and the role of K&R insurance in enabling the operation of a global economy is offered as conclusion.

The security apparatus of K&R insurance

There is no such thing as K&R insurance in nature. K&R policies are products; in fact, they are unique products which are tailored on demand and there is nothing natural about them. As François Ewald has wisely noted, 'there is no such thing as insurance in general. There are only insurance companies who are in competition with one another.'[2] The corollary of kidnap and ransom policies is kidnap risk. It is not natural either. Kidnap risk is an interpretation that results from problematizing kidnapping in terms of risk, a concept that renders reality in a particular way. Likewise, there are neither 'kidnapping prospects' nor 'kidnappers' in nature. There are only people who are speciated as specific populations with the purpose of promoting and protecting their capacity to circulate. K&R insurance, kidnap risk, kidnappers and kidnapping prospects all arise in relation to a way of problematizing reality in such a way that they constitute a security problematic for which responses are demanded: the problematic of kidnap risk.

Constituted as a security problematic, K&R insurance is presented as a sophisticated form of embracing kidnap risk that operates under a complex ensemble of technologies aimed at rendering kidnapping in as calculable a form as possible. This is done by enframing the practice of kidnapping within a calculable rationality premised upon the metrics of probabilities and expected impacts. Quantified kidnapping is then actuarialized, as the practice through which risk is transformed into probabilities is known. Actuarialized kidnapping can then be tackled through various mechanisms. A very effective one is K&R insurance, as the figures offered before demonstrate. But the problematization goes further, as the introductory story indicates: there is a particular kind of expertise mobilized around the practice of hostage recovery that becomes instrumental in constituting K&R insurance as a product. Such expertise is articulated through a deeper knowledge of the ways through which insurers identify the level of risk that potential clients bring to their insurantial pools. This is the world of risk analysis consultancy services and crisis response groups. Altogether, the problematization of kidnapping into kidnap risk, the constitution of kidnapping prospects and kidnappers as populations, the mobilization of a complex ensemble of expert knowledges and practices and the creation of a sophisticated product to respond to the problem constitute what Michel Foucault has referred to as a security *dispositif*, here used in its English translation as apparatus.[3] The security apparatus of kidnap risk is here analysed by looking at the micro-practices through which it proceeds.

According various experts in international protection services, by 2007 there were anything between 8000 and 10,000 kidnap and ransom situations globally on an annual basis. Private security services providers argued that by that year there were more than 15,000 cases a year.[4] The London-based Foreign Policy Centre estimated in 2001 that economic kidnapping was one of the fastest growing criminal industries in the world and that kidnappers globally generated a revenue of around $US500 million a year.[5] After the terrorist events of 9/11 applications for K&R insurance increased around 20 per cent as a result of heightened terrorism awareness. According to some reports, corporate policies ranged between

$US1500 and 5,000 a year for $US1 million of coverage.[6] Coverage of up to $US5 million could be arranged under certain circumstances.

The market for K&R insurance is ample and is under constant re-creation by the insurance–risk consultancy complex, which defines the problem in market terms. According to a ransom product manager at the Chubb Group, 'up to 80 percent of Fortune 500 companies had purchased K&R policies for their globetrotting executives by December 2003'.[7] An advertisement brochure from an insurer posted on the internet noted that '[m]ost kidnaps are carried out in order to obtain a ransom, and in most cases a ransom is paid. Rescues are rare, largely because the authorities in most countries recognize that the safety of the victim is paramount'. The brochure, aimed at senior executives at Fortune 500 companies, highlighted the added value of their product as the direct access to a world-leading security management consultancy. Another advert noted that the average death rate following a kidnap is 9 per cent (7 per cent are rescued, 15 per cent are released without payment, 2 per cent escape and 67 per cent are released following payment of a ransom).[8]

K&R insurance products are marketed as a necessary instrument for companies operating in environments of heighted criminal activity. As noted by various specialist risk consultancies, there are some crises that companies cannot manage on their own, whatever their size and resilience. Protecting employees and corporate assets from extortion, crime and political instability becomes an operational challenge for corporations doing business in highly volatile security environments. However, the geography and the motives of the problem are quite specific. As a consultant working in association with the AIG insurance group stated in 2007, '[d]espite the recent flurry of high profile kidnappings in the Middle East, Latin America continues to be the scene of more than 80% of all kidnaps for ransom and Colombia is still the dubious world leader with Mexico not far behind'. The main motive for kidnap remained profit.

> Even in Colombia, the kidnappers, who are traditionally highly-trained, well-organized pseudo-Marxist rebel groups, make no attempt to hide the fact their sole concern is profit. Recently, when a distraught family involved in a protracted hostage negotiation tried to determine the condition of the victim, they were promptly told, 'We are kidnappers, not murderers!'[9]

Kidnapping is also a significant problem in other regions, particularly Western Africa, the Middle East, India and Central Asia, and in most cases is related to multinational economic interests. Kidnapping in advanced liberal economies is also prominent. When a plan to abduct the youngest son of Tony Blair, then Britain's prime minister, was uncovered in 2006, it was widely advertised that 442 kidnaps had been reported in London alone in 2005, and throughout the United Kingdom the figure for 2004–05 was 2790 cases.[10] Indeed, K&R insurance can be traced back to 1932 when, following the kidnapping and murder of famed aviator Charles Lindbergh's son, Lloyd's underwriters brought the product to the scene.[11]

Kidnapping may itself be subdivided into different types, each operationalized and 'secured' against in different ways. Kidnapping for profit is different from political kidnapping, whose explicit purpose is to affect in some way or protest against governmental policies and decisions. Famous cases, such as those of 'Black September' of 1972 recreated by Spielberg in his film *Munich*, the 1996 hostage crisis at the Japanese Embassy in Lima, which ended with a police storming of the building, the Moscow theatre hostage-taking of 2002, in which gases where used in the recovery of the victims, and the Beslan school siege in North Ossetia in 2004, among others, have in common that they are perpetrated as a mechanism to exercise pressure against governmental policies or principles. This chapter is concerned solely with the analysis of kidnap for profit as described in the introductory story.

The first step in analysing this security apparatus is exploring how populations are created in the process of insuring, particularly the population of 'kidnapping prospects'. This population results from depicting kidnapping as an occupational hazard for those whose professional activities lead them to live or operate in a risky environment. Mr Smith, for example, is prone to being kidnapped owing to the nature of his job, which requires him to be where the mines are. A kidnapping event is, for Mr Smith, a professional risk that he needs to take. Such treatment, however, is not gratuitous. It results from considering the fact that the possibilities of a kidnap are highly probable and of a certain magnitude. As noted in previous chapters, risk is uncertainty made fungible, and uncertainty is made fungible because it matters for a particular purpose or form of life. For uncertainty to matter, and this is central to the processes through which risk is rendered tradable and exchangeable, it must be accounted for. The way to do this in relation to K&R insurance is by conducting a risk assessment exercise.[12] A risk assessment is a methodology intended to identify the different types of vulnerabilities of a company, an institution or an individual. Its results are later employed in the formulation of a risk management strategy. The results of these assessments are usually represented graphically, or plotted, in terms of the probability of occurrence of an event versus the impact such event would have over the affected interest. The plotting is then used to identify levels of risk upon which decision makers will have to opt for a risk aversion strategy, engage in a risk management one or decide on a risk-spreading mechanism.

A fundamental aspect of the risk assessment is the quality of information available. This relates also to the existence of specific knowledge in relation to the events being assessed, which may require some level of research. Access to existing information may involve, in some cases, ethical considerations arising out of engaging with actors, legal and illegal, who might possess knowledge about useful facts. Information on past records and historical cases is also central to the process. Knowledge developed through the analysis of cases is usually required, and experts are usually employed to provide it. Because information about particular events changes as events evolve, risk assessments become dynamic processes that demand the continuous engagement of analysts, consultants and decision-makers.

When results from the risk assessment indicate that there is a high probability of kidnapping for an individual or a corporation, protective measures will be needed to tackle the risk. There are three options: to avert the risk, to embrace it or to transfer it. Averting a kidnap would entail suspending operations and evacuating personnel. Usually, if the economic profit compensates for the price of engaging with the risk, this option is not considered. This is usually the case for mining and oil companies. If the decision is to stay, then kidnap risk must be embraced. The management of kidnap risk can include preventative measures such as guarding the anonymity of the company's agents in risky regions, attempting to make their movements unpredictable, providing them with physical protection such as armour and armed escorts, adopting a clear strategy to protect and filter information and imposing restrictions on non-essential travel. Reactive measures from medium to very high kidnap risk would most likely include some form of insurance, either self-insurance through the accumulation of cash to pay for a ransom and hostage recovery services, or K&R insurance policies as described before. Usually the process involves some form of crisis communications plans.

Kidnapping prospects are therefore the result of risk assessment exercises. It might, of course, be the case that all the officials of a multinational company operating in an area of heightened security risk are automatically considered as kidnappable. But even then the population identified as at risk of kidnap would have been constituted as the result of a risk assessment of some kind. Once the population has been identified, members of that population will be subject to the procedures and mechanisms mentioned above, that is, if the company decides to engage with the risk. Populations are here understood, of course, and in line with previous chapters, as a form of speciating individuals. Mr Smith, the chief exploration officer, is transformed into a subject of security premised upon the risk assessment that identified him as such. Mr Smith now belongs to a species of kidnappable prospects.

The speciation process of risk assessment is also related to the demand side of the kidnapping market. This is the side of the kidnappers as criminal organizations, or bandits, as many governments refer to them. Kidnapping organizations, as business actors within this equation, will be seizing opportunities arising from the geographical region or economic sector in which they specialize. To do this they would research their market to identify kidnapping prospects. They would do this based on open-source publications such as media and market reviews, on intelligence they can gather by means of infiltrating personnel within the circles in which the prospects interact, and by exploiting social, economic or cultural inequalities and grievances as a means to identify their victims. As the objective of this kidnapping activity is to generate profit, the potential value of the prospect has then to be established. If the potential victim appears to have enough money or is part of an organization that does, what follows is the implementation of well-rehearsed procedures leading to the capture: tracking the potential victim's movements, learning about his or her routines, getting to know as much as possible about the victim's family and friends, analysing his or spending habits and understanding the protective strategies that might have been put in place to deter a kidnap. A kidnap, when it occurs, it is no mere exploitation of chance; the kidnappers will have carefully chosen the day, hour and place, the people involved and weapons to be used. García Márquez vividly illustrated such procedures in his narrative of three simultaneous kidnappings in Colombia in 1990 (although such kidnappings were political).[13]

Both kidnappable prospects and kidnappers are subjects each of distinctive forms of life. Both of them are actors of forms of life devoted to profit-making. Both employ professional expertise and knowledge to make a living and to meet the economic objectives of the organizations of which they are part. Both are engaged in working to the best of their ability to promote and protect a form of life that provides them with the material resources for a particular lifestyle. However, the population of kidnappable prospects in this story is taken to be one engaged in legal economic practices and the population of kidnappers is taken to be engaged with an illegal practice. Whereas both forms of life exercise an entrepreneurial form of power to engage with risk and maximize economic benefit, one bases its business in transforming the life of kidnappable prospects into value that can be cashed in. The form of life of kidnappable prospects, on the other hand, does not depend only on being able to perform specific economic activities or provide the necessary knowledge for them. It depends heavily on the capacity to perform such activities or provide such knowledge at a given place and at a particular time. In other words, the form of life of the kidnappable prospect is defined by the availability of the subject in real time. If the availability of the subject is suspended, the actuality of that form of life is interrupted. If the kidnappable prospect is taken out of circulation and detained in its mobility, its value for the form of life of which he or she is part is affected. On the other hand, it is precisely the value of the kidnappable prospect as life in circulation that matters for the kidnapper. Getting the life of the kidnappable prospect out of economic circulation creates a negative effect in the organization that employs such a life. The value for the kidnapper is therefore related to retaining the capacity of putting that life back in circulation, keeping it alive and demonstrating its existence in order to obtain a ransom.

What the K&R insurance product promises to do is to repair the form of life of the kidnappable prospect whilst being taken out of circulation. It covers the salary of the prospect in order to protect the lifestyle of the family, but it also covers the expenses to be incurred in getting the life back in circulation, including the payment of the ransom. In so doing, the K&R policy promotes and protects the form of life that depends on the performance of the economic activity in which the kidnappable prospect is employed. It also enables the form of life of the kidnapper who depends on the availability of resources to buy back the circulation of the kidnappable prospect once the kidnap event has taken place. This constitutes the biopolitics of value involved in the K&R apparatus. Its theoretical implications will be further explored in the conclusions to this chapter.

Underwriting K&R insurance

Underwriting is the process by which an insurer analyses the levels of risk that an event related to a potential client would bring to the insurance company. Based on that level of risk, the cost of providing insurance against that event will be priced in the form of a premium. During the underwriting process, the insurer can decide if the risk is affordable to the company or if it exceeds its capacity. If such is the case, there might still be ways of insuring that risk by transferring part of it to a higher level of insurance by means of reinsurance treaties. Securitization of risks in the financial markets, as noted in Chapter 4, can also be considered. In any case, underwriting is traditionally done by means of correlating patterns of behaviour of the prospective client with records on the occurrence of the events to be insured against. These are analysed together with contingent circumstances affecting the policy. Underwriting, however, is not confined to documenting the contingent correlations of behaviour and statistics with levels of risk pre-established in actuarial tables. It is not a mechanical practice but plays an active and creative role in establishing levels of risk which overlap with the process of constituting populations at risk, such as kidnapping prospects.

An underwriter's objective is to select bad from good risks and opt for the latter if its company is to remain competitive within the business; a good risk is a low risk. However, as noted in the description of risks assessment above, risk discrimination is based on information, qualified information upon which decisions will be made. For the research leading to this chapter, I analysed 10 K&R insurance corporate application questionnaires. Central to the underwriting of K&R insurance are three major areas which will be analysed below: first, financial and management capacity; second, the type of operations undertaken by the client's line of business; and, third, the risk responsibility and risk management culture in place in the companies seeking to buy the product.

To determine their financial and management capacity, insurers ask potential clients to disclose their latest audited financial reports together with details of those responsible for its management. Companies are also asked to state the terms of coverage required and the deductible limits they are prepared to pay. This information is used to determine the solvency of potential clients as a means of assessing whether they can afford K&R policies, which are expensive products. The type and size of the company give an indication of the type of internal controls by which its management is held accountable (for example, bigger corporations are audited and held accountable by their shareholders and listed companies are subjected to additional forms of auditing). Answers to these questions are also taken to be indicative of the client's corporate responsibility, which is taken as indicative of responsible risk management.

Insurers are also concerned with the type of activities that a prospective client undertakes. Corporate application forms request detailed descriptions of the company's operations, specifying number of locations, number of employees assigned to them and their corresponding revenues. Information regarding foreign travel is particularly important and includes the position and number of people of travelling, the number of trips, the average length of stay, travelling, the means of transport and any security provisions in place. Underwriters understand that personnel based in fixed locations are at less risk than those who are constantly on the move. Travel to and within risky areas heightens the exposure to kidnapping, therefore a description of measures already in place to mitigate such risk is indicative of a responsible attitude towards risk management. By acquiring this kind of information, underwriters try to assess the level of 'moral hazard' that potential clients might represent. Moral hazard refers to the possibility that clients holding insurance policies might incur risks that they could prevent. In other words, moral hazard is the added risk that the behaviour of insured clients, intended as well as unintended, brings to the insurantial pool. Another risk that underwriters are attentive to prevent is that of 'adverse selection'. Adverse selection results from choosing clients who, because of the high level of risk they represent, are very likely to make claims. Collecting information at the maximum level of detail, especially in relation to the client's operations, contributes towards the minimizing of these two risks.

Third, insurers are concerned with assessing the potential client's understanding and management of its corporate security. A statement of the company's knowledge of 'higher than average risks' in the countries where it operates with regards to kidnapping, extortion, political instability or acts of terrorism is explicitly demanded. The information required goes as deep as requesting the disclosure of the company's security records and the outcomes of security events that could be related to the policy under application. For example, six of the forms I examined demanded the disclosure of kidnapping, extortion threats, cyber-extortion, hijacking, wrongful detention or political threats that had been discovered by the company in the past five years which could have been covered by an insurance policy. Itemized losses for each case were asked to be disclosed. The prospective client was also required to describe the risk management strategies that were already in place for the control of the identified risks. A direct question enquired about knowledge of facts or information that may have already given rise to a claim. By understanding the client's security culture, underwriters seek to learn about the company's security profile.

Finally, underwriters are concerned with learning about the potential client's strategies to protect their own and client's information and with seeking evidence of their good faith in previous contracts and activities. A request for the name of the person responsible for managing insurance plans and at times explicitly requiring the signature of the company's risk manager indicate the interest of insurers in making responsibilities as transparent as possible. This issue is of special importance in the case of K&R insurance as a disclosure of the possession of K&R cover might invalidate the policies.

The existence of a K&R policy, if made public, would motivate a kidnap demand inspired by the profit that could result from a kidnapping event. Tom Hargrove referred to this in his kidnap diary towards the end of his retention: '[k]idnapping [is] the deliberate creation and marketing of human grief, anguish and despair'.[14] Here is a dramatic example of what happens when information on K&R insurance holders is disclosed. As related by Vranckx based on Valencia,[15] between 1984 and 1989, 40 members of the Colombian Jewish community which held K&R insurance policies were kidnapped after factions of that country's guerrillas managed to infiltrate an agent amongst the insurance file-keepers.[16]

The fundamental condition for any form of insurance is the principle of utmost good faith, as demonstrated by a note included in most application forms reminding clients that concealing or providing false or inaccurate information will invalidate the policy. This fact constitutes a moral economy of which the three criteria used to collect information for the K&R insurance underwriting process noted above are part. When clients approach an insurer seeking to obtain K&R cover, they have to render themselves auditable in their behaviour and corporate structures. By opening themselves to scrutiny, transparency becomes a marker of good conduct used to certify their good faith. In a similar way, clients will approach insurers with a reputation that proves that they are capable of servicing the policies they sell. If an insurer is not willing to pay the ransom and provide the allied services included in the policy, the instrument of K&R insurance cannot be used to get the life of the kidnapped back in circulation. Even if the insurer can be taken to court to enforce the contract, it is the circulation of the kidnapped person that matters and clients would expect a quick and diligent response to a kidnap event. The moral economy on the part of the client is, of course, part of the wider process of auditability analysed at length by Power.[17] What remain relatively concealed, however, are the moral economies on the side of the K&R insurance complex, which involves not only the insurers, but also the practices of brokers and of the specialist service providers such as crisis response teams. Owing to the nature of the activities carried out by some of these services, it would not be practicable to expect a detailed account of what they do and how they do it. However, it would be expected that the effect of their practices would be felt at the level of their efficiency and how they are trusted by other service providers. If insurers and specialist K&R service providers had nothing to lose they would not be in the business of underwriting risks and repairing the consequences of kidnap events.

K&R insurance and the circulation of entrepreneurial populations

In previous chapters it has been shown how an entrepreneurial form of power has been exercised through insurance to resist the governmentalizing agency of sovereign power (Chapter 2), to assert the right of insurers to translate uncertainty into risk and trade in it even when it approaches the ethical boundaries of what are taken to be acceptable interventions in the idea of life (Chapter 3), and to entrepreneurialize the sovereign provision of security in the form of protection against environmental hazards in emerging and developing economies (Chapter 4). The exercise of entrepreneurial power at stake in this chapter, however, represents a different logic. K&R insurance, as a materialization of an entrepreneurial form of power, is created, serviced and deployed to operate in environments that escape the reach of sovereign security apparatuses. In a way, K&R insurance is devised to operate where sovereign security apparatuses of protection such as the police cannot. This area is not necessarily geographically circumscribed but it is more likely to be located in Mexico, Colombia, Iraq, Somalia, Nigeria and Eastern Europe than in London, New York and Berlin. Entrepreneurial power is employed to provide favourable conditions of operability for an enterprising form of life in places and circumstances that do not offer acceptable operational conditions.

A characteristic feature of this form of entrepreneurial security, however, is that it does not seek to ascribe itself the responsibility to protect that sovereign forms of security are charged with. Rather than replacing the state in providing an environment in which industry and enterprise can flourish, K&R insurance is used to manage a specific operational risk that might affect commercial or industrial operations in a given region. Although K&R insurance claims might trigger private military-type operations to ensure the recovery of a victim, these will never be in the form of sustained military efforts to recover for the state the monopoly of legitimate violence in a given territory. K&R insurance has been designed as a security to be employed whenever a risk assessment identifies kidnap as a realistic event in the course of operations in a given place.

The moral aspects of the very existence of K&R insurance cannot, of course, be forgotten. The use of K&R insurance has been presented since its introduction in the 1930s as an incentive for kidnapping. Some countries implement a strict policy of no negotiation with kidnappers. Others tolerate the use of K&R insurance but make it illegal to sell these products within the country. In reality, however, businesses have employed K&R to carry on with their operations around the world. As part of their operational costs, businesses exposed to hostile criminal environments involving the risk of kidnap have found ways of employing the instrument to protect their personnel and the security of their operations. On the other hand, the development of a market of K&R insurance also results in moral economies that protect against its excesses. Policies are expensive products that cannot be bought lightly. Insurers, protecting themselves from moral hazard and adverse selection, do their best to identify legitimate clients who will not increase the insurer's exposure to illegitimate claims. The secrecy surrounding the existence of the policies is in the interest not only of the insurer but also of the insured as K&R policies will repair only the financial damage deriving from the event. The psychological and emotional impact of a kidnap event will escape any form of quantification and will have lifelong effects on families, loved ones and colleagues.

K&R insurance highlights, however, an alternative moral aspect that helps to reveal the biopolitical dimension of the product and the practices that make it possible. K&R insurance is used to assign value to the potential of life to circulate, in a voluntary capacity, in relation to an economic activity. The price of a K&R insurance policy relates to the cost of getting a kidnapped person out of a criminal space and back in circulation in an area of ethically acceptable sovereign protection. However, the purpose of such policies is not just to recover the individual as a productive asset of a corporation, but to fulfil a corporate responsibility to protect those who work for the company. Indeed, it could be argued that a company's failure to provide K&R cover for employees exposed to kidnap risk could render employers liable for damages caused to a victim during a kidnap event. In this sense, K&R insurance policies would be the means by which employers protect themselves from accusations of exposing employees to an unsafe environment. Whatever the legal implications of this idea, what this represents is a curious interaction between an entrepreneurial form of power and the extension of a state's sovereign responsibility to protect the life, property and culture of an individual. In this respect, then, K&R insurance becomes a biopolitical instrument through which the form of life of an individual is promoted and protected beyond the geographical reach of traditional sovereign security apparatuses such as the police and the military. K&R insurance becomes yet another effect of the interaction between sovereign and entrepreneurial power highlighted in previous chapters.

In this respect, technical aspects described in this chapter, such as the corporate risk assessments and the insurance underwriting processes, acquire a deeper biopolitical dimension. Whereas merchants were challenged by the Church in the medieval Renaissance for trading in something that could not be demonstrated in its existence (uncertainty), both insurers and employers can now be charged for not having identified and taken action against risks that expose their employees to unacceptable danger. Just as the Church forced merchants to make evident the uncertainty they were trading in, the state and employees can expect employers and insurers to be able to demonstrate how risks were identified, prioritized, managed and priced. Because the entrepreneurial activity of employers and insurers has effects on the security of the lifestyles of employees and their dependants, instruments such as K&R insurance, in their design and operation, become sites of biopolitical significance from which to hold entrepreneurial forms of power accountable for the protection and promotion of life.

This introduces the controversial issue of judging the rightfulness of the price of insurance, which is intrinsically related to the value assigned to life by insurance practices. When actuaries sit down to design the stochastic models upon which to calculate the price of premiums for specific insurance products, and when underwriters collate information to identify the level of risk a client might bring to an insurantial pool, the last thing that might come to their mind is that they are putting a valuation on the lives of those covered by the policy. However, technical processes such as stochastic model design and underwriting procedures will have an impact upon the likelihood of getting an individual back in circulation when things go wrong. An accurate valuation of the price incurred in getting these individuals back in circulation might compromise the very possibility of recovering a victim. It would be reasonable to expect, then, that processes of this nature would be exposed to a degree of public scrutiny in the form of state regulatory action or some other form of public accountability, especially in societies where irresponsible risk-taking is increasingly seen as unacceptable behaviour. This would, however, open up the K&R insurance industry, a remarkably discreet one, and expose its market strategies, procedures and operations to a public which might not even be interested. After all, K&R insurance is an instrument to cope with an operational risk that employers should know how to handle.

Nonetheless, the usefulness of this instrument in enabling the operations of companies beyond areas protected by sovereign forms of security highlights another biopolitical effect. The use of K&R insurance helps to globalize a rationality of risk management as the Western way of coping with security phenomena. When the analysis of a security environment is made in terms not of threats but of risks, what is intrinsically entailed is that such situation can be rendered manageable by using professional tools and expertise to that purpose. Indeed, the economic success of risk consultancies operating around the world is premised on this very idea. A situation is not necessarily hostile. Situations can be managed through expert knowledge that is available at a price. Mining diamonds in Congo and ensuring the security of supply to Western markets entails not necessarily imposing a sovereign security environment in the region but employing the right kind of expertise based on the right kind of risk assessment and risk management, as well as risk-spreading strategies. Conducting petroleum-prospecting operations in Colombia might not require ensuring the capacity of the national government to exercise the sovereignty of the state in the totality of the country's territory. It involves, instead, a programmed risk management strategy that adapts to the shifting circumstances of the region where the company seeks to operate and managing the risks as they arise. K&R insurance is, of course, part of that strategy with all the considerations mentioned in the early parts of this chapter. Meanwhile, the exercise of sovereign power by states where these commercial enterprises take place carries on and, even if the security situation can be affected by the payment of ransoms through K&R policies, states profit from the foreign investment and knowledge transfer that is expected to result from these commercial operations. In the process, the knowledge transfer that derives from the implementation of risk management strategies of foreign, mainly Western, corporations operates an interaction with the security forces and the political structures of investment-recipient states which provides them with elements to understand how to operate risk management structures of their own. In so doing, the wider strategies that deploy K&R insurance as a security instrument contribute towards the globalization of a rationality of risk management in coping with adverse circumstances for entrepreneurial ventures.

Ascribing value to the circulatory capacity of life through K&R insurance instruments entails another element touched on in Chapter 4 and worth revisiting in light of the ideas noted here. It has to do with the possibility of a form of power rendering life 'bare' or raw. Does K&R insurance transform the lives of individuals into bare assets prone to be exchanged in a commercial transaction? If the quote from Tom Hargrove's kidnap diary noted before is to be taken seriously, does K&R insurance transform life into an asset and contribute to the 'deliberate creation and marketing of human grief, anguish and despair'? Would that human grief, anguish and despair be the result of having secured life in relation to its circulatory dimension? The answer would be yes, of course, as once the kidnappable prospect becomes a kidnapped individual his or her mere existence acquires a commercial dimension, the existence of a human asset to be traded for money. Does this context, then, constitute a situation whereby entrepreneurial power transforms human life into bare life? The debate moves beyond Agamben's original formulation of sovereign power utilizing biopolitical strategies to render life bare. It poses a question of entrepreneurial power having the capacity to reduce an individual's life to commercial value. What to do then with grief, anguish and despair? They have not been priced within the circulatory value of life that K&R

insurance apparatuses deal with. They do matter, however, for the non-circulating Mr Smith, for Mrs Smith and the children, as well as for loved ones and colleagues. So, what is to happen with human conditions such as grief, anguish and despair when they operate as the excess in the equation of valuing life in terms of the circulatory dimension of a body in relation to the capacity to generate value for a commercial enterprise? Human grief, anguish and despair, as Agamben and Hannah Arendt illustrated in various ways, have also been the remainder of sovereign interventions through biopolitical strategies. How is the valuation of the circulatory capacity of life that K&R insurance operate different from sovereign interventions?

The answer is perhaps to be found in the exploitation of feelings to market a life out of circulation. A human life is not an item to be warehoused but needs to be kept alive and shown in despair as a way of accelerating the payment of a ransom. In so doing captured life represents investment capital that is to be transformed into cash. However, capitalizing life is not a new phenomenon. The capitalization of life that results from the development and operation of life insurance instruments analysed in Chapter 2, an operation at the very core of the liberal capitalist society of many Western countries, also markets a form of economic circulation of life to transform it into present investment capacity. Whereas the kidnapping industry profits from getting a life out of circulation and charging a ransom for its return, life insurance exacerbates the already circulating life and uses it as a collateral security to access credit. The distinction that Marx made between exchange and use-value helps to clarify the difference. In the first case, the value of kidnapped life is that of a commodity to be exchanged for a particular sum of money. In the second, the life of insured lives is used to perform a role of promoting and protecting a specific lifestyle by enabling access to credit. Would life as a commodity then be life reduced to the price of its circulation and therefore stripped from its human conditions?

This leads back to the debate on the biopolitics of values mentioned before. If employers resort to the use of K&R insurance policies as part of their risk management strategies to operate in violent environments, and in a way they do so because they have a legal responsibility to provide their employees with a safe environment in which to work, employers together with insurers are exercising an entrepreneurial form of power to promote and protect the value that individuals represent to their enterprises. On the other hand, individual conditions expressed through feelings and affect that escape the pricing of the risks of life being taken out of commercial circulation are also valuable. The problem is that they cannot be quantified or 'valued' in the ways in which the risk of kidnap is. What is at stake, then, is a tension between two forms of life in the body of a single person. And this is indeed one of the curious characteristics of insurance operated on lives. Insurance products underwrite life in relation to events to be insured against, for which an insurable interest must be made evident to justify the investment. However, lives can be insured against multiple events in relation to various insurable interests which would be underwritten in different ways. The case of K&R insurance illustrates the case clearly. The insurer and employer are interested in the value of the life of Mr Smith in terms of his capacity to circulate. The loveable Mr Smith, his family and his friends value his life not only for his capacity to generate revenue for an employer and a family, but also for his human conditions. These values are however not insurable precisely because they cannot be made fungible, that is rendered in exchangeable and tradable form.

6 Insurance and the securitization of global maritime circulation[1]

On 6 August 2001, the Joint War Committee (JWC) of the Lloyd's Market Association (LMA), together with the War Risks Rating Committee (WRRC) – another LMA committee looking after the interest of cargo – announced a decision to include Sri Lanka in its circular of listed areas of heightened maritime risk related to war (the War List). The announcement followed an attack on 24 July 2001 on Colombo's Bandaranaike International Airport by the Liberation Tigers of Tamil Eelam. The attack resulted in the destruction of three airliners and eight military aircraft and damage to a further three aeroplanes with a total insured value of around $US576 million. This was not an isolated case. By the time of the attack, Sri Lanka, along with Iraq, Angola, Israel, Lebanon, Libya, Eritrea, Somalia, Congo, Sierra Leone and Yugoslavia, was already on the Lloyd's Market War Risk Trading Warranties list of countries posing heightened security risks for insurers. The JWC-WRRC decision, however, had as a consequence the imposition of war risk surcharges on all air and seaborne shipping to Sri Lana, which presented serious economic implications for the country. The additional war surcharge was payable by exporters/importers and led to a reduction in the traffic of vessels, increased freight rates, a reduction in container transhipment, uncompetitive exports and general economic compromise.[2] Owing to the gravity of the situation, Sri Lankan shipping agents asked their principals to inform marine underwriters that the additional premium was totally unjustifiable as the security of the port was not compromised by the attack on the airport.[3] The government of Sri Lanka made representations against the decision to the JWC in London on 11 August.[4] Six days later, a meeting between the Sri Lankan High Commission in London and the Lloyd's Market Association followed and a statement was made to the effect that 'rating improvements may become available to ship-owners in respect of vessels calling at Sri Lankan ports'.[5] That same day it was announced that 'the Sri Lankan government agreed to pay a bond of $US50 million against any claims that might be lodged for damage to vessels heading for or in Sri Lankan waters'.[6]

In October 2001, Pakistan was added to the JWC list. In this case, the committee decided to recommend surcharges on shipments to and from Pakistan because it feared that they could become targets of reprisals by Islamic radicals in the context of the recently launched War on Terror.[7] The Pakistani government made an immediate reply arguing that the extra charges were 'totally uncalled for and unjustified as Pakistan [was] not at war'.[8] The statement was followed by an announcement that government officials were seeking an urgent meeting with Lloyd's of London to ask its member firms to abstain from imposing loaded charges.[9] Presenting the United States as its ally, the government argued that, if anything, 'Pakistan's ships are safer than before because they [were] protected by the presence of US naval ships in the Arabian Gulf'.[10] Government officials also noted that even at the height of the 10-year Soviet occupation of Afghanistan, when Pakistani ports and airports were under imminent threat of being bombed, the country was never declared a war zone by the JWC.[11] Neil Smith, then chairman of the JWC, clarified that the circumstances of 9/11 had led to higher rates all around the world and that Pakistan was not an exception. He explained that after the September events Pakistan was categorized as needing 'trading warranties', which meant that 'shippers had to inform their underwriters of every cargo rather than relying on annual insurance cover'.[12] As a result of pressure from the Pakistani government, the JWC met with the Pakistani ambassador to London on 16 October and a resultant statement read that 'there [was] an understanding of each other's positions'.[13] Arguing Pakistan's economic reliance on exports, the minister of communications and railways of the country later announced that his government 'was thinking of giving a sovereign guarantee to all the ships visiting Pakistan'.[14]

A third notable case took place on 20 June 2005 when Singapore, together with the whole region of the Strait of Malacca, was added to the list.[15] Singapore's prime minister, Lee Hsien Loong, expressed his concerns to Lord Levene, chairman of Lloyd's of London, over the decision. Singapore's complaints where echoed by Indonesia and Malaysia. The committee responded that its decision was based on evidence of heightened piracy risk in the region.[16] Earlier that year, the International Maritime Bureau announced in its yearly report that 138 pirate attacks were recorded in the Malacca Strait in 2004.[17] This information was taken into consideration by a consultant providing expert information services to the committee who recommended that the whole region be included in the list. Following the littoral states' complaints, the chairman of the JWC attended a meeting with representatives from the maritime industry in Singapore and agreed that if alternative information proved the heightened risk assessment to be inaccurate such information could be taken into consideration to modify the committee's decision. The Singapore Maritime Foundation then commissioned a report by the London-based International Institute for Strategic Studies (IISS) on the threat of maritime terrorism in the Malacca Strait. The report suggested a global trend of falling piracy and, in particular, that the number of incidents in Malacca Strait was likely to fall despite the fact that pirates in that region were relatively better armed and organized.[18] The report was sent to the JWC for review in December 2005, although its findings did not affect the committee's decision.[19] However, on 2 August 2005, Indonesia, Malaysia and Singapore signed an agreement in Kuala Lumpur to expand their coordinated naval controls in the Strait by introducing air assets to the security scheme.[20] Within the scope of the agreement,

Malaysia conducted a network-centric warfare exercise on its exclusive economic zone with other littoral states using P4 ATM, a video and communication tool, to integrate the operations of 1,500 naval personnel and 1,000 airmen, 20 naval vessels and 25 fighter-jets.[21] As a consequence of these joint maritime operations, the JWC announced on 7 August 2006 that '[t]he Committee [was] now of the opinion that the evidence has shown that not only has the situation improved within the area, but the measures are long-term'. They will lead to resolving 'the long-standing security threat in the area'. Consequently, the Malacca Strait was removed from the list.[22]

The three cases described above illustrate a very particular role of insurance that affects the behaviour of sovereign states in relation to specific geopolitical security environments. As a committee representing the interests of hull marine underwriters in the Lloyd's marketplace, the JWC provides guidance to its members on what areas of the world represent a higher than normal security risk. Underwriters who sit on the committee are interested in advising members on how to balance a market of heightened security risks with higher than average insurance premiums. The aim of this service is to facilitate the profitable operation of a global marine insurance market; national interests are of no concern to members of the JWC. However, the committee's decisions could have negative economic consequences for the countries and regions involved. This results in the situation that the decisions of an economic actor, in its entrepreneurial role, have significant sovereign effects. These sovereign effects influence military decisions, as in the case of the littoral states of the Strait of Malacca, and financial effects, as noted in the cases of Sri Lanka and Pakistan.

However, and of great importance to the general argument of this book, the effects that decisions made at Lloyd's have on the behaviour of sovereign states result from an interaction between different forms of power. On the one hand, the entrepreneurial form of power exercised by Lloyd's is affected by the sovereign power of the British state. This happens in various forms, for example through competition law. On the other hand, the entrepreneurial power of Lloyd's can have geopolitical consequences affecting the exercise of sovereign power by states. This entrepreneurial–sovereign power interaction has a biopolitical effect that is in fact the security outcome that is the subject of this chapter. This effect is the securitization of global maritime circulation and relates directly to the form of life promoted and protected by marine insurance. Such a form of life, central to the operation of a global capitalist economy, depends to a great extent on the capacity of vessels to circulate the globe.

As will be explained later, the role that the JWC plays in relation to the promotion and protection of circulation in the high seas is analysed in this chapter as one of stewardship. Stewardship relates not to the allocation of rights to circulate or a territorial administration of waters but, rather, to the role of facilitating the circulation of vessels. Circulation in this sense is understood as a resource that enables the connectivity of various nodes within a highly complex networked economy. It becomes a condition of possibility for a capitalist economy in which, according to various sources, over 77 per cent of the total world trade measured in terms of volume is seaborne.[23] Circulation becomes, therefore, a central referent for the promotion and protection of a global capitalist economy that relies on the capacity to trade globally. In this capacity, circulation also becomes the central biopolitical security element for the analysis offered in this chapter.

The work presented in this chapter is divided into three parts. First, based on the cases already described, an analysis of the processes involved in the making of the War List is offered. Second, piracy is analysed in relation to the risk it poses to global circulation. Third, the stewardship role performed by the JWC to insure ocean space is discussed. Finally, the relationship between the stewardship role of the JWC is analysed in relation to entrepreneurial power, sovereignty and biopower.

The making of the list of the Joint War Committee at Lloyd's

The Joint War Committee has a history that goes back at least to the Second World War, although no public records are available to trace its evolution.[24] The committee comprises a group of underwriters from the Lloyd's Market Association (LMA) and members of the International Underwriting Association (IUA), who write marine policies in various parts of the world. Their remit is to analyse the 'war' risks associated with the hulls of vessels travelling the world and to produce a list to guide members on geographical regions that pose higher than normal levels of 'war' risks. War, however, is widely interpreted as a condition of heightened security risks related to social, political and economic unrest.

Insurance on vessels comprises policies on marine perils as well as separate policies covering war and related risks. In the case of the latter, the committee produces 'the list' officially entitled the Hull War, Strikes, Terrorism and Related Perils List. As a means to encompass the volatile nature of marine risks, underwriters on the JWC have established a mechanism whereby they can advise members on areas warranting higher than normal maritime premiums owing to their higher than normal security risks. The list is expected to encompass changes in levels of risk that will affect underwriting decisions and, although members are not obliged to follow the committee's advice, they regularly do so.[25] The geographical location of vessels and cargo, in relation to the security environment through which they circulate, affects the level of risk that a client's shipping represents to the insurer. The marine underwriter is therefore expected to match the right level of risk of a particular shipping venture with the right premium. The list becomes a source of trusted information for this purpose. Because changes in a particular security environment can affect the levels of risk for which policies are written, underwriters, following certain procedures, can at any time load policies based on the recommendations of the list. This has been the case for maritime policies covering shipping to Sri Lanka, Pakistan and the Strait of Malacca, as the examples noted in the introduction illustrate.

The compiling of the list, as will be elaborated below, is itself the result of negotiation in two major areas of conflict. The first is related to the governmentalization of the state noted by Foucault and referred to in previous chapters. The governmentalization of the state is a continued reassertion of the role of the state through, for example, methods of regulating markets. The second is a tension between competing commercial interests within the industry. These tensions become evident in discussions about the kind of information used for making JWC decisions and the providers of this information. As a way of dealing with this situation, the JWC sought a way of institutionalizing a system that would provide fairness and transparency in the eyes of regulators and objective professional advice in a competitive market environment. This led to the JWC in 2004 issuing an open invitation to tender to for independent professional consultancy and the provision of security information. Aegis Defence Services Ltd, a London-based consultancy firm, was selected.

Prior to the 2005 reform, the LMA had in place a process that allowed ‘general notices of cancellation’ to be issued whenever the list was published. The purpose of this instrument was to cancel all marine hull war policies currently in place, allowing for a seven-day expiration period, after which the policy cover would reattach automatically with the implications of the new list.[26] This procedure resulted from a previous agreement with the London Market Brokers Association (LMBA), which stipulated that the list had to be processed in exactly the right format and at exactly the right time. The advantage was that the new list would automatically apply to existing insurance contracts. However, because the Lloyd’s marketplace is under scrutiny in regards to competition law, the LMA’s legal advisers questioned whether that process was still legally acceptable under the new regulations.[27] The scheme was therefore examined and the following statement accompanied the list of 20 June 2005:

> The Joint War Committee has been reviewing the use of procedures in relation to amendments to war risk areas utilised on marine hull war risk contracts. As a result of these deliberations, and being cognisant of the legal and commercial aspects, the JWC has adopted the following approach:
>
> The JWC will, in conjunction with an independent third-party security consultant, publish, from time to time, a list of areas of perceived enhanced risk in relation to hull war, strikes, terrorism and related perils. Port, places and coasts which feature on the list will have been assessed by the independent consultants to exceed an enhanced risk benchmark established by them. This list will be published on the LMA and IUA websites and will be freely accessible to all.[28]

A central objective of the reform was to instil transparency in the process. As stated by Neil Smith, the fact that the information is published on the Internet allows anybody around the world to access it.[29] Whether or not the loaded premiums suggested in the list apply to a specific policy is a matter of negotiation between the client and the particular underwriter. The effect of the reform, however, was that under pressure from state regulation, in this case in the form of competition law, decisions from the JWC became governmentalized. However, such governmentalization does not imply state interference in the JWC’s decision-making processes. Its effect is directly related to guaranteeing market fairness within the industry, one of the cornerstones of a capitalist economy.

The second conflict, the tension between competing commercial interests within the industry, gave rise to the development of a knowledge regime premised upon independent professional security advice. Before 2005, the JWC would make decisions based on the information shared by members. As related by Smith, 'members sitting in the Committee would have their own private security analysts so whenever they came to the meetings they had already been briefed on the latest developments in terms of marine security worldwide'.[30] A member would request a report from its security advisor about a specific area or risk concern and then inform the committee on the outcome. However, as Smith also explained, such a scheme proved to be quite problematic.

> Since marine underwriters run an international business and are in competition with each other, members' involvement and interests in some places differed from each other and affected the global risk perceptions of the committee.
>
> This brought difficulties with regards to the ways in which members saw particular problems. Discussions about the local, regional, or global implications of certain facts depended on the involvement of members of the JWC in that area. The criticism that arose from this practice was that the committee was operating in a reactive mode and could only respond by including regions in the list once events had taken place. The process became very cumbersome and required a more solid procedure. The kind of information provided would also proceed from different sources and this made it difficult to compare like with like.[31]

These tensions were negotiated through the decision to hire the services of an independent advisor. A tender process was initiated in 2004 with the aim of awarding the contract to the security analysis provider best able to address the JWC's specific concerns.[32] According to Smith, all tendering companies had significant experience in various areas of the world and had developed expertise on specific risks by having worked in this area for various clients for a period of time. They were all well-established security consultancies selling information products to businesses around the globe. Such expertise was taken into consideration as part of the selection process.

When Aegis Defence Services Ltd was selected, it was charged with providing the committee with a regular updated listing of the areas it regarded as more volatile than others in terms of security risks. The company's knowledge was not only technical but supported by a range of senior expertise in the military and political sectors. According to the company's website, senior executives and non-executive staff in 2006 comprised high-profile individuals including retired officers of the British armed services, a British member of parliament and a former national security adviser to President Reagan in the United States.[33] Aegis's advice was reviewed by the committee to generate the updated list to be made publicly available on the LMA website.[34]

Part of Aegis's remit was to monitor the world on a daily basis and provide the JWC with specific information that could lead to accurate and timely underwriting of hull risks.[35] As part of the agreed methodology, Aegis was specifically charged with the responsibility for developing and implementing a risk assessment model. The aim of this model was to provide a system that would allow worldwide comparisons of risk levels, a common baseline for decision-making at committee level.[36]

The current model is expected to ensure transparency and provide a common neutral ground for the competing commercial interests of members of the industry. Based on the information provided through the model, the committee meets representatives of the consultancy firm on a quarterly basis to discuss the latest analysis on areas of concern. However, the contract allows for the possibility of meetings at short notice if an event affecting the soundness of the list arises.[37]

The 2005 reform of the knowledge base used by the JWC to configure the list can be interpreted as an attempt to legitimize the role of the committee as a fair and neutral entity seeking to enhance the soundness of the global maritime insurance industry worldwide. Its contribution comes in the form of advising members of the LMA and the IUA on guidelines to achieve the right premium for the right level of risk.

Decision-making within the committee is, however, the result of intense negotiations among members based on the evidence provided by the security consultancy. Because of the neutral nature of the committee, decisions must be reached by consensus. As put by its chairman:

> the List is not produced to make media headlines or to 'stir things up'. There is always a very tractable basis for decisions. Because it is politically sensitive and because the JWC knows that decisions affect the trade of countries, all efforts are done to assess the real risks as accurately as possible. We are in the business of supporting trade. We are not in the business of adding areas to the List unless it is particularly necessary. We have to go through a very robust sort of process which involves lots of discussion and negotiation within the Committee before decisions to add or even remove areas from the List.[38]

Decisions by the JWC have an immediate global reach owing to the networked nature of international trade. The impact, however, is also a complex one. Historically, the addition of an area to the list has resulted in local resentment because of the political, economic and social consequences that derive from this action. The list is a categorization of risks that causes people, governments and traders all kinds of difficulties. When an area is added, the local authorities will invariably suggest that the circumstances that led to the inclusion were misunderstood. Governments usually state that there is no such state of 'war' that would justify a heightened risk and that the committee lacks a local and regional understanding of the issues. This was indeed the situation with Sri Lanka, Pakistan and the littoral states of the Malacca Straits. The JWC replied to these comments by arguing that the strategic environment since 9/11 had shifted. War risks are not necessarily related to or caused by specific situations in one country but depend on a complex international system. The 2005 reform of the committee's decision-making process, as explained before, sought to deflect such criticisms by disclosing the evidence upon which the list is based. From an underwriting point of view, this pressure to conduct an evidence-based decision-making process has led underwriters to undertake much more risk analysis and obtain expert advice before offering quotes. It is no longer acceptable to offer standard rates until the regional security environment has been normalized.

In practice, as was the case of the inclusion of the Malacca Strait in the list, there was a consensual view that the increase in piracy posed a significantly enhanced risk that had to be charged for accordingly.[39] However, 'it was clear from the outset that criticism deriving from this decision would be received due to the strategic importance of this area for global and particularly Asian trade'.[40] Consequently, it did not come as a surprise that the littoral states implemented concert actions to cope with the fact that there was indeed a heightened security risk that affected the security of hulls and cargo. 'When the Committee was approached by government representatives the decision was comfortably explained because of the thought processes that the Committee and Aegis had gone through.'[41] When the IISS report commissioned by the littoral states to challenge the committee's decision was considered, it was judged irrelevant to the facts that led to the loading of premiums. It was only after coordinated governmental action was taken on the matter that a reduction in pirate attacks in the region was observed and the Strait was removed from the list.

'Piracy' as a risk for global circulation

The piracy events that led to the inclusion of the Strait of Malacca in the list are, however, a particular reading of the problem.[42] Piracy is a contested concept with different legal definitions and various social implications. Quantifying the risk of piracy is therefore controversial and depends on the definition of pirate events, how are they assessed, and for what purpose. Moreover, as a social and economic phenomenon, piracy is interconnected with certain criminal actions, and this can lead to more politicized interpretations of pirate events, for example as acts of terrorism.[43] Thus, presenting criminality in the Malacca Strait waters as piracy was not a politically neutral act. It was the result of encompassing the situation through a rationality that insurers are well experienced in dealing with: risk management. By assuming criminality in the Malacca waters as piracy, and by employing a risk management approach to understand its consequences for the insurance industry, insurers detailed piracy as a matter of heightened security risks that demanded a rise in premiums to match the circumstances.

Chapter 101 of the United Nations Convention on the Law of the Sea defines piracy as acts of violence or detention committed for private ends by the crew or passengers of a private ship, against another vessel, or against persons and property on board such vessels. Acts of piracy under this definition take place outside the jurisdiction of any state.[44] However, this definition escapes the operational requirements of the criminal environment of the Malacca Strait as all so-called pirate actions have taken place within the territorial waters of the littoral states. In this respect, criminal activities in these waters fall within these states' domestic law. To compensate for the shortfall in the legal definition, the International Maritime Bureau (IMB), a subsection of the International Chamber of Commerce's Commercial Crime Services, understands piracy as 'an act of boarding or attempting to board any ship with the intent to commit theft or any other crime and with the intent or capability to use force in the furtherance of that act'. The IMB has a Piracy Reporting Centre (PRC) based in Kuala Lumpur, where a record of all declared acts of piracy falling within this definition are kept. The PRC is a key piracy statistics provider and influences policy-making and insurance decision-making around the world. The decision by the JWC to include the region of the Strait of Malacca in its list was heavily influenced by PRC statistics.

The piracy that the PRC records, however, has a recent history.[45] It is not the romantic history of adventures and men wearing eye patches storming the high seas. According to Eklöf, piracy reappeared in the Malacca Strait region in the 1990s after having been all but extinct for over a century.[46] This re-emergence of criminal activity in this geostrategic chokepoint has posed a difficult political problem to the littoral governments, stretching their police and military capabilities to the limit. As Eklöf explained in relation to Indonesia, the situation is not easy.

> [W]ith a coastline twice as long as the circumference of the earth, and with no more than a few dozen operating vessels to patrol its territorial waters, there are a range of more important problems for the Indonesian navy and maritime police to tackle. Many of these, including the smuggling of people and goods, illegal fishing and degradation of the maritime environment due to human activity, have grown to alarming proportions in recent decades.[47]

Piracy as a phenomenon has been analysed from a criminological perspective by scholars such as Fréçon and Liss, who have investigated the how and why of the perpetrators.[48] 'It is, by and large, a sadly familiar and not very romantic story of socially and economically disadvantaged young men making the most of criminal opportunities in fast-changing and socially unstable regions.'[49] Contemporary piracy, as indeed could be argued for other forms of historical piracy, is an economic activity that seeks to deprive others of their property. Be it in the desert or on roads or sea lanes, criminologists constantly remind policy makers of the social nature of the problem.[50] However, criminal activity in the Malacca waters, because of the very geopolitical nature of the region, has been constituted into an international security concern.

With an annual transit rate of over 50,000 vessels, the Malacca Strait is a strategic maritime chokepoint that links the oil fields of the Middle East with the growing production economies of East Asia. As disruption of maritime circulation in this region would seriously affect the security of the whole Asia-Pacific, a militarization of the problem was initially explored. Since the 1990s Japan has favoured the creation of a multinational force to patrol the area. In 1999, Prime Minister Keizo Obuchi called for a regional coastguard body.[51] In late 2001 and early 2002, the US and Indian navies conducted joint anti-piracy exercises with some of the regional state's security forces.[52] In 2004, US Admiral Fargo, commander in chief of the US Pacific Command, revealed that the Pentagon 'was formulating a Regional Maritime Security Initiative to combat piracy, maritime terrorism and sea-trafficking in people and narcotics'.[53] Such an initiative was openly supported by Singapore but opposed by the governments of Malaysia and Indonesia, which argued that security was the responsibility of the coastal states.[54] Some forms of cooperation have been explored around the American initiative.

Military initiatives to jointly police the Malacca waters met considerable political resistance from the regional states. Issues of sovereignty and conflicts of economic and political interests in the exclusive economic zones made it increasingly difficult to reach an agreement on how to tackle the issue and, indeed, how to develop the regional military capabilities to face the challenge. However, in 2003, an alternative treatment of the issue began to emerge. Rather than approaching criminality in the Strait as a geopolitical problem, the issue began to be problematized as an issue of risk management. The conditions to facilitate such an approach were already present. As is normal in problematizations of this kind (see Chapter 5), it all began with the provision of reputable statistics. In October that year, the IMB's quarterly report highlighted a 'spate of attacks on small tankers by heavily armed pirates using fast craft as well as fishing vessels, and suggested that separatist rebels from the Free Aceh Movement (GAM) were often behind the attacks in the Malacca Strait'.[55]

> During February and March 2003, marauders armed with assault rifles attacked three chemical tankers in the Strait. In one case, they disabled the ship's radio, took the helm and apparently experimented with steering the vessel at various speeds. In another particularly serious incident in August 2003, pirates claiming membership of GAM attacked a fully laden oil tanker 19km from Port Klang in Malaysia, forcing the vessel into Indonesian waters and taking its captain and other crew members as hostages.[56]

In that same document, the IMB reported that attacks on ships in the Malacca Strait increased from 16 in 2002 to 28 in 2003. Attacks in the region that year accounted for roughly one-third of the worldwide total.[57]

A second element in the presentation of maritime crime in the Malacca Strait as piracy was an active process of securitization, in this particular case the profiling of piracy through political discourse.[58] The narrative of the problem was heavily circumscribed within the rhetoric of the War on Terror.[59] Later on it was further securitized as 'maritime terrorism'.[60] In October 2003, the defence minister of Singapore warned that terrorists might turn 'supertankers, LPG [liquid petroleum gas], LNG [liquid natural gas], or chemical carriers into floating bombs'.[61] Another Singaporean minister spoke about the 'almost military precision' of the attacks.[62] As always, such securitizations are not politically neutral. Statements by high-level Singaporean officials, as will be evident later, responded to an alignment of the city-state's security with the American interest in patrolling the area.

The third element in the problematization of the issue and its further securitization within the context of the wider War on Terror was related to technical authorization. In 2005, a report prepared by Aegis for the JWC stated that there was a potential close link between piracy in the Malacca region and terrorist activities. It argued that the modus operandi and weaponry employed resembled those by used by Islamist organizations in the area. 'Pirates in the Strait are now largely indistinguishable from terrorists in terms of tactics employed, as well as their potential to cause significant damage to shipping.'[63] It explicitly identified the Strait as a potential target for the Jemaah Islamiah, which had shown interest in Strait traffic. The report concluded that sinking or damaging vessels in this sea lane would seriously disrupt global maritime trade with significant economic and political consequences for the global economy.[64]

The Aegis report, supported by IMB statistics, provided sanctioned knowledge that could potentially be translated into the evidence required to defend the inclusion of the whole of the Malacca Strait region in the list, as indeed happened in June 2005. As noted in the previous section, the shift towards an evidence-based decision-making process supported by third-party authoritative knowledge contributed to the legitimization of the process in the eyes of competition law and rival insurers. The problematization of maritime crime as a piracy issue and its translation into an insurance issue allowed for the problem to be operated upon by the inclusion of the Malacca region in the list. It was therefore treated as a risk for global circulation, a risk that the stewardship role of the JWC, as will be explained below, could manage through its entrepreneurial form of power.

Insuring ocean space

> In postmodern capitalism, capital denies the existence of the sea as a distinct place or environment (even as its actual use of the sea continues to grow). The spatial ideology of postmodern capital is one of flexibility, speed, and global coverage, and the ocean has a special place within this spatial ideology as a seemingly friction-free surface across which capital can move without hindrance.[65]

The role of the JWC in securitizing maritime crime as a risk management problem should be analysed, it is suggested, within the context of a deeper security problematic: the security of global circulation. Circulation is here taken not simply as a descriptor for a flow; it is a 'quasi-transcendental' for life. This category is clearly opposed to a Kantian 'transcendental' that denotes a teleology of human nature,[66] a category of a teleological unity of reason that presupposes 'an organised totalisation of truths'.[67] A quasi-transcendental, instead, operates as an enabler for life that does not predetermine a destination or a horizon. It helps to describe an ongoing process that 'makes life possible'. Life is, of course, understood as a non-predetermined venture.

The circulation of global trade is one of the necessary conditions for the promotion and protection of a global capitalist economy. The security of circulation is in this respect a biopolitical category of analysis that helps understand the deployment of alternative security practices different from those of, for example, defence and diplomacy. This is precisely the case of the use of maritime insurance as a means to operationalize a problematization of piracy as a risk management challenge. Methodologically speaking, contemplating the security of circulation as a biopolitical category of analysis falls within what Michel Foucault called doing the 'history of the present'.[68]

The use of maritime insurance to securitize global maritime circulation is not fortuitous. Its usefulness relies on the fact that both insurance as a technology and circulation as a quasi-transcendental for liberal life are understood by resorting to spatio-temporal analysis. Insurance is a technology of risk that operates on spatio-temporal dimensions presented as *events*. Contrary to what the layperson might assume, insurance is a security technology that does not seek to securitize assets. Insurance operates on the security of events which are always interpreted *in relation to* insurable interests: that which is insured (see Chapter 2). These events are spatially and temporally enframed and their formulation demands precise descriptors as to what constitutes their location and time.[69]

The deployment of maritime insurance is therefore aimed at securing circulation as an *event*. The security of a hull is circumscribed to its function as mobile vessel for goods and people, but also as the depiction of a transportation service required for maritime trade. Any obstruction to maritime transport services constitutes an event of circulation (in)security. Inadvertently, then, the security of maritime circulation as event becomes the security of a quasi-transcendental of liberal life that materializes places and periods of time.

However, when insurance technologies are deployed to tackle the security of circulation in the ocean, ocean space cannot be taken for granted. If maritime insurance practices operate upon spatio-temporally defined events, then ocean space needs to be understood as a space for circulation. Of course, such a statement needs to be circumscribed to the operation of maritime insurance. It follows then that maritime insurance practices perform ocean space as a global security site. The ocean is the materialization of spaces of circulation. Ocean space becomes a biopolitical security site and the JWC plays an active securitizing role. This role, as will be explained later, is that of a global maritime stewardship.

The JWC has been successful in problematizing ocean space as a space for circulation prone to be managed through technologies of risk. This problematization entails an understanding of the ocean as a resource, a circulation resource. The ocean is taken to be a space that connects nodes within a global trading network. Indeed, according to the LMA, 77 per cent of global trade by volume is transported by sea. Hence, ensuring maritime circulation becomes a strategic imperative. What maritime insurance does through the services of the JWC is problematize ocean-space under a rationality of risk. According to such a rationale, any obstacle to maritime circulation will be subject to management through technologies of risk, in this case maritime insurance.

Steinberg, in *The Social Construction of the Ocean*, provided a ground-breaking analysis of different *constructions* of ocean space. He argued ‘that each period of capitalism, besides having a particular spatiality on land, has had a complementary – if often contrapuntal – spatiality at sea, with specific interest groups during each period promoting specific constructions of ocean-space’.[70] What he elaborated as the construction of ocean space is understood in this chapter as *problematizations* of ocean space. The difference is not only semantic but epistemological. Whereas a problematization seeks to make ‘facile gestures difficult’, a construction focuses on the actor–social agency relationship and aims at explaining phenomena as the result of intended actions. If the output of the latter is an object, the outcome of the former is a problem space. A problem space is here seen as the result of challenging the integrity of the social and the individual. The subject of forms of life is already a power/knowledge construct.

Steinberg argued that throughout the industrial capitalist era ‘the ocean was idealised as the antithesis of land-space’.[71] Based on classical and neoclassical doctrines of the period it was believed that ‘nations should seek power not by controlling trade but by wisely investing the resources for which they possessed a comparative advantage’.[72] If nations could trade freely amongst themselves, wealth and happiness would follow.[73] Ocean space was, then, idealized ‘as an empty transportation surface, beyond the space of social relations, and projection of power in the deep sea was perceived as legitimate only when applied toward the end of destroying obstacles to free navigation’.[74] ‘The sea was constructed, like money or markets, as without social “roots” – beyond society, politics or other “artificial” social constructs that could interfere with the “natural” free flow of capital’.[75]

The construction of ocean space changed in the post-industrial capitalist era. Steinberg provides some in-depth analysis of the context in which this happens, but his main point is that it is now *incessant circulation* what defines spaces of all kinds.[76] Speed is characteristic of this era.

> In their effort to identify, create, and satisfy new consumer identities in specific world-regions and in specific, globally dispersed social strata, enterprises have developed increasingly sophisticated transportation, communications and logistical systems for rapidly transmitting capital, information, components and products among far-flung production facilities and markets.[77]

As argued by him, this makes it difficult to accept ‘the great void idealisation of transportation/communication space as an asocial, formless surface traversed by goods and information, generated in the static places of “society” ’.[78] However, his thesis is that postmodern capitalism, ‘for all its outward differences from industrial capitalism, maintains a spatiality on land and on sea not unlike that of the industrial era'.[79] Places are important as locations for fixed investments. Movement of goods (and money and information) between these places is also important. To a greater degree than ever before, the speed of this movement is also important.[80] What has radically changed, however, is the degree of intensification in the identification of special spaces of stewardship, spaces suitable for 'systemic regulation but to be insulated from state appropriation and territorial enclosure'.[81] However, this chapter argues that another change to this process is the emergence of stewardship roles from non-state to non-international organization actors such as the JWC.

Marine stewardship is not a new security practice. In its contemporary form it is an application of the Roman understanding of the concept. As described by Steinberg:

> the Romans constructed the Mediterranean as a space within their sphere of influence, but they never deigned actually to claim it as the territory of the state. Indeed, they emphasised this distinction by governing the sea according to *jus gentium* (common law, or the law of the peoples) as opposed to Roman civil law, which applied only in the land-space of the empire.[82]
>
> In effect, Rome constructed the Mediterranean as a 'force-field', a placeless surface that belonged to no one but upon which powerful states could intervene so as to steward its resources for the national interest. Since the sea primarily was used as a surface for the movement of troops and goods, interventions in this space centred on ridding the space of pirates and other oppositional forces that could impede the flow of goods and people.[83]

The role of the JWC, as described in the cases provided in the first part of the chapter, is to perform a novel form of stewardship which securitizes ocean space as a circulation resource, a resource that enables the connectivity of various nodes within a highly complex networked capitalist economy. Building on Steinberg's insightful work, the suggestion of this chapter is that this is clearly not a construction of ocean space. It is a biopolitical problematization of spaces of circulation as a necessary condition for the liberal way of life. Such problematization provides the possibility for intervening in the promotion and protection of a liberal form of life.

The stewardship performed by the JWC is a site of interrogation for students of global politics. It adds to Steinberg's interpretation of contemporary stewardship under conditions of incessant circulation. In fact, the real conditions are more accurately described as exacerbated circulation that demands the provision of active and highly adaptive forms of security. Whereas Steinberg's postmodern marine stewardship concerns relate mainly to natural resources,[84] the role of the JWC illustrates an active role of stewardship in the securitization of global circulation through the problematization of ocean space as a circulation resource. The intricacies of this role and of the form of security it performs, however, exceed the aim of this chapter and will be the material for a later publication.

By definition, the insurance industry operates under conditions of uncertainty; a certain world would not require the development of insurance. For the JWC and its stakeholders, global insecurity in the seas is a challenge that means business. Insurance technologies, as noted throughout this book, have historically been developed to cope with the uncertainties related to specific activities and changes in forms of life. The re-emergence of piracy in the Malacca Strait in recent years does not pose a threat to insurers. Quite the contrary. It represents the possibility of developing better ways of affecting the environment and in so doing reducing the financial exposure of member companies.

It has been argued in this chapter that the role of the JWC is one of marine stewardship. This stewardship proceeds through a non-territorial securitization of ocean space. When the JWC included the Strait of Malacca in its list, it was not its intention to exercise sovereignty over the littoral states. Rather, the desired result was that the sovereign littoral states would effectively police and patrol their waters. This could, of course, be analysed as a conspiracy of the market upon the sovereign. However, the problem space that results from the role of the JWC is much more complicated and interesting than that.

The JWC's role as marine steward is giving away a complex reality. Liberal security practices exceed the state–legitimate violence complex. Security practices are not solely circumscribed to the national state. Security practices are not restricted to military and police operations. Private security practices are not the privilege of private military corporations. Liberal security practices, instead, are to be explored in the everyday technologies that make liberal life possible. Insurance is a case in point, and the same could be argued for any technology of risk. What is interesting, however, is that the conditions of possibility for liberal life exceed the rigid conditions of statehood established, for example, in the Montevideo Convention and, yet, the state as security provider is still required within a global political economy of risk management.

Security practices aimed at providing the security of global circulation are demanding the deployment of ever more complex security technologies. The degree of sophistication of these technologies is visible only through the effects they generate. For example, the fact that insurance achieved what the United States and Japan could not from a sovereign perspective indicates the relevance of conducting deeper studies into insurance practices. However, the analysis runs the 'risk' of becoming a study of the technological rationality under which, allegedly, insurance operates. The way out is to circumscribe insurance practices into a biopolitical security framework that immediately relates them to the study of the promotion and protection of a liberal way of life. Future work on the relationship between insurance and war will be required to further explore the biopolitical security outcome of the use of insurance in securitising global circulations. Such work will be the subject of a future volume.

7 Valuation–subjectivity–security

The cases presented in this book have documented and analysed how insurance practices ascribe value to 'life' and in so doing produce insurance instruments as securities to promote and protect ways of life. Historically, insurance techniques and practices have been deployed to develop instruments to secure lives characterized by the uncertain conditions under which they evolve. In this respect, insurance, as a technology, operates a valuation of life contingent on lifestyles and livelihoods.

An idea that is central to the ways in which insurance ascribes value to life and produce securities is that of uncertainty. Uncertainty has been here understood in the context of *events* related to the ways of life sought to be secured. However, the philosophy of the event involved in this process is not a single eventalness but a complex reflection that foregrounds temporality as an actant rather than a context. It brings a potentiality of life to a present of actualized life.[1] From this perspective, the conjuncture of time and space as events initiates dynamic relationalities rather than end states. In this context, a focus on events to be insured against helps problematize security in terms of the regulation of forms of life under continuous formation. Forms of life, as noted throughout the book, are emergent and should not be taken for granted as givens of preformed subjects and preformed objects of security. They operate instead as referents of promotion and protection.

Uncertainty in relation to evental life-forms is mediated through conceptions of risk. Risk, however, results from the different strategies through which the need to secure a form of life is framed. Risk becomes an ethos that allows the transformation of uncertainty into matter amenable to trade and exchange. The performative role of the event is, then, to effect a valuation of the potentiality of life into fungible uncertainty as risk. Risk is therefore presented as a commodification of contingency expressed as a valuation of life. This commodification is enabled through various strategies, one of them being the mathematized probabilization of events, which always leaves a level of indeterminacy as the open opportunity for chance. But the commodification of contingency precedes and also goes beyond the limits of probabilities and involves all sorts of legal and financial manoeuvres that enable technologies of insurance to operate. Instead of focusing on an outcome or a plan, a principle or a cause,[2] resorting to risk continuously opens up the possibility for developing political economies of security. The notion of risk as ethos and risk as technique on which this book has been written is deeply indebted to the central notion of event.

Insurance–security–temporality

A main feature of the political economy of security opened up by this notion of risk is the creation of an infinite market for and of security instruments and strategies. By means of insuring against events, insurance actualizes life in the form of a continuous present. The production of this contingent time through the interaction of multiple forms of power performs a teleology of security in which individuals and their lifestyles will never be secured enough. This teleology operates an asymptotic logic. Following the metaphor of this geometrical concept, whereby a curve strives to meet the axis infinitely but will never reach it, life and lifestyles will always be in demand of novel forms of insurantial protection. The higher the revenue produced by a life, the more capital there will be in need of protection. The more an individual earns, the higher the cost of promoting and protecting a lifestyle. Because of the cumulative logic of capitalist lifestyles, capitalist lives will always be in demand of higher insurance and lifestyles will never be insured enough. The intermediation between such demands for security and the provision of instruments and strategies to provide it constitutes, in the process, political economies of security.

The possibility for developing political economies of security through the commodification of contingency, together with the teleological character of insurance, constitutes the context in which insurance instruments and practices become biopolitical security effects. As effects, insurance instruments and practices are produced and performed by insurers, which exercise power in the expectation of generating a profit. As noted throughout the book, this form of power has been described as entrepreneurial. In very specific expressions which will be detailed later, this entrepreneurial form of power, in interaction with traditional sovereign expressions of power such as the rule of law, has been employed in ascribing value to life and making it fungible as risk.

A central moment for the insurantial ascription of value to life can be understood as that of vital valuation. In any form of insurance there is a moment in which insurers operate a classification of lives and lifestyles. Any form of insurance involves the constitution of risk pools, which are used to determine the price of risk. Risk pools are the result of identifying particular features of clients or groups of individuals in relation to the level of risk they represent to the insurer with regards to an insurable event. The constitution of risk pools involves risk assessments which engage individual decision-making and mechanical procedures employing stochastic models. However, and here lies the fundamental biopolitical effect of insurance underwriting, every process of valuation through risk assessment involves making decisions on what to consider valuable or invaluable life. When landless gentlemen were accepted to an insurance pool in mid-eighteenth-century Britain, not only did they access an instrument with which to collateralize a debt and protect their lifestyle and that of their families in case of death, but they also got a certification of the value of their lives. Their lives were valued on their capacity to continue to generate an income within a given period of time. Valuable lives were insurable lives. The value of the lives of those who, owing to ill-health or character traits, were considered to be unable to continue to generate revenue was a non-value that translated into uninsurable life. Another case in point is provided in Chapter 3. When insurers in Britain in the early twenty-first century and at the peak of a wave of hype about genetic determinism were challenged on the potential use of genetic information for life and health underwriting, what was at stake was the very possibility of assessing the value of life on 'objective' markers. Although it became clear that genetic information was not relevant for underwriting practices, the simple idea that underwriting genes could lead to an uninsurable genetic underclass was enough to mobilize a whole semiregulatory state apparatus. The fear that the biopolitical effect of insurers using genetic information would equate to excluding individuals from insurance cover, understood already as a necessary condition for liberal life, highlights the popular understanding of insurance as a technology that can render life as valuable or invaluable.

However, and contrary to a public imaginary, life rendered uninsurable through risk assessments is not invaluable life. On the contrary, uninsured lives represent a condition of possibility for insurance practice. What exceeds processes of risk classification, or the remainder of risk assessments, plays two particular roles. On the one hand, it becomes the frontier towards which insurance can expand in its quest to render the uninsurable insurable. It becomes the frontier of the incalculable, which could be seen as catastrophic, as noted in Chapter 4, where insurantial and financial innovation can be developed in order to transform the uncertain into an opportunity for profit. On the other hand, the invaluable becomes the space of resistance to specific forms of insurantial security. That which has been excluded from insurance cover nonetheless depicts a vital circulation which is an expression of life and could potentially be insured. The claim of the Multiple Sclerosis Society noted in Chapter 3 in relation to the insurability of the lives of its members illustrates the point. It was a claim for the development of more creative forms of underwriting to encompass the heterogeneity and complexity of life and rejected a standard tradition of underwriting. The process of vital valuation is therefore not a sovereign exclusionary practice but the result of the insurantial imaginary that employs an entrepreneurial form of power capable of developing the conditions of possibility for an ever-growing insurance market.

What needs to be challenged, then, is the rationality through which life is classified as valuable or invaluable. It is so in relation to a utilitarian perspective that anchors the capacity of a life to generate revenue with the possibility of owning property, accessing credit and investing capital. There is nothing natural about that rationality, and it is the result of a history of a liberal–capitalist tradition of accumulation, of liberal governance and of liberal societies. It is a powerful and influential rationality that, at the risk of making a gross generalization, constitutes a liberal way of life. But it is not the only way of life, and the fact that nearly 80 per cent of the world's population remains uninsured, as noted in the introduction to the book, proves the point. There is, however, something quite particular that helps understand why the liberal rationality of insurance has been so pervasive within the Western world and why it has been so successful in its interaction with sovereign forms of power. Processes of valuation on which insurantial risk assessments rely operate a curious and widely under-researched aspect of the constitution of individual subjectivity. The individual whose life is being insured in relation to an event, or the form of life which is sought to be promoted and protected in relation to a given scenario, does not assume the individual as a totality or a permanent whole. An individual can be simultaneously assessed for various types of risks and be assigned to differing levels of risks in each case. This is what will be analysed in the closure of these conclusions, as the multiple/simultaneous subjectivities of insurance.

Insurance as a biopolitical effect

As noted throughout the book, insurance products are biopolitical effects that result from the interaction between sovereign and entrepreneurial forms of power. This interaction, although productive, is constantly haunted by governmentalizing attempts to bring insurance and insurers under the strict regulation of states. Insurers have historically resisted these processes, and although cohabitation seems to be possible, as in the case of insurance against catastrophic environmental events, and also in cases not discussed in this book, such as motor and employer's liability insurance, insurers have always claimed and fought for their right to underwrite. Central to this tense, but fruitful, interaction have been aspects of knowledge and knowledge provision, as well as administrative and legal structures that deserve some attention.

Insurers, in their quest for profit, have always been quick to explore forms of knowledge that will enable the valuation of lives. Be it in the form of the knowledge supporting legal resources in the rudimentary and complex forms of third-party contracts, in the adoption of systems of calculation and ways of assessing probabilities, in exploring opportunities deriving from the life sciences and research on the human genome, in learning about the opportunities for profit in the context of climate change, in the demands for protection against operational security risks in emerging and developing economies, as well as in expert knowledge in relation to issues of piracy in the world seas, insurers have adopted, developed or produced specific forms of knowledge to support their trade. In some cases, this knowledge has emerged out of rationalities of government such as that of 'political arithmetick' in the seventeenth and eighteenth centuries in Britain. In others, it has been adopted from academic or private intellectual developments funded by states, individuals or the private sector. Regardless of the origin of such knowledge, insurers have displayed an incredible capacity to absorb whatever evidence might be useful to refine their underwriting processes in order to expand the horizon of insurability. Cases such as the one analysed in Chapter 3 in relation to the use of predictive genetic testing for insurance products highlight the intense interaction between the use of accepted forms of knowledge in insurance decisions that can have significant social and political effects. Although pressure for state regulation in such cases has been strong, insurers have been cautious in warning against knowledge hypes that might affect the way in which they provide everyday security for individuals and collectivities.

A second front on which sovereign and entrepreneurial depictions of power have been in constant interaction is that of the legal and administrative structures required for the operation of an insurance market. As insurance policies are contracts enforceable by law, insurers always require some form of legal system to be able to conduct their operations. As simple as this might appear, however, this relationship highlights an overlapping of a traditional sovereign form of security, the rule of law, with an entrepreneurial form of security, insurance. Although the form of security provided by insurance is private in nature, its effects are public, and looking at how these two forms of power interact to produce security instruments as biopolitical effects allows for an investigation of the blurring of the traditional public–private divide so prominent within political theory, as well as economic and security studies. The case noted in Chapter 4 of insuring against levels of rain in Ethiopia through a complex international public–private arrangement is a case in point. The scheme involved employing a new form of underwriting originally developed for insuring against environmental hazard in the United States, adapting it to the case of insuring against parameters of rain in a developing country in order to protect the livelihood of small-scale farmers, enabling an insurance role for the Ethiopian government through the role of an agency of the United Nations, developing a strategy of risk transfer through a global reinsurer, which then required the securitization of risk in the financial markets. Separating the public from the private in such schemes not only ceases to make sense but is also an impossible venture.

In relation to the knowledge base and the administrative and legal structures through which sovereign/entrepreneurial forms of power interact in producing insurance, the role of expertise is also being transformed. In an age of calculations, but also in an age of creative calculations on how to consider something as an event to be insured against, expertise contributes to further denaturalize the private–public divide. As evidenced in the last four chapters of the book the provision of expertise for generating and underwriting insurance products is not academically disciplined. Neither does it necessarily follow the knowledge-base of traditional professions. It operates instead as bricolage, as an art of creatively combining available bits of knowledge taken from any necessary source, and putting it to work in relation to a specific problem. The emergence of security consultancies employed in the underwriting of special risks such as kidnap and ransom insurance, the use of specialized firms to provide authoritative knowledge on maritime security to the Joint War Committee of the Lloyd's Market Association, the creation of new specialized figures such the nominated genetic underwriter in the British life insurance industry, and the invention of the role of the embedded chief risk officer by Swiss Re to liaise between local governments and insurers in dealing with environmental hazards, are just an illustration of these new ensembles of expertise. The new roles, although in many cases performed by experienced underwriters or defence professionals, are characterized by the emerging requirements of practices of risk management. Risk management, as the practice of securing emerging forms of life, demands a great degree of flexibility from these professionals in encompassing new empirical and theoretical findings generated by private and public institutions on how individuals relate to themselves, to each other, to nature and to institutions such as the state and markets. Perhaps best characterized as useful knowledge, the expertise of security professionals is put to the service of state administrative structures and of insurance underwriters to ensure a fruitful interaction between sovereign and entrepreneurial power. When, for example, the state demands from insurers to reveal the evidence base on which insurantial decisions with clear social and political effects are made, as in the case of predictive genetic testing in Britain, and when insurers demand that the state adapt its legal and administrative structures to enable novel insurance–government partnerships to operate, as in the case of earthquake insurance in Mexico, a bricolage of knowledge is employed in providing alternative strategies or solutions to the problems. Expertise in this age of creative calculations is therefore attuned with what Foucault referred to as a logic of strategy, not as prescriptive planning, but as an art of contingent combinations.[3]

Analysing insurantial security by looking at how sovereign and entrepreneurial forms of power interact does matter a great deal when researching the ways in which life and forms of life are secured. It moves the emphasis away from the juridical which restrains the analysis to legal forms and legal orders, both domestic and international. It moves away from realist accounts of security that focus on the projection of power by state entities in the form of the military, diplomatic services, international organizations and lobby groups. It also moves away from traditional international political economy perspectives that focus on state restrictions to trade, the role of states coordinating economic processes and labour relations, and conditions of oppression in economic systems. Instead, it opens up the possibility of thinking insurance politically, as a security problem that brings together the sovereign, the juridical, the economical and the social. Although insurance operates in relation to forms of life, the question for insurance is not what forms of life it promotes and protects, but what happens in the process of doing so. This is the question that has supported the different chapters of the book.

Securing multiple/simultaneous subjectivities beyond the bareness of life

By looking at the cases explored in this book, it is possible to recognize differences in the subjectivities that result from traditional sovereign exercises of power from those that result from the interactions of entrepreneurial and sovereign power in the form of insurance. For example, although it is fundamentally important for states to *identify* individuals by a name, a nationality, a domicile, an economic activity, an ethnic origin, amongst other categories, for insurers all these aspects become relevant only in so far as they help classify the level of risk a client represents. Although the subjectivity of an individual in relation to the state is circumscribed to categories such as that of a citizen, the subjectivity of the individual with regards to insurance can be multiple and simultaneous. For example, a female aged 62 years may represent a very low level of risk for motor insurance because of her age group, postcode and type of car; a relatively high level of risk for health insurers owing to a family history of breast cancer; a relatively low level of risk for home contents insurance because of her postcode and a history of no claims; and a heightened level of risk for travel insurance because of her skiing holidays. She remains a single individual, but insurers will provide her with securities in relation to the four different events against which she is being insured.

Although the subject of security for the sovereign appears to be monolithic, the subject of security for the insurer remains a multiplicity of combinations, a pluripotential complex suitable to simultaneous and multifarious forms of underwriting. The sovereign identifies the individual in the singularity of its body (e.g. date and place of birth, body measurements, abnormalities) as well as through its activities (e.g. occupation/profession, driving and travel histories, income and expenditure records, recorded actions). The insurer, in contrast, identifies the individual in relation to the events against which he or she is being insured. Although the biopolitical categories through which sovereign powers constitute populations matter, other criteria will also be considered (e.g. health history, family health history, use of drugs, drinking and smoking habits, credit risk records, history of past insurance claims, performance of dangerous activities). Insurers, in summary, are interested in any information on the life of the client relevant to the event to be insured against. The effect of insurance on the individual will relate specifically to the form of circulation being insured and will not have totalizing effects such as incarceration of the body. The 62-year-old woman mentioned above might be denied health cover because of a heightened level of breast cancer risk, but she will very likely remain insurable for motor activities. This client will be subjectified in different simultaneous forms and her way of life will be affected in various ways by the moral economies that result from insurance practices.

Traditional sovereign security practices have difficulties adapting to the fact that individuals might resist identification and monolithic subjectification – take, for example, the case of citizens with dual nationality or of multiple or modified gender. Although these abnormalities in the categories of sovereign identification become problematic for the state, people in such circumstances are still individuals whose lives can be insurantially valued. In this respect, the way in which insurers operate subjectivities contrasts with the sovereign idea of identity analysed by Connolly as established in relation to differences fixed and regulated through sovereign security apparatuses.[4] The subjectivity that results from insurance practices corresponds more to the Nietzschean hypothesis of facing the subject as a multiple entity: the subject as multiplicity.[5] Whereas sovereign actors contribute to the constitution of singular identities and their security depends on their capacity to subjectify identified individuals, insurers contribute to the identification of the individual's complex intersubjectivities and profit from providing the securities through which simultaneous expressions of being can be promoted and protected. Whereas states pursue an agenda for securing the identification of individuals through biometrics, insurers continue to speciate individual lives as multiple subjectivities expressed in terms of levels of risk in relation to multiple insurable events.

In both cases there is a biopolitical effect, the promotion and protection of life through the subjectification of the individual, in either singular or multiple ways. As simple as this phenomenon might appear, however, its analysis marks a difference in the ways in which security has been traditionally studied. If biopolitical securities are to be understood in relation to the function they perform and the ways of life they are designed to promote and protect, it is necessary to transcend the study of linear cause–effect relations and concentrate on analysing the logics of strategy. This implies a clear move from the transcendental idea of an 'object' of security towards an emphasis on the 'referent' to be promoted and protected. Such referent, as constantly emergent, is therefore defined not by fixed observable features which can be traced back in history or explained through sanctioned forms of knowledge, but by its pluripotent and heterogeneous character.

It is this pluripotent and heterogeneous uncertain character of life which resists any form of theorization as 'bare'. Although ways of depicting life and forms of life are always biopolitical effects, biopolitical effects are not the logical result of the agency of preformed political bodies such as a sovereign. The inscription of value into life, the classification of life as valuable or invaluable as a result of its insurability and the production of securities through the capitalization of life subjectify individuals in relation to their circulations and not on some natural necessary basis. The distinction that Agamben made between *bios* and *zoe* in order to conduct a politico-juridical analysis of the political character of life falls short of providing elements for understanding how the securitization of life in the modern period became a function of processes of capitalization. More importantly, it fails to consider that life can always be depicted otherwise and that the multiple subjectivities that Nietzsche hinted at become at the same time sites for subjectification of the individual as well as sites of resistance to unidirectional sovereign designs. What unfolds from the analysis offered in this book is that there is no sovereign, but only governmentalizing practices; that there is no entrepreneurial, but only practices of capitalization; and that there is no life and no preformed ways of life, but only emerging ways of being in the world. If this is so, then it is possible to suggest that there is no such thing as 'the inclusion of bare life in the political realm [constituting] the original – if concealed – nucleus of sovereign power'.[6] It is also possible to suggest that that 'the production of a biopolitical body' is not 'the original activity of sovereign power',[7] simply because there is no resulting biopolitical body but forms of subjectification. The nucleus of sovereign power referred to by Agamben will remain within his own politico-juridical analysis. In the analysis offered in this book, sovereign power is a function of governmentalizing practices that interact with entrepreneurial processes of capitalization in relation to emergent forms of life. There is no origin from which to fix and regulate identities *in* life, but power practices through which value is ascribed *to* life. Security is the ultimate expected effect. But security is asymptotic.

Moral economies as the entrepreneurial effects of insurance

A curious, and usually ignored phenomenon at the core of the operation of insurance practices is that of confession. As noted in various chapters, individuals or entities seeking insurance are expected to reveal to the best of their knowledge any information that might affect the assessment of their level of risk. Indeed, and without wishing to intervene in issues of law, insurers operate on the principle of utmost good faith. Apart from a legal precept, utmost good faith enshrines a moral imperative, but, most interestingly for this book, its implementation affects the conduct of individuals and collectivities. Trust between insurer and insured is a fundamental value, in fact a condition of possibility of insurance relations. When clients complete questionnaires or reply to questions formulated during the underwriting process, they are reminded that any false or concealed information might invalidate the policy. When clients make a claim, the insurer will try to verify the validity of the claim against the information provided by the client when the policy was issued. Insurers argue that if false or incomplete information was provided by the client, the event to be insured against was not exactly the one for which the policy was issued. If the level of risk does not correspond to the price noted in the policy, and if this discrepancy relates to inaccurate information instead of actuarial mistake, then the policy does not cover the contingency insured as an event. This relates to the problem discussed in Chapter 1 in relation to the liceity of insuring against uncertain events and which continues to constitute a foundation for contemporary insurance. If the event against which insurance is being offered cannot be made evident (see Chapters 2–5), then insurance is either a way of gambling or a form of usury and both of them are prescribed as sins by the Church and legislated against in various modern legal systems. If the policy – as the insurance contract – is accurate in describing the event against insurance is being bought, by specifying the contingency, the period of cover and the specific conditions of the clients, then that policy is transforming uncertainty into risk. When uncertainty is rendered as risk it is being made fungible and therefore amenable to trade and exchange. Whatever resources are employed in defining and calculating the risk, insurers will always seek to prevent adverse selection, risks which will probably result in claims not compensated for in the price of the premium, and moral hazard, the failure to anticipate adverse behaviours by clients.

Confession traditionally relates to the Christian practice of admission of one's guilt in front of God, either directly or through an intermediary. It takes the form of a practice between a confessor and a priest, a confessor and a congregation or a confessor in direct communication with God. Whereas this form of confession results from an internal examination of one's own conscience and performs a role of individual repentance, the form of confession that takes place through the process of insurance underwriting is slightly different. For a start, clients are not obliged to buy insurance – except in the cases of motor and employer liability compulsory in some countries. When clients approach an insurer, they do so seeking to obtain a form of financial protection in relation to specific events. In that capacity, and if acting in utmost good faith, clients will help insurers by providing the necessary information for an accurate calculation of risks. It would, in principle, be in the interest of the client and the insurer to match information with risk and agree on the right price. In a market environment, however, the right price would also depend on economies of scale, efficiencies and the entrepreneurial creativity of insurers and clients. An insurer might be in a position of offering a better quote to a client because of its own market position. In any case, clients are free to shop around the insurance market to find an acceptable quote.

The second difference lies in the fact that clients do not admit guilt to insurers but reveal facts that can be transformed into information to be used in the underwriting process. There is no fault in admitting one's propensity to a particular disease based on a family history. There is no guilt involved in revealing one's professional activity and place of work. The fault in the relationship, and it is a fault to the principle of utmost good faith, is the concealment of information that can be useful in assessing a level of risk. However, not declaring information that one is not aware of is not a fault, for example not declaring a family history of a particular disease that one learns about only after the event has materialized. This idea is linked to the relational character of insurance. It can be argued than any insurance policy is an agreement between two parties supported by the principle of mutual trust. If either of the parties conceals relevant information from the other party, there is no insurance *relationship*. This is particularly important in as much as it is the relationship that will enter into force in case of a claim. What insurers do in the process of claims adjustment that follows a claim is first to determine if there is any fault on the part the client in failing to reveal information relevant to the event insured against. They then assess if the materialization of the event had anything to do with the unacceptable behaviour on the part of the client. If there is evidence of fault, the insurer will refuse to pay and will probably report the client as having concealed information or having made a false claim. Both faults would be seen as invalidating the insurance relationship and could have legal consequences.

However, and what matters most for the analysis offered in this book, is that the security dimension of the role of insurance as a biopolitical security technology arises from this insurance relationship. The effects of the confession the client made to the insurer, the ways in which insurers employ information generated throughout the underwriting process and the ways in which both clients and insurers behave in relation to the insurance relationship instantiate moral economies. These economies of behaviour are directly related to the point made before in relation to insurance creating multiple and simultaneous subjectivities. The truth about the client or, better put, the information provided by the client and the truth-value of this information under the obligation of the principle of utmost good faith becomes the key to access a technology of reparation provided through insurance. If the confession of the client appears to be false, access to reparation is denied and with it the possibility of promoting and protecting a lifestyle. The consequences of this act, in an age of digitalized information and virtual circulation, are quite significant. The client will not only be denied payment on a claim arising out of the insured event but also be added to a database which other insurers can use to make decisions on future insurance policies. An individual reported to have violated the principle of utmost good faith would therefore be considered, for a period of time (depending on market practices or legislation on this area), an uninsurable subject. However, this might not affect all forms of insurance and, within the context of multiple/simultaneous subjectivities, the individual might still be eligible for some forms of cover.

The client's confession of truth, although a voluntary decision, is already mediated and enframed by the insurer. Consequently, the enquiry does not amount to a fact-finding exercise and is far from problematic. A client will be asked to disclose information only in relation to questions formulated by the insurer, in many cases through a pro-forma. The truth-value of such information will be circumscribed to the specific question and context and might relate to a different truth when the question changes. The question, therefore, enframes the truth within a particular instrumental reasoning enabling the underwriting process. Although clients might also be asked if there is any other information that they could consider relevant to the underwriting of the policy, they could always claim their ignorance on the process and in light of it withhold information. However, this truth-telling process remains central to the understanding of the production of subjectivities in advanced liberal economies where the use of insurance is a fundamental feature for the security of everyday life. The task and obligation of truth-telling about oneself is inserted within the procedure indispensable for insurability, within techniques for the protection and promotion of the individual's form of life, and within a technology of security that proceeds through the rendering of uncertainty fungible as risk. This last sentence paraphrases one written by Foucault in 1982 when referring to the role of confession within the Christian tradition as 'an absolutely crucial moment in the history of subjectivity in the West'.[8] Foucault was trying to make sense of the role of confession in the context of a hermeneutic enquiry of the subject. Although an insurance client is not seeking the salvation of a soul or the admission of guilt for a particular action or thought, the insurer does seek to identify factors that might help classify the client within specific risk groups. These factors can be related to the conditions of the life or lifestyle of the client, but also to the likelihood of the client seeking to cheat on the insurer. Therefore, the underwriter's questions are informed by a narrative that presupposes a moral order that operates as the benchmark against which the client will be underwritten. A distance from such moral order, expressed in the form of normal deviations, would be represented in higher or lower than standard risk ratings.

What underwriters do, then, is ascribe value to lives in terms of levels of risk. It will therefore be in the interest of clients to disclose accurate information, but also to modify their behaviour and as far as possible their life and lifestyles to affordable insurable levels. Changing the locks on doors and windows to a higher security specification might reduce house contents insurance premiums. Going to the gym three times a week might render some lives insurable and reduce premiums for health insurance. Driving a particular type of vehicle, having no points on one's driving licence and living within certain postcode areas might make motor insurance more affordable. Reducing the risk of accidents in the workplace by removing obstacles to circulation might improve employers' liability quotes. Improving fire detectors and water-sprinkler systems as well as updating fire doors might make fire insurance cheaper. But at the same time, adopting the administrative and risk assessment systems required to implement parametric insurance schemes against environmental hazards might allow countries and regions to buy cover for otherwise catastrophic events. In short, assessing lives and lifestyles in relation to expected standard conditions and moral behaviours contributes to shaping subjectivities of risk. The effect of adapting lives and lifestyles to more favourable conditions of insurability constitutes insurantial moral economies which underlie the provision of security through insurance practices.

These moral economies, however, differ from the Kantian moral imperatives of the Enlightenment. Responsible risk-embracing, as a condition of possibility for contemporary (neoliberal) entrepreneurial life, demands flexibility in the assessment of risk. Instead of moral doctrines, insurers trawl the markets and mine databases. Instead of prescriptive dogmas of identity, insurers underwrite multiple and simultaneous circulations. The morality of the biopolitical economy of security produced through insurance is a fluid one that adapts to the continuous transformation and change of lives and lifestyles and operates in relation to sovereign forms of security. But the detailed analysis of these moral economies will be the subject of subsequent work.

Notes

Introduction

1 Figures taken from Swiss Re, 'World Insurance in 2007: Emerging Markets Leading the Way', *Sigma* 3, 2008, pp. 33, 35.
2 Rata based on figures taken from the above and IISS, 'Chapter Nine: Country comparisons – commitments, force levels and economics', *The Military Balance* 109, no. 1, 2009, pp. 447–53.
3 Geneva Association, 'Special Issue on G-20 Summit', *Geneva Association Information Newsletter*, April 2009, p. 6.
4 For some notable exceptions, see V. Haufler, *Dangerous Commerce: Insurance and the Management of International Risk*, Ithaca: Cornell University Press, 1997; C. Aradau and R. van Munster, 'Governing Terrorism through Risk: Taking Precautions, (un)Knowing the Future', *European Journal of International Relations* 13, no. 1, 2007, pp. 89–115; M. Paterson, 'Risky Business: Insurance Companies in Global Warming Politics', *Global Environmental Politics* 1, no. 4, 2001, p. 18; S. Strange, *The Retreat of the State*. Cambridge: Cambridge University Press, 1989; R. Deuchars, 'The Emergence of Statistical Knowledge', in *The International Political Economy of Risk*. Aldershot: Ashgate, 2004, pp. 32–54; and M. de Goede, *Virtue, Fortune, and Faith: A Genealogy of Finance*. Minneapolis: University of Minnesota Press, 2005.
5 F. Ewald, 'Insurance and Risk', in Graham Burchell (ed.) *The Foucault Effect: Studies in Governmental Rationality*. Hemel Hempstead: Harvester Wheatsheaf, 1991, p. 198.
6 See also M. Dean, *Governmentality: Power and Rule in Modern Society*. London: Sage, 1999; M. de Goede, 'Beyond Risk: Premediation and the Post-9/11 Security Imagination', *Security Dialogue* 39, no. 2–3, 2008, pp. 155–76; M. Dillon, 'Underwriting Security', *Security Dialogue* 39, no. 2–3, 2008, pp. 309–32; P. O'Malley, 'Uncertain Subjects: Risk, Liberalism and Contract', *Economy and Society* 29, no. 4, 2000, pp. 460–84; P. O'Malley, *Risk, Uncertainty and Government*. London: Glasshouse Press, 2004; I. Hacking, *The Emergence of Probability*, Cambridge: Cambridge University Press, 2006; I. Hacking, *The Taming of Chance*, Cambridge: Cambridge University Press, 1990; P. Miller and N. Rose, 'Political Power beyond the State: Problematics of Government', *British Journal of Sociology* 43, no. 2, 1992, pp. 173–205; N. Rose, 'The Politics of Life Itself', *Theory Culture Society* 18, no. 6, 2001, pp. 1–30; N. Rose, *Powers of Freedom*, Cambridge: Cambridge University Press, 1999; and R. Ericson, A. Doyle and B. Dean, *Insurance as Governance*. Toronto: University of Toronto Press, 2003.
7 Dean, *Governmentality: Power and Rule in Modern Society*, p. 177.
8 For example, G. Gigerenzer, Z. Swijtink, T. Porter, L. J. Daston, J. Beatty and K. Kruger, *The Empire of Chance*. New York: Cambridge University Press, 1989; I. Hacking, *The Emergence of Probability*. Cambridge: Cambridge University Press, 2006; G. Poitras,

The Early History of Financial Economics, 1478–1776. Cheltenham: Edward Elgar Publishing, 2000; T. Porter, *Trust in Numbers: The Pursuit of Objectivity in Science and Public Life*. Princeton, NJ: Princeton University Press, 1995; and L. Daston, *Classical Probability in the Enlightenment*. Princeton, NJ: Princeton University Press, 1988.

9 Daston, *Classical Probability in the Enlightenment*, p. 19.
10 Hacking, *The Emergence of Probability*, p. 12.
11 F. Knight, *Risk, Uncertainty and Profit*. Boston: Houghton Mifflin, 1921, p. 233.
12 Ewald, 'Insurance and Risk', p. 198.
13 For a further discussion on an understanding of insurance technology as the 'how to' of insurance, see T. Baker and J. Simon, *Embracing Risk: The Changing Culture of Insurance and Responsibility*. Chicago: University of Chicago Press, 2002, p. 8.
14 J. Dodson, *The Mathematical Repository*. London, 1753, vol. II, p. viii.
15 For a theoretical elaboration on this idea in relation to the biopolitical imaginary of species being, see M. Dillon and L. Lobo-Guerrero, 'The Biopolitical Imaginary of Species Being', *Theory Culture Society* 26, no. 1, 2009, pp. 1–23.
16 Baker and Simon, *Embracing Risk: The Changing Culture of Insurance and Responsibility*, p. 1.
17 Ibid.
18 See F. Ewald, *L'Etat Providence*. Paris: P. Grasset, 1986; and Baker and Simon, *Embracing Risk: The Changing Culture of Insurance and Responsibility*, pp. 3–7.
19 T. Baker, 'Embracing Risk, Sharing Responsibility', *Drake Law Review* 56, no. 2, 2008, pp. 561–70, especially p. 568.
20 See D. A. Moss, *When All Else Fails: Government as the Ultimate Risk Manager*. Cambridge, MA: Harvard University Press, 2002.
21 Baker, 'Embracing Risk, Sharing Responsibility', p. 568.
22 M. Duffield, *Development, Security and Unending War: Governing the World of Peoples*. Cambridge: Polity, 2007, p. 16.
23 Ibid., p. 17.
24 See G. Agamben, *Homo Sacer: Sovereign Power and Bare Life*, Stanford, CA: Stanford University Press, 1998, p. 6. For a discussion on this topic see Chapter 7 of this book.
25 K. Knorr-Cetina, 'Sociality with Objects: Social Relations in Postsocial Knowledge Societies', *Theory, Culture and Society* 14, no. 1, 1997, pp. 1–30.
26 H.-J. Rheinberger, *Toward a History of Epistemic Things: Synthesizing Proteins in the Test Tube*. Stanford, CA: Stanford University Press, 1997, p. 28.
27 Ibid., p. 28.
28 Ibid., p. 28.
29 Ibid. See M. Serres, *Statues: le second livre des fondations*. Paris: Bourin, 1987, p. 191.
30 For example, M. Foucault, *The History of Sexuality*, Vol. 1, *The Will to Knowledge*. London: Penguin, 1998; M. Foucault, *Society Must Be Defended*. London: Penguin Books, 2003; M. Foucault, *Security, Territory, Population*. Basingstoke: Palgrave Macmillan, 2007; M. Foucault, *The Birth of Biopolitics*. London: Palgrave Macmillan, 2008; G. Agamben, *Homo Sacer: Sovereign Power and Bare Life*; M. Hardt and A. Negri, *Empire*. Cambridge, MA: Harvard University Press, 2000; M. Hardt and A. Negri, *Multitude: War and Democracy in the Age of Empire*. New York: Penguin, 2005; R. Esposito, *Bios: Biopolitics and Philosophy*. Minneapolis: University of Minnesota Press, 2008; and P. Virno, *A Grammar of the Multitude*. Los Angeles: Semiotext(e), 2004.
31 P. Virno, *A Grammar of the Multitude*.

1 Making uncertainty fungible

1 G. Ceccarelli, 'Risky Business: Theological and Canonical Thought on Insurance from the Thirteenth to the Seventeenth Century', *Journal of Medieval and Early Modern Studies* 31, no. 3, 2001, p. 611.

2 Ibid.
3 Ibid., p. 610.
4 Ibid.
5 Ceccarelli explains his use of *liceity* by arguing that he preferred it to *lawfulness* or *licitness* as his way of translating the Latin term *liceitas* (ibid., footnote 5, p. 634).
6 Usury was treated in two loci in the decretum: Part 1, Distinction 46, chs 8–10, and Distinction 47, chs 1–5; Part 2, Causa 14, Questions 1–6, the core definition being found in II C. 14, q. 3; A. Friedberg (ed.) *Corpus Iuris Canonici*. Leipzig: Tauchnitz, 1879, I, 169–71, 732–42. For the development of canonist usury theory, see T. P. McLaughlin, *The Teaching of the Canonists on Usury (XII, XIII and XIV centuries)*, *Mediaeval Studies* 1, 1939, pp. 81–147; 2, 1940, pp. 1–22). Cited by J. L. O'Donovan, 'The Theological Economics of Medieval Usury Theory', *Studies in Christian Ethics* 14, no. 1, 2001, p. 50.
7 Ibid., p. 50.
8 Ibid., p. 50.
9 Ibid., p. 50.
10 Ibid., p. 50.
11 P. G. Pesce, 'La dottrina degli anichi moralisti circa la liceitá del contratto di assicurazione', *Assicurazione (Rome)* 33, 1966, pp. 36–66.
12 C. Bergfeld, 'Die Stellungnahme der spanischen Spätscholastiker zum Versicherungsvertrag', in Paolo Grossi (ed.) *La Seconda scolastica nella formazione del diritto privato moderno: incontro di studio, Firenze 16–10 ottobre, 197*. Milan: Giuffré, 1973, pp. 457–71.
13 E. Spagnesi, 'Aspetti dell'assicurazione medievale', in Associazione nazionale fra le imprese assicuratrici (ed.) *L'assicurazione in Italia fino all'Unità: Saggi storici in onore di Eugenio Artom*. Milan: Giuffré, 1975, pp. 3–189.
14 C. F. Trenerry, *The Origin and Early History of Insurance, Including the Contract of Bottomry*. London: P.S. King & Son, Ltd., 1926, Part I, Chapter III, pp. 61–71.
15 Ibid.
16 B. Benfield, *Life Insurance Company Management*. Los Angeles: Primary Asset Administrative Services, 2005.
17 Trenerry, *The Origin and Early History of Insurance, Including the Contract of Bottomry*, pp. 50–60.
18 Ibid.
19 Ibid.
20 Ibid., p. 54.
21 See F. E. de Roover, 'Early Examples of Marine Insurance', *Journal of Economic History* 5, 1945, footnote 2 on p. 173.
22 Benfield, *Life Insurance Company Management*, Ch. 1.
23 Ibid.
24 Trenerry, *The Origin and Early History of Insurance, Including the Contract of Bottomry*. For a description of 'Life Assurance as Known to the Romans', see Chapter VIII.
25 Ibid., p. 135.
26 See W. M. Howard, 'A Note on Mortality Tables and Interest Rates', *Journal of Insurance* 24, no. 2, 1957, pp. 88–92.
27 E. Halley, 'An Estimate of the Degrees of the Mortality of Mankind, Drawn from Curious Tables of the Births and Funerals at the City of Breslaw; With an Attempt to Ascertain the Price of Annuities upon Lives', *Philosophical Transactions (1683–1775)* 17, 1693.
28 Ceccarelli, 'Risky Business: Theological and Canonical Thought on Insurance from the Thirteenth to the Seventeenth Century', p. 609.
29 De Roover, 'Early Examples of Marine Insurance'.
30 P. Perdikas, 'Die Entstehung der Versicherung im Mittelalter: Geschichtliche

Grundlagen im Verhältnis zu Seedarlehen, Überseekauf, Commenda und Bodmerei', *Zeitschrift für die gesamte Versicherungswissenshaft* 55, 1966, pp. 425–509.

31 L. A. Boiteaux, *La Fortune de mer. Le besoin de sécurité et les débuts de l'assurance maritime*, Paris: SEVPEN, 1968.

32 Ceccarelli, 'Risky Business: Theological and Canonical Thought on Insurance from the Thirteenth to the Seventeenth Century', p. 609. Emphasis added.

33 O'Donovan, 'The Theological Economics of Medieval Usury Theory'.

34 O. Langholm, *Economics in the Medieval Schools: Wealth, Exchange, Value, Money, and Usury, according to the Paris Theological Tradition 1200–1350*. Leiden: E.J. Brill, 1992.

35 J. Noonan, *The Scholastic Analysis of Usury*. Cambridge, MA: Harvard University Press, 1957.

36 Ibid.

37 See J. Le Goff, *Your Money or Your Life: Economy and Religion in the Middle Ages*. New York: Zone Books; MIT Press [distributor], 1988.

38 Ibid.

39 Ceccarelli, 'Risky Business: Theological and Canonical Thought on Insurance from the Thirteenth to the Seventeenth Century', pp. 613–14.

40 For specific examples on this double concern of the Church, see Le Goff, *Your Money or Your Life: Economy and Religion in the Middle Ages*.

41 De Roover, 'Early Examples of Marine Insurance'.

42 Ibid.; C. B. Hoover, 'The Sea Loan in Genoa in the Twelfth Century', *Quarterly Journal of Economics* 40, no. 3, 1926, pp. 495–529.

43 M. Foucault, *Security, Territory, Population: Lectures at the College de France 1977–1978*. Basingstoke: Palgrave Macmillan, 2007, p. 165.

44 Ibid., p. 165.

45 Ibid., p. 166.

46 See all of lecture seven, 22 February 1978, ibid., pp. 163–90.

47 Ibid., p. 167.

48 Ibid., p. 235.

49 Ibid.

50 Ibid.

51 Ibid.

52 Ibid.

53 Ibid.

54 Ibid., p. 236.

55 See R. Lopez, *The Commercial Revolution of the Middle Ages: 950–1350*. Englewood Cliffs, NJ: Prentice-Hall, 1971.

56 Ibid., pp. 1–56.

57 Ibid., p. 56.

58 De Roover, 'Early Examples of Marine Insurance', pp. 173–4.

59 Ibid., p. 174.

60 Ibid.

61 Ibid.

62 Ibid.

63 De Roover notes that the word 'factors' had a special meaning in the Middle Ages. The term was used mainly for salaried employees who served a merchant as agents abroad. Ibid. footnote 5.

64 Ibid., p. 174.

65 H. Bernardelli, 'The Origins of Modern Economic Theory', *The Economic Record* no. 37, 1961, p. 320, p. 17.

66 B. Rotman, *Signifying Nothing: The Semiotics of Zero*, New York: St. Martin's, 1987, p. 4.

67 Ibid., p. 5.

68 Langholm, *Economics in the Medieval Schools: Wealth, Exchange, Value, Money, and Usury, according to the Paris Theological Tradition 1200–1350*, pp. 17–18.
69 Ibid., p. 18. See also Rotman, *Signifying Nothing: The Semiotics of Zero*, p. 8.
70 Kantorowicz, *Frederick the Second, 1194–1250*. London: Constable and Co., 1931.
71 Langholm, *Economics in the Medieval Schools: Wealth, Exchange, Value, Money, and Usury, according to the Paris Theological Tradition 1200–1350*; C. T. Maier, *Preaching the Crusades: Mendicant Friars and the Cross in the Thirteenth Century*. Cambridge: Cambridge University Press, 1999; G. H. Sabine, *A History of Political Theory*. London: George G. Harrap & Co., 1961 [1937], p. 244; J. I. Catto (ed.) *The History of the University of Oxford*, Vol. 1, *The Early Oxford Schools*. Oxford: Clarendon Press, 1984.
72 Sabine, *A History of Political Theory*, p. 244; O. Langholm, *Economics in the Medieval Schools: Wealth, Exchange, Value, Money, and Usury, according to the Paris Theological Tradition 1200–1350*.
73 Sabine, *A History of Political Theory*, pp. 244–6.
74 Ibid., p. 244.
75 Ibid., p. 245.
76 Ibid.
77 Ibid.
78 Ibid., p. 247.
79 Langholm, *Economics in the Medieval Schools: Wealth, Exchange, Value, Money, and Usury, according to the Paris Theological Tradition 1200–1350*, p. 1.
80 Ibid.
81 Ibid.
82 Gregory IX, *Decretal Naviganti of Pope Gregory IX*. GREG.LIB. V. TIT. XIX. CAP. XIX, 1236.
83 Ceccarelli, 'Risky Business: Theological and Canonical Thought on Insurance from the Thirteenth to the Seventeenth Century', p. 614.
84 Ibid., p. 613.
85 According to Ceccarelli, the difference was between 'profit in a partnership and gains obtained by loans on the basis of the ownership of the goods invested, property which, in the mind of medieval masters, is determined by the incidence of risk. In a *mutuum*, ownership and *periculum* are transferred, and therefore any profit is due to the skill and labour of the borrower. In a partnership, by contrast, property is not transferred, and thus just as the risks are shared, the probable gains may be divided by the partners'. Ibid., p. 613, based on J. Kirshner, 'Preface to Raymond de Roover', in Julius Kirshner (ed.) *Business, Banking, and Economic Thought in Late Medieval and Early Modern Europe*. Chicago: Chicago University Press, 1974, pp. 31–2.
86 Langholm, *Economics in the Medieval Schools: Wealth, Exchange, Value, Money, and Usury, according to the Paris Theological Tradition 1200–1350*.
87 Ibid.
88 Ibid., p. 1.
89 Ibid., p. 1.
90 Ibid., p. 10.
91 Ibid., p. 24.
92 J. Le Goff, *Saint Francis of Assisi*. London: Routledge, 2004.
93 J. H. Smith, *Francis of Assisi*. London: Sidgwick & Jackson, 1972; Langholm, *Economics in the Medieval Schools: Wealth, Exchange, Value, Money, and Usury, according to the Paris Theological Tradition 1200–1350*.
94 Smith, *Francis of Assisi*.
95 On Peter Olivi, see Langholm, *Economics in the Medieval Schools: Wealth, Exchange, Value, Money, and Usury, according to the Paris Theological Tradition 1200–1350*, pp. 345–74.

96 Ceccarelli, 'Risky Business: Theological and Canonical Thought on Insurance from the Thirteenth to the Seventeenth Century', p. 614.
97 Ibid.
98 Langholm, *Economics in the Medieval Schools: Wealth, Exchange, Value, Money, and Usury, according to the Paris Theological Tradition 1200–1350*, pp. 352–4.
99 J. Le Goff, *Time, Work, and Culture in the Middle Ages*. London: University of Chicago Press, 1982, p. 29.
100 Ibid., p. 30.
101 Ibid.
102 Le Goff, *Your Money or Your Life: Economy and Religion in the Middle Ages*, p. 48.
103 Le Goff, *Time, Work, and Culture in the Middle Ages*, p. 48, emphasis in original.
104 Le Goff, *Your Money or Your Life: Economy and Religion in the Middle Ages*, p. 50.
105 Ibid., p. 50.
106 Le Goff *Time, Work, and Culture in the Middle Ages*, p. 50.
107 Ibid.
108 Le Goff, *Your Money or Your Life: Economy and Religion in the Middle Ages*, p. 50.
109 See M. Foucault, *Security, Territory, Population*. Basingstoke: Palgrave Macmillan, 2007, p. 167.
110 F. E. de Roover, 'Early Examples of Marine Insurance', *Journal of Economic History* 5, no. 2, 1945, p. 175.
111 Hoover, 'The Sea Loan in Genoa in the Twelfth Century', p. 495.
112 Ibid., p. 497.
113 de Roover, 'Early Examples of Marine Insurance', p. 174.
114 Hoover, 'The Sea Loan in Genoa in the Twelfth Century', pp. 498–9.
115 Ibid., pp. 498–9.
116 Ibid., p. 499.
117 de Roover, 'Early Examples of Marine Insurance', p. 175.
118 Hoover, 'The Sea Loan in Genoa in the Twelfth Century', p. 499.
119 Ibid., p. 499.
120 Ibid., p. 499.
121 G. O'Brien, *An Essay on Medieval Economic Teaching*. New York: Longmans, 1920, p. 178.
122 Ibid., p. 178.
123 Ibid., p. 178.
124 Hoover, 'The Sea Loan in Genoa in the Twelfth Century', p. 501.
125 Ibid., footnote 1, p. 499.
126 Ibid., p. 499.
127 De Roover, 'Early Examples of Marine Insurance', p. 176.
128 See, for example, E. Briys and D. Joos de ter Beerst, 'The Zaccaria Deal: Contract and Options to Fund a Genoese Shipment of Alum to Bruges in 1298', presented at XIV International Economic History Congress (Helsinki, August 2006), 2006, p. 79.
129 De Roover, 'Early Examples of Marine Insurance', p. 176.
130 Ibid., p. 176.
131 Hoover, 'The Sea Loan in Genoa in the Twelfth Century', pp. 527–9.
132 M. Kohn, 'Risk Instruments in the Medieval and Early Modern Economy', Department of Economics, Dartmouth College, Hanover, Working Paper No. 99-07, 1999.
133 De Roover, 'Early Examples of Marine Insurance', p. 176.
134 Ibid., p. 176.
135 A. P. Usher, 'The Origin of the Bill of Exchange', *Journal of Political Economy* 22, no. 6, 1914, pp. 566–76.
136 Ibid.
137 Ibid.
138 Ibid., p. 570.
139 Ibid., p. 570.

140 Ibid., pp. 569–70.
141 Some examples are provided in Usher's article which are useful illustrations of this fact.
142 Usher, 'The Origin of the Bill of Exchange', p. 571.
143 Ibid., p. 572.
144 De Roover, 'Early Examples of Marine Insurance', p. 177.
145 Ibid., p. 177.
146 M. Kohn, 'Payments and the Development of Finance in Pre-Industrial Europe', Department of Economics, Dartmouth College, Hanover, Working Paper 01-15, 2001, p. 13.
147 Ibid., pp.13–14.
148 Ibid.
149 Ibid.
150 De Roover, 'Early Examples of Marine Insurance', p. 180.
151 R. Zeno, *Documenti per la storia del diritto marittimo nei secoli XIII e XIV*, Turin, 1936, pp. 229–30, no. 190. Cited by de Roover, 'Early Examples of Marine Insurance', p. 183.

2 Securing by capitalizing life

1 J. Dodson, *The Mathematical Repository*. London, 1753, vol. II, p. viii.
2 Hacking has rightly pointed out that the phrase 'law of large numbers' was coined by Poisson in 1835. The concept, however, was in use during the eighteenth century and owing to the explanatory value of the phrase it is used in this chapter. See I. Hacking, *The Taming of Chance*. Cambridge: Cambridge University Press, 1990, p. 95.
3 There is a growing literature on the history of probabilities and early financial instruments that sheds light on how risk became increasingly measurable and directly applicable to the calculation of annuities. It analyses the significance of the discoveries of Fermat and Pascal, followed by Huygens, and the bills of mortality of John Graunt and Edmond Halley in the second half of the seventeenth century. See L. Krüger, L. Daston and M. Heidelberger (eds.) *The Probabilistic Revolution*, Vol. 1: *Ideas in History Cambridge*. MA: MIT Press, 1987; P. Bernstein, *Against the Gods: The Remarkable Story of Risk*. New York: John Wiley & Sons, 1998; J. Daston Lorraine, *Classical Probability in the Enlightenment*. Princeton, NJ: Princeton University Press, 1988; G. Gigerenzer *et al.*, *The Empire of Chance*. New York: Cambridge University Press, 1989; I. Hacking, *The Emergence of Probability*; Cambridge: Cambridge University Press, 1975; and G. Poitras, *The Early History of Financial Economics, 1478–1776*, Cheltenham: Edward Elgar Publishing, 2000.
4 See S. M. Stigler, *The History of Statistics: The Measurement of Uncertainty before 1900*. Chicago: Chicago University Press, 1986.
5 M. de Goede, *Virtue, Fortune, and Faith: A Genealogy of Finance*. Minneapolis: University of Minnesota Press, 2005, chapter 3.
6 A. O. Hirschman, *The Passions and the Interests: Political Arguments for Capitalism before its Triumph*. Princeton: Princeton University Press, 1977.
7 G. Clark, *Betting on Lives: The Culture of Life Insurance in England, 1695–1775*. Manchester: Manchester University Press, 1999, p. 13.
8 For example, R. S. Smith, 'Life Insurance in Fifteenth-Century Barcelona', *Journal of Economic History* 1, no. 1, 1941, pp. 57–9, which suggests that the notarial archives of the city might keep valuable resources for the understanding of life insurance in pre-modern times.
9 Cleirac, *Les Us et Coutumes de la Mer. Divesees en troit parties. i. De la Navigation. II. Du Commerce Naval et Contrats Maritimes. III. De la Jurisdiction de la Marine, Avec un traitte des Termes de Marine, &c.*, Bordeaux, 1661.
10 F. Hendriks, *Contributions to the History of Insurance, and of the Theory of Life*

Contingencies, with a Restoration of the Gran Pensionary De Wit's Treatise on Life Annuities. London: C&E Layton, 1851, chapter XVI, paras 1–5.

11 Clark, *Betting on Lives: The Culture of Life Insurance in England, 1695–1775*, pp. 13–16.

12 Ibid., p. 14.

13 Ibid.

14 Ibid.

15 Ibid.

16 Ibid.

17 Ibid.

18 Ibid., p. 16.

19 Ibid., p. 17.

20 Ibid., p. 48.

21 Ibid., p. 48.

22 Ibid., p. 48.

23 Ibid., p. 60.

24 Ibid., p. 62.

25 Ibid., p. 53.

26 Clark, *Betting on Lives: The Culture of Life Insurance in England, 1695–1775*, p. 20.

27 Great Britain, 'An Act for Regulating Insurances on Lives', 14 Geo III c. 48, 1774.

28 Clark, *Betting on Lives: The Culture of Life Insurance in England, 1695–1775*, p. 22.

29 P. G. M. Dickson, *The Financial Revolution in England: A Study in the Development of Public Credit, 1688–1756*. Aldershot: Gregg Revivals, 1993, p. 7.

30 C. Wright and C. E. Fayle, *A History of Lloyd's: From the Founding of Lloyd's Coffee House to the Present Day*. London: published for the Corporation of Lloyd's by Macmillan and Co. Ltd, 1928, p. 91.

31 Ibid.

32 Ibid.

33 Hirschman, *The Passions and the Interests: Political Arguments for Capitalism Before its Triumph*, p. 48.

34 See I. Kant, *Perpetual Peace: A Philosophical Essay*. London: Garland, 1972.

35 Hirschman, *The Passions and the Interests: Political Arguments for Capitalism before its Triumph*, p. 20.

36 Ibid.

37 Ibid., p. 26.

38 Ibid.

39 A. Ferguson, *An Essay on the History of Civil Society*. Cambridge: Cambridge University Press, 1996.

40 See M. Foucault, 'Governmentality', in James Faubion (ed.) *Michel Foucault: Power, the Essential Works 3*. London: Allen Lane The Penguin Press, 1994, p. 221.

41 Dickson, *The Financial Revolution in England: A Study in the Development of Public Credit, 1688–1756*, p. 12. On the financial revolution see H. Roseveare, *The Financial Revolution, 1660–1760*. Harlow: Pearson Education, 2001; and D. R. Weir, 'Tontines, Public Finance, and Revolution in France and England, 1688–1789', *Journal of Economic History* 49, no. 1, 1989, pp. 95–124.

42 E. L. Jones, *Agriculture and Economic Growth in England, 1650–1815*. New York: Barnes & Noble, 1967; E. Kerridge, *The Agricultural Revolution*. London: Allen & Unwin, 1967; and C. More, 'Agriculture and Rural Society', in *The Industrial Age: Economy and Society in Britain, 1750–1995*. London: Longman, 1997, pp. 3–11.

43 Hacking, *The Emergence of Probability*, p. 103.

44 T. G. McCormick, 'Transmutation, Inclusion, and Exclusion: Political Arithmetic from Charles II to William III', paper presented at the conference 'Without Let or Hindrance: Inclusion and its Subversion from the Medieval to the Modern', Department of History, Lancaster University, 7–9 July 2006, p. 2.

45 K. S. Bottigheimer, *English Money and Irish Land: The 'Adventurers' in the Cromwellian Settlement of Ireland*. Oxford: Oxford University Press, 1971.
46 P. Buck, 'Seventeenth-Century Political Arithmetic: Civil Strife and Vital Statistics', *Isis* 68, no. 1, 1977, pp. 67–84. See also McCormick, 'Transmutation, Inclusion, and Exclusion: Political Arithmetic from Charles II to William III'.
47 McCormick, 'Transmutation, Inclusion, and Exclusion: Political Arithmetic from Charles II to William III'.
48 Ibid., p. 2.
49 W. Petty, *The Political Anatomy of Ireland*, London, 1691, as referred to by McCormick, 'Transmutation, Inclusion, and Exclusion: Political Arithmetic from Charles II to William III', p. 3.
50 W. Petty, *Political Arithmetick*. London: printed for Robert Clavel at the Peacock, and Hen. Mortlock at the Phoenix in St. Paul's Church-yard, 1690 (http://socserv2.socsci.mcmaster.ca/~econ/ugcm/3ll3/petty/poliarith.html).
51 Petty, *The Political Anatomy of Ireland*, as cited by McCormick, 'Transmutation, Inclusion, and Exclusion: Political Arithmetic from Charles II to William III', p. 3.
52 C. Davenant, 'The Political and Commercial Works of that Celebrated Writer Charles D'Avenant', in C. Whitworth (ed.) *The Works of Sr William D'Avenant Kt*, 1771, Vol. I, p. 178. Cited by J. Hoppit, 'Political Arithmetic in Eighteenth-Century England', *Economic History Review* 49, no. 3, 1996, p. 517.
53 'Political Arithmetic', in *Encyclopaedia Britannica*, 3rd edn, Vol. XV, 1797–1801, p. 318.
54 Hoppit, 'Political Arithmetic in Eighteenth-Century England', p. 517.
55 W. Petty, *Political Arithmetick*. London: printed for Robert Clavel at the Peacock, and Hen. Mortlock at the Phoenix in St. Paul's Church-yard, 1690 (http://socserv2.socsci.mcmaster.ca/~econ/ugcm/3ll3/petty/poliarith.html). Emphasis added.
56 See Hoppit, 'Political Arithmetic in Eighteenth-Century England', pp. 517–18.
57 Ibid., pp. 517–18.
58 Dickson, *The Financial Revolution in England: A Study in the Development of Public Credit, 1688–1756*, Chapter 8. Cited by Hoppit, 'Political arithmetic in eighteenth-century England', p. 520.
59 Hoppit, 'Political Arithmetic in Eighteenth-Century England', pp. 517–18.
60 M. Foucault, *The History of Sexuality*, Vol. 1: *The Will to Knowledge*. London: Penguin, 1998, Part 5.
61 G. C. Bowker and S. L. Star, *Sorting Things Out: Classification and its Consequences*. Cambridge, MA: MIT Press, 1999, p. 10. Emphasis in original.
62 Ibid., p. 10. Emphasis in original.
63 Ibid., p. 10.
64 I. Hacking, 'Making up People', in T. Heller, M. Sosna and D. Wellberry (eds.) *Reconstructing Individualism*. Stanford, CA: Stanford University Press, 1986, pp. 222–36; I. Hacking, 'Biopower and the Avalanche of Printed Numbers', *Humanities in Society* 5, 1982, pp. 222–36.
65 J. Graunt, *Natural and Political Observations Mentioned in a Following Index, and Made upon the Bills of Mortality*, London: printed by Tho. Roycroft, for John Martin, James Allestry, and Tho: Dicas, at the Sign of the Bell in St. Paul's, 1662.
66 Bowker and Star, *Sorting Things Out: Classification and its Consequences*; see Gaunt's tables on pp. 22–3.
67 See M. Foucault, *The Order of Things*. London: Routledge, 1989.
68 Graunt, *Natural and Political Observations Mentioned in a Following Index, and Made upon the Bills of Mortality*, conclusions.
69 E. Halley, 'An Estimate of the Degrees of the Mortality of Mankind', *Philosophical Transactions* no. 196, 1693, pp. 596–610.
70 Ibid.
71 Ibid.

72 'Motion for a Bill to Take an Annual Account or Register of the People', *Gentleman's Magazine* 1753, as noted by P. Buck, 'People Who Counted: Political Arithmetic in the Eighteenth Century', *Isis* 73, no. 1, 1982, p. 32, footnote 16.
73 Ibid.
74 'Motion for a Bill to Take an Annual Account or Register of the People', p. 499, as cited by Buck, 'People Who Counted: Political Arithmetic in the Eighteenth Century', p. 35.
75 Buck, 'People Who Counted: Political Arithmetic in the Eighteenth Century', p. 35.
76 Here Buck makes reference to 'Richard Forster to Thomas Birch, 2 Dec. 1760, in D.V. Glass, *Numbering the People*. Farnborough: Saxon House, 1973) p. 88; 'An Account of the Proceedings in Parliament, on the Bill to Number the People', *Gentleman's Magazine*, 1753, no. 23, pp. 550–551, on p. 550; Frederick Morton Eden, *An Estimate of the Number of Inhabitants in Great Britain and Ireland* (London: 1800), title page. See ibid., footnote 1, p. 29.
77 Buck, 'People Who Counted: Political Arithmetic in the Eighteenth Century', p. 29.
78 Ibid., p. 29.
79 G. Alter and J. Riley, 'How to Bet on Lives: A Guide to Life Contingent Contracts in Early Modern Europe', *Research in Economic History* 10, 1986, p. 3.
80 M. E. Ogborn, *Equitable Assurances: The Story of Life Assurance in the Experience of the Equitable Life Assurance Society, 1762–1962*. London: Allen & Unwin, 1962, p. 121.
81 Ibid., p. 20.
82 Ibid.
83 Clark, *Betting on Lives: The Culture of Life Insurance in England, 1695–1775*, p. 20.
84 Ibid., p. 124.
85 Ibid.
86 Ibid.
87 Ogborn, *Equitable Assurances: The Story of Life Assurance in the Experience of the Equitable Life Assurance Society, 1762–1962*, p. 125.
88 Ibid., p. 23.
89 Ibid.
90 Ibid.
91 Ibid., p. 130.
92 Ibid.
93 Ibid.
94 Ibid.
95 Ibid.
96 As cited by Ogborn, ibid.
97 Ogborn, *Equitable Assurances: The Story of Life Assurance in the Experience of the Equitable Life Assurance Society, 1762–1962*, p. 131.
98 Ibid., p. 30.
99 Ibid.
100 Society for Equitable Assurances, 'A Short Account of the Society for Equitable Assurances on Lives and Survivorships; Established by Deed, Inrolled in his Majesty's Court of King's Bench', in David Jenkins and Takau Yoneyama (eds.) *The History of Insurance*. London: Pickering & Chatto, 2000 (1762), Vol. III, p. 36.
101 Ibid., p. 363.
102 Ibid., p. 364.
103 Ibid., pp. 364–5.
104 Ibid.
105 Ibid.
106 Ibid.
107 Ibid., p. 366.
108 Ibid.

109 Ibid., p. 367. See also fn. 109.
110 Ibid., p. 368.
111 Ibid., p. 368.
112 Ogborn, *Equitable Assurances: The Story of Life Assurance in the Experience of the Equitable Life Assurance Society, 1762–1962*, p. 372.
113 Ibid.
114 Ibid., p. 48.
115 Ibid., pp. 48–9.
116 Dodson, *The Mathematical Repository*, pp. 377–87.

3 The quest for insurability in the molecular age

1 Anonymous, 'Leaders: Insurance in the Genetic Age', *The Economist* no. 357, 2000, 21 October, pp. 1–2.
2 Ibid.
3 Ibid. Emphasis added.
4 See Anonymous, 'Leaders: Insurance in the Genetic Age'.
5 S. D. Taylor, 'Predictive Genetic Test Decisions for Huntington's Disease: Context, Appraisal and New Moral Imperatives', *Social Science & Medicine* 58, no. 1, 2004, pp. 137–49.
6 Anonymous, 'Leaders: Insurance in The Genetic Age'.
7 Ibid.
8 See Multiple Sclerosis Society, *MS and Insurance*. London: Multiple Sclerosis Society, 2006.
9 O. O'Neill, *Genetics, Insurance and Discrimination*. Manchester: Manchester Statistical Society, 1998.
10 Ibid., p. 8.
11 This phrase is borrowed from J. Mittra, '"Genetic Exceptionalism" and Precautionary Politics: Regulating for Uncertainty in Britain's Genetic and Insurance Policy Process', *Science and Public Policy* 33, no. 8, 2006, p. 598.
12 HCSTC, *Human Genetics: The Science and its Consequences. House of Commons Science and Technology Committee. Third Report*. London: Her Majesty's Stationery Office, 1995.
13 Ibid.
14 Ibid.
15 R. J. Pokorski, 'A Test for the Insurance Industry', *Nature* 391, no. 670, 1998, pp. 835–6; S. Raeburn, 'Implications of Genetic Testing for the Insurance Industry: The UK Example', *Community Genetics* no. 5, 2002, pp. 102–9.
16 UK Government, *Government Response to the Fifth Report of the House of Commons Select Committee on Science and Technology, 1996–97*. London: The Stationery Office, 1997.
17 Ibid.
18 ABI, *Life Insurance and Genetics: A Policy Statement*. London: Association of British Insurers, 1997.
19 Ibid.
20 Mittra, '"Genetic Exceptionalism" and Precautionary Politics: Regulating for Uncertainty in Britain's Genetic and Insurance Policy Process', p. 590.
21 Ibid., p. 590.
22 HGAC, *The Implications of Genetic Testing for Insurance*. London: HGAC, 1997.
23 A. Macdonald, 'How Will Improved Forecasts of Individual Lifetimes Affect Underwriting?', *Philosophical Transactions of the Royal Society*, B, 352, 1997, pp. 1067–75.
24 HGAC, *The Implications of Genetic Testing for Insurance*.
25 ABI, *Life Insurance and Genetics: A Policy Statement*.

26 Ibid.
27 UK Government, *Government Response to the Fifth Report of the House of Commons Select Committee on Science and Technology, 1996–97*.
28 Ibid.
29 Ibid.
30 Ibid.
31 Wellcome Trust, *Letter to Second Clerk of the Committee, Science and Technology Committee, House of Commons*, London: Wellcome Trust, 15 August 2001 (www.wellcome.ac.uk/stellent/groups/corporatesite/@policy_communications/documents/web_document/wtd.pdf; accessed 8 February 2010).
32 L. Low, S. King and T. Wilkie, 'Genetic Discrimination in Life Insurance: Empirical Evidence from a Cross-sectional Survey of Genetic Support Groups in the United Kingdom', *British Medical Journal* 317, no. 7173, 1998, pp. 1632–5.
33 Wellcome Trust, *Letter to Second Clerk of the Committee, Science and Technology Committee, House of Commons*.
34 HCSCST, *House of Commons Select Committee on Science and Technology – Fifth Report: Genetics and Insurance*. London: House of Commons Science and Technology Select Committee, 2001.
35 Ibid.
36 Ibid.
37 HGC, *The Use of Genetic Information in Insurance: Interim Recommendations of the Human Genetics Commission*. London: Human Genetics Commission, 2001.
38 Ibid., p. 1.
39 UK Department of Health, *Government Response to the Report from the House of Commons Science and Technology Committee: Genetics and Insurance*. London: Department of Health, 2001.
40 See Swiss Re Life & Health Ltd, *The Insurance Report 1998 – Life Results*, 1998, as cited in Wellcome Trust, *Responses to the 'Whose Hands on Your Genes?' Human Genetics Commission Consultation*, London, 2001, footnote 9 (www.hgc.gov.uk/Client/Content_wide.asp?ContentId=475; accessed 6 February 2010).
41 Wellcome Trust, *Letter to Second Clerk of the Committee, Science and Technology Committee, House of Commons*.
42 Department of Health and Association of British Insurers, *Concordat and Moratorium on Genetics and Insurance*. London: Department of Health–Association of British Insurers.
43 Ibid.
44 Ibid.
45 On the social role of insurance see ABI, *The Social Value of General Insurance*. London: Association of British Insurers, 2005.
46 E. M. Neumann-Held and C. Rehmann-Sutter, *Genes in Development: Re-reading the Molecular Paradigm*. Durham, NC: Duke University Press, 2006.
47 Ibid.
48 Neumann-Held and Rehmann-Sutter, *Genes in Development: Re-reading the Molecular Paradigm*. See especially chapter 3, Sahotra Sarkar, 'From Genes as Determinants to DNA as Resource'.
49 Ibid., p. 3.
50 Ibid.
51 Ibid.
52 Ibid.
53 Ibid.
54 Ibid.
55 M. Cooper, *Life as Surplus: Biotechnology & Capitalism in the Neoliberal Era*. Seattle: Washington University Press, 2008.
56 Ibid., p. 127.

57 E. H. Davidson, 'The Sea Urchin Genome: Where Will it Lead us?', *Science* 314, 2006, pp. 939–40. I am grateful to Professor Christoph Rehmann-Sutter from the University of Basle, Switzerland, for introducing this case to me at the 'Life at the Margins' international workshop organized by the Life, Science, Governance Research Platform, University of Vienna, Vienna, 27–28 November 2006.
58 Ibid., p. 939.
59 Ibid., p. 939.
60 Ibid., p. 939.
61 Ibid., p. 939.
62 Ibid., p. 939.
63 L. Kay, *Who Wrote the Book of Life?: A History of the Genetic Code*. Stanford, CA: Stanford University Press, 2000.
64 Christoph Rehmann-Sutter, 'Life at the Margins', international workshop organized by the Life, Science, Governance Research Platform, University of Vienna, Vienna, 27–28 November 2006.
65 Davidson, 'The Sea Urchin Genome: Where Will it Lead us?'
66 Ibid., p. 940.
67 Ibid.
68 M. Tyers and M. Mann, 'From Genomics to Proteomics (insight overview)', *Nature* 422, 2003, pp. 193–7.
69 Ibid.
70 See P. Glasner, 'Beyond the Genome: Reconstituting the New Genetics', *New Genetics and Society* 21, no. 3, 2002, pp. 267–77.
71 R. McNally and P. Glasner, 'Beyond the Human Genome Project: Genomics, Proteomics and Systems Biology', manuscript, 2007. See also V. Regenmortel, 'A Paradigm Shift is Needed in Proteomics: "Structure Determines Function" Should be Replaced by "Binding Determines Function" (Editorial)', *Journal of Molecular Recognition* no. 15, 2002, pp. 349–51.
72 V. Regenmortel, 'A Paradigm Shift is Needed in Proteomics: "Structure Determines Function" Should be Replaced by "Binding Determines Function" (Editorial)'.
73 L. Lobo-Guerrero, interview with Professor Angus Macdonald, Heriot-Watt University, Edinburgh, 11 November 2005.
74 A. Macdonald, 'Modeling the Impact of Genetics on Insurance', *North American Actuarial Journal* 3, no. 1, 1999, pp. 83–105; A. S. MacDonald, 'Moratoria on the Use of Genetic Tests and Family History for Mortgage-related Life Insurance,' *British Actuarial Journal* 9, no. 1, 2003, pp. 217–37.
75 ABI, *Genetic Testing: Code of Practice*. London: Association of British Insurers, 1999.
76 ABI, *Life Insurance and Genetics: A Policy Statement*.
77 ABI, *Genetic Testing and Insurance: ABI Code of Practice on Genetic Testing Compliance Report and Data Analysis for 2003*, London: Association of British Insurers, 2005.
78 Confidential interview: GAIC member 1, 16 November 2006. Henceforth, numbered interviews correspond to confidential interviews.
79 Nominated genetic underwriter interview 1, 17 January 2007.
80 Nominated genetic underwriter interview 3, 16 November 2007.
81 Nominated genetic underwriter interview 4, 1 March 2007.
82 Nominated genetic underwriter interview 6, 19 January 2007.
83 ABI and BMA, *Agreement between the ABI and BMA on General Practitioner's Reports and Medical Fees*. London: Association of British Insurers–British Medical Association, 2002.
84 ABI, *General Practitioner's Report, Cover Letter, Covering Letter Enclosure, and Official Format*, unpublished document: ABI, 2002. A copy of this document was provided by the ABI to the author.

85 Ibid.
86 Nominated genetic underwriter interview 1, 19 January 2007.
87 Nominated genetic underwriter interview 4, 19 January 2007.
88 Nominated genetic underwriter interview 4, 19 January 2007.
89 Nominated genetic underwriter interview 5, 19 January 2007.
90 For example, P. Bellerose, *Reinsurance for the Beginner*. London: Witherby & Co., 1998.
91 Reinsurer's interview 1, 15 March 2007.
92 On operational risk see M. Power, *The Invention of Operational Risk*. London: Centre for Analysis of Risk and Regulation, 2003; M. Power, *Organized Uncertainty: Designing a World of Risk Management*. Oxford: Oxford University Press, 2007.
93 A. Butterworth, *Temporal Trends in ABI Genetic Testing Data 2002–2005: A Report on the ABI Annual Questionnaire Responses since 2002 with Comparison to National Genetic Testing Data*. London: unpublished manuscript, p. 5.
94 Nominated genetic underwriter interview 5, 19 January 2007.
95 Butterworth, *Temporal Trends in ABI Genetic Testing Data 2002–2005: A Report on the ABI Annual Questionnaire Responses since 2002 with Comparison to National Genetic Testing Data*.
96 M. Foucault, 'The Birth of Biopolitics', in Paul Rabinow (ed.) *Michel Foucault: Essential Works of Foucault 1954–1984*, Vol. 1: *Ethics*. London: Penguin, 1994, p. 74.
97 See B. Godin, *Measurement and Statistics on Science and Technology: 1920 to the Present*. London: Routledge, 2005.
98 T. Porter, 'Objectivity and Authority: How French Engineers Reduced Public Utility to Numbers', *Poetics Today* 12, no. 2, 1991, p. 252.
99 Gigerenzer, Swijtink, Porter, Daston, Beatty and Kruger, *The Empire of Chance: How Probability Changed Science and Everyday Life*, p. 2.
100 L. Daston, *Classical Probability in the Enlightenment*. Princeton, NJ: Princeton University Press, 1988; L. J. Daston, 'The Domestication of Risk: Mathematical Probability and Insurance 1650–1830', in Lorenz Krüger, Lorraine J. Daston and Michael Heidelberger (eds.) *The Probabilistic Revolution*. Cambridge, MA: MIT Press, 1987, pp. 237–60; L. J. Daston, 'Mathematical Probability and the Reasonable Man of the Eighteenth Century', *Annals of the New York Academy of Sciences* 412, issue 'History and Philosophy of Science: Selected Papers', 1983, pp. 57–72; Gigerenzer *et al.*, *The Empire of Chance*.
101 O. Langholm, *The Aristotelian Analysis of Usury*. Bergen: Universitetsforlaget AS, 1984; O. Langholm, *Economics in the Medieval Schools: Wealth, Exchange, Value, Money, and Usury, According to the Paris Theological Tradition 1200–1350*. Leiden: E.J. Brill, 1992.
102 See A. Gamble, *The Spectre at the Feast: Capitalist Crisis and the Politics of Recession*. Basingstoke: Palgrave Macmillan, 2009.
103 See I. Hacking, 'Risk and Dirt', in Richard Ericson and Aaron Doyle (eds.) *Risk and Morality*. Toronto: University of Toronto Press, 2003, pp. 22–47.
104 Ibid., p. 30.
105 M. Power, 'Risk Management and the Responsible Organisation', in Richard Ericson and Aaron Doyle (eds.) *Risk and Morality*. Toronto: University of Toronto Press, 2003, pp. 145–64; Hacking, 'Risk and Dirt', p. 30.
106 P. O'Malley, *Risk, Uncertainty and Government*. London: Glasshouse Press, 2004, p. 26.
107 M. Power, *The Risk Management of Everything: Rethinking the Politics of Uncertainty*. London: Demos, 2004, p. 11.
108 Power, 'Risk Management and the Responsible Organization'. See also Power, *The Risk Management of Everything: Rethinking the Politics of Uncertainty*.
109 Power, *Organized Uncertainty: Designing a World of Risk Management*.

110 Power, *The Risk Management of Everything: Rethinking the Politics of Uncertainty*, pp. 10–11.
111 Power, *The Invention of Operational risk*, pp. 24–31.
112 Power, 'Risk Management and the Responsible Organization'.
113 Z. Bodie and R. Merton, *Finance*. Englewood Cliffs, NJ: Prentice Hall, 1999, p. 257.
114 For a theorization on this form of governance, see, for example, N. Rose and P. Miller, 'Political Power beyond the State: Problematics of Government', *British Journal of Sociology* 43, no. 2, 1992, pp. 173–205.
115 M. Dillon and L. Lobo-Guerrero, 'The Biopolitical Imaginary of Species Being', *Theory Culture Society* 26, no. 1, 2009, pp. 1–23.
116 M. Dean, 'Putting the Technological into Government', *History of the Human Sciences* 9, no. 3, 1996, p. 48.
117 Ibid.
118 Multiple Sclerosis Society, *MS and Insurance*, p. 1.
119 G. Agamben, *Homo Sacer, Sovereign Power and Bare Life*. Stanford, CA: Stanford University Press, 1998.
120 M. Foucault, *The Order of Things*. London: Routledge, 1966 (1989), p. xxi.
121 Ibid., p. xxiv.
122 Ibid., p. xxiv.
123 Ibid.
124 M. Heidegger, *The Concept of Time*. Cambridge, MA: Blackwell, 1992.
125 T. Lemke, 'From Eugenics to the Government of Genetic Risks', in Robin Bunton and Alan Petersen (eds.) *Genetic Governance: Health, Risk and Ethics in the Biotech Era*. London: Routledge, 2005, pp. 95–105; M. Cooper, 'Resuscitations: Stem Cells and the Crisis of Old Age', *Body Society* 12, no. 1, 2006, pp. 1–23.
126 J. Fries, 'The Compression of Morbidity', *Milbank Quarterly* 83, no. 4, 2005, pp. 801–23; J. F. Fries, 'Measuring and Monitoring Success in Compressing Morbidity', *Annals of Internal Medicine* 139, no. 5, 2003, pp. 455–9; J. Fries, 'Frailty, Heart Disease, and Stroke: The Compression of Morbidity Paradigm', *American Journal of Preventive Medicine* 29, no. 5, Supplement 1, 2005, pp. 164–8.
127 N. S. Rose, *The Politics of Life Itself: Biomedicine, Power, and Subjectivity in the Twenty-first Century*. Princeton, NJ: Princeton University Press, 2007, p. 7.
128 C. Waldby, 'Umbilical Cord Blood: From Social Gift to Venture Capital', *BioSocieties* 1, no. 1, 2006, p. 15. See also N. S. Rose, *The Politics of Life Itself: Biomedicine, Power, and Subjectivity in the Twenty-first Century*, p. 19.
129 Rose, *The Politics of Life Itself: Biomedicine, Power, and Subjectivity in the Twenty-first Century*, p. 6.
130 R. Helfenstein and T. Holzheu, 'Securitisation – New Opportunities for Insurers and Investors', *Sigma* 7, 2006, pp. 1–42.
131 Ibid., p. 3.
132 Ibid., p. 3.
133 Ibid., p. 3.

4 Securitizing catastrophic environments, insuring uninsurable lives

1 C. Fleming and J. Lyons, 'Mexico's $160 Million Bond Issue to Insure against Earthquakes', *Wall Street Journal – Eastern Edition*, 247, no. 111, 2006.
2 See P. Bougen, 'Catastrophe Risk', *Economy and Society* 32, no. 2, 2003, pp. 253–74; A. Zanetti and S. Schwartz, 'Natural Catastrophes and Man-made Disasters in 2006: Low Insured Losses', *Sigma* 2, 2007, pp. 1–40.
3 F. R. Skees and B. Collier, 'The Potential of Weather Index Insurance for Spurring a Green Revolution in Africa', paper prepared for the Alliance for Green Revolution in Africa Policy Workshop (Nairobi, Kenya, 23–25 June 2008).
4 F. Ghesquiere and O. Mahul, 'Sovereign Natural Disaster Insurance for Developing

Countries: A Paradigm Shift in Catastrophe Risk Financing', *Policy Research Working Paper, The World Bank* 4345, no. 4345, 2007 (www-wds.worldbank.org/external/default/WDSContentServer/IW3P/IB/2007/09/10/000158349_20070910112223/Rendered/PDF/wps4345.pdf).

5 For a description of this situation, see Zanetti and Schwartz, 'Natural Catastrophes and Man-made Disasters in 2006: Low Insured Losses'.

6 Ibid.

7 V. Cardenas, 'Mexico Cat Bond: Lessons to be Learned', paper presented at the Sovereign Debt Management Forum, World Bank, Washington, DC, 23–25 October 2006.

8 P. O'Malley, 'Risk, Uncertainty and Government', in *Risk, Uncertainty and Government*. London: Glasshouse Press, 2004, p. 8.

9 R. Ericson, 'Governing through Risk and Uncertainty', *Economy and Society* 34, no. 4, 2005, p. 663.

10 T. Baker and J. Simon, 'Embracing Risk', in Tom Baker and Jonathan Simon (eds.) *Embracing Risk: The Changing Culture of Insurance and Responsibility*. Chicago: University of Chicago Press, 2002, pp. 1–26; T. Baker, 'Embracing Risk, Sharing Responsibility', *Drake Law Review* 56, no. 2, 2008, pp. 561–71; F. Ewald, 'The Return of Descartes's Malicious Demon: An Outline of a Philosophy of Precaution', in Tom Baker and Jonathan Simon (eds.) *Embracing Risk: The Changing Culture of Insurance and Responsibility*. Chicago: University of Chicago Press, 2002, pp. 273–301; B. Glenn, 'Risk, Insurance and the Changing Nature of Mutual Obligation', *Law and Social Inquiry* 28, 2003, pp. 295–314; P. O'Malley, 'Risk, Uncertainty and Freedom', in *Risk, Uncertainty and Government*. London: Glasshouse Press, 2004, pp. 174–81; N. Rose, 'Governing Liberty', in Richard Ericson and Nico Stehr (eds.) *Governing Modern Societies*. Toronto: University of Toronto Press, 2000, pp. 141–76; N. Rose, 'The Politics of Life Itself', *Theory Culture Society* 18, no. 6, 2001, p. 663.

11 See R. Ericson, A. Barry and A. Doyle, 'The Moral Hazards of Neoliberalism: Lessons from the Private Insurance Industry', *Economy and Society* 29, no. 4, 2000, pp. 532–58.

12 O'Malley, *Risk, Uncertainty and Government*, p. 533.

13 Bougen, 'Catastrophe Risk'.

14 See G. B. Jones, 'Alternative Reinsurance: Using Catastrophe Bonds and Insurance Derivatives as a Mechanism for Increasing Capacity in the Insurance Markets', *CPCU Journal* 52, no. 1, 1999, pp. 1–6.

15 See F. Black and M. Scholes, 'The Pricing of Options and Corporate Liabilities', *Journal of Political Economy* 81, no. 3, 1973, pp. 637–54; Bodie and Merton, *Finance*.

16 For a debate on different understandings of financial derivatives and the theory of money, see D. Bryan and M. Rafferty, *Capitalism with Derivatives: A Political Economy of Financial Derivatives, Capital and Class*. Basingstoke: Palgrave Macmillan, 2006; and M. Pryke and J. Allen, 'Monetized Time–Space: Derivatives – Money's "New Imaginary"?', *Economy & Society* 29, no. 2, 2000, pp. 264–84.

17 Pryke and Allen, 'Monetized Time–Space: Derivatives – Money's "New Imaginary"?', p. 267.

18 D. Bryan and M. Rafferty, 'Financial Derivatives and the Theory of Money', *Economy & Society* 36, no. 1, 2007, p. 136.

19 Pryke and Allen, 'Monetized Time–Space: Derivatives – Money's "New Imaginary"?'; Bryan and Rafferty, 'Financial Derivatives and the Theory of Money'; G. Ingham, 'Fundamentals of a Theory of Money: Untangling Fine, Lapavitsas and Zelizer', *Economy & Society* 30, no. 3, 2001, pp. 304–23; E. LiPuma and B. Lee, 'Financial Derivatives and the Rise of Circulation', *Economy & Society* 34, no. 3, 2005, p. 136.

20 Bryan and Rafferty, 'Financial Derivatives and the Theory of Money'.

21 D. MacKenzie, 'The Material Production of Virtuality: Innovation, Cultural

Geography and Facticity in Derivatives Markets', *Economy & Society* 36, no. 3, 2007, p. 359.
22 Bougen, 'Catastrophe Risk', p. 262.
23 Ibid., pp. 262–3.
24 M. Foucault, 'Governmentality', in James Faubion (ed.) *Michel Foucault: Power, the Essential Works 3,* London: Allen Lane The Penguin Press, 1994, pp. 201–2; N. Rose, *Powers of Freedom*. Cambridge: Cambridge University Press, 1999, pp. 262–3.
25 Foucault, ibid.
26 Zanetti and Schwartz, 'Natural Catastrophes and Man-made Disasters in 2006: Low Insured Losses', p. 35.
27 U. Beck, *Risk Society: Towards a New Modernity*. London: Sage, 1992; U. Beck, W. Bonss and C. Lau, 'The Theory of Reflexive Modernization: Problematic, Hypotheses, and Research Programme', *Theory, Culture and Society* 20, no. 2, 2004, pp. 1–33.
28 D. Laster and C. Schmidt, 'Innovating to Insure the Uninsurable', *Sigma* 4, 2005, pp. 1–36.
29 Lloyd's, *360 Risk Project: Climate Change, Adapt or Bust?* London: Lloyd's of London, 2006.
30 Ibid.
31 Ibid., p. 5.
32 Ibid., p. 21.
33 Personal conclusions derived from the final debate of the forum. Ibid.
34 Ibid., p. 21.
35 Ibid.
36 Ibid.
37 Ibid.
38 R. Ferguson, 'Luncheon Speech: The Risk and Opportunity of Climate Change – a Reinsurer's Perspective', paper presented at the Large Cities Climate Summit, Essex House, New York City, New York, 16 May 2007, p. 21.
39 For a critique on this perspective, see M. Paterson, 'Risky Business: Insurance Companies in Global Warming Politics', *Global Environmental Politics* 1, no. 4, 2001, pp. 18–42.
40 Lloyd's, *360 Risk Project: Climate Change, Adapt or Bust?*, p. 3.
41 Ibid.
42 Ibid., p. 5.
43 Ferguson, 'Luncheon Speech: The Risk and Opportunity of Climate Change – a Reinsurer's Perspective', p. 8.
44 Ibid., p. 8.
45 Ibid., p. 8.
46 Ibid., p. 8.
47 Ibid., p. 8.
48 UNEPFI, *Insuring for Sustainability: Why and How the Leaders are Doing It – Inaugural Report of the UNEPFI*. Geneva: UNEPFI, 2007, p. 13.
49 Ibid., p. 6.
50 Ibid., p. 6.
51 Ibid., p. 6.
52 Ibid., p. 7.
53 Ibid., p. 10.
54 Ibid., p. 10.
55 Ibid., p. 7.
56 Ibid., p. 7.
57 See Laster and Schmidt, 'Innovating to Insure the Uninsurable', p. 7.
58 For a critique, see, for example, M. Paterson and S. Dalby, 'Empire's Ecological Tyreprints', *Environmental Politics* 15, no. 1, 2006, pp. 1–22.

59 UNEPFI, *Insuring for Sustainability: Why and How the Leaders are Doing It – Inaugural Report of the UNEPFI*, p. 12.
60 Ibid.
61 H. Ibarra and R. Mechler, 'Innovative Risk Financing Instruments', *Agriculture and Rural Development – IIASA Conference*. Manila: World Bank–IIASA, 2006.
62 Ibid.
63 Ibid.
64 Ibid.
65 In relation to their use in agriculture, see D. V. Vedenov, J. E. Epperson and B. J. Barnett, 'Designing Catastrophe Bonds to Securitize Systemic Risks in Agriculture: The Case of Georgia Cotton', *Journal of Agricultural and Resource Economics* 31, no. 2, 2006, pp. 318–38.
66 Ibarra and Mechler, 'Innovative Risk Financing Instruments'.
67 Ibid.
68 Ibid.
69 Ibid.
70 Ibid.
71 Zanetti and Schwartz, 'Natural Catastrophes and Man-made Disasters in 2006: Low Insured Losses'.
72 World Food Programme, 'World's First Humanitarian Insurance Issued', 6 March 2006 (www.wfp.org/node/598; accessed 10 February 2010).
73 Ibid.
74 Reuters, 'Insurers Eye Opportunities in Poorest Nations', *Reuters On-line*, 13 November 2006 (accessed 7 February 2010).
75 Ibid.
76 UNEPFI, *Adaptation and Vulnerability to Climate Change: The Role of the Finance Sector*. Geneva: UNEPFI, 2006.
77 Ibid.
78 Ibid.
79 Ibid.
80 Cardenas, 'Mexico Cat Bond: Lessons to be Learned'.
81 Ibid.
82 Ibid., p. 7.
83 Ibid.
84 Ibid., p. 8.
85 Ibid., p. 7.
86 See J. J. Fernandez-Duran and M. M. Gregorio-Dominguez, 'Actuarial Valuation of Cat Bond for Natural Disasters in Mexico', *Trimestre Economico* 72, no. 288, 2005, pp. 877–912.
87 On the actuarial modelling for the Mexican cat bonds see AIR, *CLAS: Catastrophe Loss Analysis Service*, Applied Insurance Research Worldwide Corporation, 2007 (www.air-worldwide.com/_public/html/consult_serv.asp; accessed 19 January 2010).
88 Ibid., p. 2.
89 Ibid.
90 The role of modelling agencies such as AIR is evidencing a shift in the ways in which industries approach catastrophic risk. Until recently catastrophe modelling services were used as a supplement to analyse catastrophe risk; now catastrophe modelling is evolving into a critical component of an organization's risk management. See ibid.
91 J. J. Fernandez-Duran and M. M. Gregorio-Dominguez, 'Actuarial Valuation of Cat Bond for Natural Disasters in Mexico', p. 2.
92 Ibid.
93 Ibid.
94 CCH Inc., 'Ground-up Loss', *Wolters Kluwer Financial Services On-line Glossary*

(www.insource.nils.com/gloss/GlossaryTerm.asp?tid=2741; accessed 19 January 2010).

95 Cardenas, 'Mexico Cat Bond: Lessons to be Learned'.
96 Ibid.
97 Ibid.
98 Ibid., p. 20.
99 Ibid., p. 20.
100 C. Fleming, C. Fleming and J. Lyons, 'Mexico's $160 Million Bond Issue to Insure against Earthquakes', *Wall Street Journal – Eastern Edition* 247, no. 111, 2006, p. 17.
101 Cardenas, 'Mexico Cat Bond: Lessons to be Learned'.
102 Ibid.
103 Ibid.
104 Laster and Schmidt, 'Innovating to Insure the Uninsurable'.
105 See G. B. Jones, 'Alternative Reinsurance: Using Catastrophe Bonds and Insurance Derivatives as a Mechanism for Increasing Capacity in the Insurance Markets', *CPCU Journal* 52, no. 1, 1999, p. 50.
106 Cardenas, 'Mexico Cat Bond: Lessons to be Learned'.
107 R. Ferguson, 'Solutions for Emerging Markets', paper presented at the Economic Forum, London, 5 December 2006, p. 8.
108 Jones, 'Alternative Reinsurance: Using Catastrophe Bonds and Insurance Derivatives as a Mechanism for Increasing Capacity in the Insurance Markets'.

5 Kidnap and ransom insurance

1 Parts of this chapter were published in Luis Lobo-Guerrero, 'Biopolitics of Specialist Risk: Kidnap and Ransom Insurance', *Security Dialogue* 38, no. 3, 2007, pp. 315–34.
2 F. Ewald, 'Genetics, Insurance and Risk', in T. McGleenan, U. Weising and F. Ewald (eds.) *Genetics and Insurance*. Oxford: Bios, 1999, p. 21.
3 M. Foucault, *Security, Territory, Population*. Basingstoke: Palgrave Macmillan, 2007, p. 21.
4 Kroll, *Kidnap for Ransom* brochure, 2006 (www.krollworldwide.com/library/brochures/Kidnap%20for%20Ransom.pdf; accessed 12 February 2010).
5 R. Briggs, *The Kidnapping Business*. London: The Foreign Policy Centre, 2001, p. 1.
6 A. Wong, *Insurers Meet Rising Demand for Kidnap and Ransom Insurance*. Columbia News Service, Columbia University, Graduate School of Journalism, 2004.
7 Ibid., p. 5.
8 References for these sources are kept confidential at the request of their providers.
9 T. Clayton, 'Companies Expanding Abroad Must Protect Employees', *San Fernando Valley Business Journal*, 19 November 2006.
10 A. Rice, 'Captive Market', *BBC News Magazine*, 19 November 2006.
11 J. A. Bogardus and R. H. Moore, *Spreading the Risks: Insuring the American Experience*. Maryland: Posterity Press, 2003.
12 Information provided in these two paragraphs is based on the author's experience as risk and security advisor for an energy corporation operating in South America between 2000 and 2002. For a general view on corporate security risk assessment and risk management see, for example, C. Roper, *Risk Management for Security Professionals*. Woburn, MA: Butterworth-Heinemann, 1999.
13 G. Garcia Marquez, *Noticia de un Secuestro*. Barcelona: Grijalbo Mondadori, 1996.
14 'Tom Hargrove's improvised kidnap diary, day 325 of 334, 1994, somewhere in Colombia'. Cited by Kroll, *Kidnap for Ransom* brochure (www.krollworldwide.com/library/brochures/Kidnap%20for%20Ransom.pdf).
15 Leon Valencia is at the time of writing an analyst for the Colombian non-governmental organization Corporación Nuevo Arco Iris.

16 A. Vranckx, *Private Security Services in the Colombian Context*. Antwerp: International Peace Information Service 2001, p. 12.
17 See M. Power, *Organized Uncertainty: Designing a World of Risk Management*. Oxford: Oxford University Press, 2007.

6 Insurance and the securitization of global maritime circulation

1 Parts of this chapter have been published as L. Lobo-Guerrero, 'Pirates, "Stewards" and the Securitization of Global Circulation', *International Political Sociology* 2, no. 3, 2008, pp. 219–35.
2 Government of Sri Lanka, 'Sri Lanka to Make Representations against Negative Risk Assessment', *Sri Lanka Current Affairs*, 2001 (www.priu.gov.lk/news_update/Current_Affairs/ca200108/20010811SL_representations_against_negative_risk_assessment.htm; accessed 19 January 2010).
3 Ibid.
4 Ibid.
5 Lloyd's, 'Joint Statement Issued on Behalf of the Sri Lankan High Commission and Lloyd's Underwriter's Association', *Lloyd's Press Releases*, LL59/01, no. 17, August 2001.
6 A. M. Kokna, 'Piracy and Terrorism are Joining Forces and Creating Troubled Waters for the Maritime Industry', *Security Management On-line*, June 2004 (www.security-management.com/library/001617.html; accessed 2 May 2007).
7 BBC, 'Pakistan War Insurance Plea', *BBC News*, 17 October 2001 (http://news.bbc.co.uk/1/hi/business/1604120.stm; accessed 10 January 2010).
8 Ibid.
9 Ibid.
10 Ibid.
11 DAWN Wire Service, 'War Risk Surcharge: Pakistan Likely to Suffer $200m Loss', 8 October 2001 (www.lib.virginia.edu/area-studies/SouthAsia/SAserials/Dawn/2001/oct0601.html#warr; accessed 8 February 2010).
12 BBC, 'Pakistan War Insurance Plea'.
13 Ibid.
14 Ibid.
15 Joint War Committee, 'JWC Hull War, Strikes, Terrorism and Related Perils Listed Areas', *Lloyd's Market Association*, JWLA-001, 20 June 2005.
16 Ibid.
17 International Maritime Bureau, 'Global Worldwide Piracy Incidents Show a Decline', *Cargo Security International*, 2005 (www.cargosecurityinternational.com/channeldetail.asp?cid=9&caid=4282; accessed 7 January 2010).
18 As noted in J. Chen, 'Reversing the Joint War Committee's (JWC) War Risk Decision in the Malacca Straits: An Interim Review', *Singapore Institute for International Affairs News*, no. 6, March 2006 (http://siiaonline.org/?q=reversing-joint-war-committee%E2%80%99s-jwc-war-risk-decision-malacca-straits-an-interim-review; accessed 10 January 2010).
19 FP, 'Key Malacca Strait Route Not a War Risk: Industry', Agence France Presse, 29 December 2005.
20 Jane's, 'Strait of Malacca to be Given Air Protection', *Jane's Defence Weekly*, no. 10, August 2005.
21 Maritime Institute of Malaysia, 'Combined Navy, Air-Force High-Tech Exercise', *Maritime Institute of Malaysia's News Flash*, Week 1 & 2, no. 1, 12 August 2006.
22 Joint War Committee, 'JWC Hull War, Strikes, Terrorism and Related Perils Listed Areas', Lloyd's Market Association, JWLA005, 7 August 2006.
23 For example, Lloyd's MIU, 'Seaborne Trade Accounts for 77% of Total World Trade',

Lloyd's MIU, 2007 (www.lloydsmiu.com/lmiu/article/200174859999/index.htm; accessed 23 December 2009).

24 The archives that contained the historical records of the London Maritime Association of which the JWC is part disappeared in various fires, most recently the Iron Mountain fire of 12 July 2006 in London.

25 N. Smith and N. Roberts, interview by the author, 2007.

26 Ibid.

27 Ibid.

28 Joint War Committee, 'JWC Hull War, Strikes, Terrorism and Related Perils Listed Areas'.

29 Smith and Roberts, interview by the author, 2007

30 Ibid.

31 Ibid.

32 Ibid.

33 See www.aegisworld.com/management.htm (accessed 12 January 2010).

34 See www.the-lma.com (accessed 12 January 2010).

35 Smith and Roberts, interview by the author, 2007.

36 Ibid.

37 Ibid.

38 Ibid.

39 Ibid.

40 Ibid.

41 Ibid.

42 For a detailed description of the issue of piracy in South-East Asia, see D. Johnson and M. Valencia, *Piracy in Southeast Asia: Status, Issues, and Responses*. Amsterdam: International Institute for Asian Studies/Singapore: Institute of Southeast Asian Studies, 2005; A. Young, *Contemporary Piracy in Southeast Asia: History, Causes, and Remedies*. Amsterdam: International Institute for Asian Studies/Singapore: Institute of Southeast Asian Studies, Singapore, 2007.

43 See M. Murphy, 'Contemporary Piracy and Maritime Terrorism: The Threat to International Security', *Adelphi Paper*, AP 388, 2007.

44 United Nations, *United Nations Convention of the Law of the Sea*. Montego Bay, Jamaica, 1982, article 101.

45 For a description of the long-standing history of piracy in the region before the twentieth century, see, for example, E. Velthoen, 'Sailing in Dangerous Waters: Piracy and Raiding in Historical Context', *IIAS Newsletter*, no. 36, 2005, p. 8; and R. Antony, 'Piracy in Early Modern China', *IIAS Newsletter*, no. 36, 2005, p. 7.

46 S. Eklöf, 'Piracy: a Critical Perspective', *IIAS Newsletter*, no. 36, 2005, p. 12.

47 Ibid., p. 12.

48 C. Liss, 'Maritime Piracy in Southeast Asia', in *Southeast Asian Affairs 2003*. Singapore Institute of Southeast Asian Studies, 2003; E. Frécon, *The Resurgence of Piracy in Southeast Asia*. Paris: IRASEC Occasional Paper No. 5, 2008.

49 S. Eklöf, 'Piracy in Southeast Asia', *IIAS Newsletter*, no. 40, 2006, p. 29.

50 See P. Chalk, 'Low Intensity Conflict in Southeast Asia', *Conflict Studies*, Research Institute for the Study of Conflict and Terrorism no. 305/306, 1998; P. Chalk, *Non-Military Security and Global Order*, London: Macmillan Press, 2000; J. Vagg, 'Rough Seas?', *British Journal of Criminology*, 35, no. 1, 1995, pp. 63–80; C. Liss, 'Maritime Piracy in Southeast Asia', in P. Chalk (ed.) 'Contemporary Maritime Piracy in Southeast Asia', *Studies in Conflict and Terrorism*, no. 21, March 1997.

51 A. Ward and J. Hacket, 'Piracy and Maritime Terror in Southeast Asia: Dire Straits', *IISS Strategic Comments* 10, no. 6, 2004, p. 2.

52 Ibid., p. 2.

53 Ibid., p. 2.

54 Ibid.

55 Ibid., p. 1.
56 Ibid., p. 1.
57 Ibid., p. 1.
58 Securitization is being used following the work of Ole Wæver. See O. Wæver, 'Securitisation and Desecuritisation', in Ronnie Lipschutz (ed.) *On Security*. New York: Columbia University Press, 1995, pp. 46–86.
59 See J. Engels, 'Floating Bombs Encircling Our Shores: Post-9/11 Rhetorics of Piracy and Terrorism', *Cultural Studies–Cultural Methodologies* 7, no. 3, 2007, pp. 326–49.
60 See M. Greenberg, P. Chalk, H. Willis, I. Khilko and D. Ortiz, *Maritime Terrorism: Risk and Liability*. Santa Monica, CA: RAND Corporation, 2006.
61 Ward and Hacket, 'Piracy and Maritime Terror in Southeast Asia: Dire Straits', p. 1.
62 Ibid.
63 Anon., 'Malacca Strait Littoral Navies Ponder Agreement on Strait Cross-border Patrols', *Jakarta Post*, 19 August 2005.
64 Ibid.
65 P. Steinberg, *The Social Construction of the Ocean*. Cambridge: Cambridge University Press, 2001, p. 165.
66 I. Kant, *Critique of Pure Reason*. New York: St. Martins, 1965.
67 I borrow this expression from J. Derrida, *Rogues: Two Essays on Reason*. Stanford, CA: Stanford University Press, 2005, p. 128.
68 This phrase is, of course, Foucault's. See M. Foucault, *Discipline and Punish: the Birth of the Prison*, London: Penguin Books, 1991, p. 31. For a useful description of this phrase, see D. Campbell, *Writing Security: United States Foreign Policy and the Politics of Identity*. Manchester: Manchester University Press, 1992, pp. 5–6.
69 There is a discussion to be had in respect to the space constituted through insurance, particularly in relation to maritime insurance. The heterotopias constituted by the ship as space, as noted by Foucault in M. Foucault, 'Of Other Spaces', *diacritics* 16, no. 1, 1986, provides a rich thought to begin with. I am grateful to an anonymous referee for pointing this out.
70 Steinberg, *The Social Construction of the Ocean*, p. 6.
71 Ibid., p. 113.
72 Ibid.
73 Ibid.
74 Ibid., p. 113.
75 Ibid., p. 114.
76 Ibid.
77 Ibid., p. 116.
78 Ibid., p. 201.
79 Ibid.
80 Ibid., p. 162.
81 Ibid., p. 163.
82 Ibid., p. 65.
83 Ibid., p. 66.
84 Ibid., pp. 176–80.

7 Valuation–subjectivity–security

1 See G. Deleuze, *The Logic of Sense*. London: Continuum, 2003.
2 See F. Dastur, *Telling Time: Sketch of a Phenomenological Chronology*. London: Continuum, 2000.
3 M. Foucault, *The Birth of Biopolitics*. London: Palgrave Macmillan, 2008, p. 42.
4 W. Connolly, *Identity/Difference: Democratic Negotiations of Political Paradox*. Minneapolis: University of Minnesota Press, 1991.

5 F. Nietzsche, *The Will to Power*. New York: Random, Vintage, 1968, paragraph 490, p. 270.
6 G. Agamben, *Homo Sacer: Sovereign Power and Bare Life*. Stanford, CA: Stanford University Press, 1998, p. 6.
7 Ibid., p. 6. Emphasis from original has been removed
8 M. Foucault, *The Hermeneutics of the Self*. New York: Picador, 2005, p. 364.

Bibliography

ABI, *Life Insurance and Genetics: A Policy Statement*. London: Association of British Insurers, 1997.

——, *Genetic Testing: Code of Practice*. London: Association of British Insurers, 1999.

——, *General Practitioner's Report, Cover Letter, Covering Letter Enclosure, and Official Format*, unpublished document, 2002.

——, *Genetic Testing and Insurance: ABI Code of Practice on Genetic Testing Compliance Report and Data Analysis for 2003*. London: Association of British Insurers, 2005.

——, *The Social Value of General Insurance*. London: Association of British Insurers, 2005.

ABI and BMA, *Agreement between the ABI and BMA 2002 on General Practitioner's Reports and Medical Fees*. London: Association of British Insurers–British Medical Association, 2002.

Agamben, G., *Homo Sacer: Sovereign Power and Bare Life*. Stanford, CA: Stanford University Press, 1998.

AIR, *CLAS: Catastrophe Loss Analysis Service*. Applied Insurance Research Worldwide Corporation, 2007 (http://www.air-worldwide.com/_public/html/consult_serv.asp; accessed 10 February 2010).

Alter, G. and Riley, J., 'How to Bet on Lives: A Guide to Life Contingent Contracts in Early Modern Europe', *Research in Economic History* 10, 1986, pp. 1–53.

Anon., 'Leaders: Insurance in the Genetic Age', *The Economist* no. 357, 2000, p. 23.

Anon., 'Strait of Malacca to be Given Air Protection', *Jane's Defence Weekly* no. 10, August 2005.

Anon., 'Malacca Strait Littoral Navies Ponder Agreement on Strait Cross-border Patrols', *Jakarta Post*, 2005 (http://www.thejakartapost.com/news/2005/08/19/navies-ponder-agreement-strait-crossborder-patrols.html; accessed 10 February 2010).

Antony, R., 'Piracy in Early Modern China', *IIAS Newsletter* no. 36, 2005, p. 7.

Aradau, C. and van Munster, R., 'Governing Terrorism through Risk: Taking Precautions, (un)Knowing the Future', *European Journal of International Relations* 13, no. 1, 2007, pp. 89–115.

Baker, T., 'Embracing Risk, Sharing Responsibility', *Drake Law Review* 56, no. 2, 2008, 561–70.

Baker, T. and Simon, J., *Embracing Risk: The Changing Culture of Insurance and Responsibility*. Chicago: University of Chicago Press, 2002.

BBC, 'Pakistan War Insurance Plea', *BBC News*, 17 October 2001 (www.news.bbc.co.uk/1/hi/business/1604120.stm; accessed 10 February 2010).

Beck, U., *Risk Society: Towards a New Modernity*. London: Sage, 1992.

Beck, U., Bonss, W., and Lau, C. 'The Theory of Reflexive Modernization: Problematic, Hypotheses, and Research Programme', *Theory, Culture and Society* 20, no. 2, 2004, pp. 1–33.

Bellerose, P., *Reinsurance for the Beginner*. London: Witherby & Co., 1998.

Benfield, B., *Life Insurance Company Management*. Los Angeles: Primary Asset Administrative Services, 2005.

Bergfeld, C., 'Die Stellungnahme der spanischen Spätscholastiker zum Versicherungsvertrag', in Paolo Grossi (ed.) *La Seconda scolastica nella formazione del diritto privato moderno: incontro di studio, Firenze 16–10 ottobre, 1972*. Milan: Giuffré, 1973, pp. 457–71.

Bernardelli, H., 'The Origins of Modern Economic Theory', *The Economic Record* no. 37, 1961, pp. 320–38.

Bernstein, P., *Against the Gods: The Remarkable Story of Risk*. New York: John Wiley & Sons, 1998.

Black, F. and Scholes, M., 'The Pricing of Options and Corporate Liabilities', *Journal of Political Economy* 81, no. 3, 1973, p. 637.

Bodie, Z. and Merton, R., *Finance*. Englewood Cliffs, NJ: Prentice Hall, 1999.

Bogardus, J., *Spreading the Risks: Insuring the American Experience*. Chevy Chase, Maryland: Posterity Press, 2003.

Boiteaux, L. A., *La Fortune de mer. Le besoin de sécurité et les débuts de l'assurance maritime*. Paris: SEVPEN, 1968.

Bottigheimer, K. S., *English Money and Irish Land: The 'Adventurers' in the Cromwellian Settlement of Ireland*. Oxford: Oxford University Press, 1971.

Bougen, P., 'Catastrophe Risk', *Economy and Society* 32, no. 2, 2003, 253–74.

Bowker, G. C. and Star, S. L., *Sorting Things Out: Classification and its Consequences*. Cambridge, MA: MIT Press, 1999.

Briggs, R., *The Kidnapping Business*. London: The Foreign Policy Centre, 2001.

Briys, E. and Joos de ter Beerst, D. 'The Zaccaria Deal: Contract and Options to Fund a Genoese Shipment of Alum to Bruges in 1298', presented at XIV International Economic History Congress, Helsinki, August 2006.

Bryan, D. and Rafferty, M., *Capitalism with Derivatives: A Political Economy of Financial Derivatives, Capital and Class*. Basingstoke: Palgrave Macmillan, 2006.

——, 'Financial Derivatives and the Theory of Money', *Economy & Society* 36, no. 1, 2007, pp. 134–58.

Buck, P., 'Seventeenth-Century Political Arithmetic: Civil Strife and Vital Statistics', *Isis* 68, no. 1, 1977, pp. 67–84.

——, 'People Who Counted: Political Arithmetic in the Eighteenth Century', *Isis* 73, no. 1, 1982, pp. 28–45.

Butterworth, A., *Temporal Trends in ABI Genetic Testing Data 2002–2005: A Report on the ABI Annual Questionnaire Responses since 2002 with Comparison to National Genetic Testing Data*. London, unpublished manuscript, 2006.

Campbell, D., *Writing Security: United States Foreign Policy and the Politics of Identity*. Manchester: Manchester University Press, 1992.

Cardenas, V., 'Mexico Cat Bond: Lessons to be Learned', paper presented at the Sovereign Debt Management Forum, World Bank, Washington, DC, 23–25 October 2006.

Catto, J. I. (ed.), *The History of the University of Oxford*, Vol. 1, *The Early Oxford Schools*. Oxford: Clarendon Press, 1984.

CCH Inc., 'Ground-up Loss', *Wolters Kluer Financial Services On-line Glossary*, 2007 (http://insource.nils.com/gloss/GlossaryTerm.asp?tid=2741; accessed 10 February 2010).

Ceccarelli, G., 'Risky Business: Theological and Canonical Thought on Insurance from the Thirteenth to the Seventeenth Century', *Journal of Medieval and Early Modern Studies* 31, no. 3, 2001, pp. 607–58.

Chalk, P., 'Contemporary Maritime Piracy in Southeast Asia', *Studies in Conflict and Terrorism* 21, no. March 1997, pp. 87–112.

——, *Low Intensity Conflict in Southeast Asia. Conflict Studies* no. 305/306. Leamington Spa: Research Institute for the Study of Conflict and Terrorism, 1998.

——, *Non-Military Security and Global Order*. London: Macmillan Press, 2000.

Chen, J., 'Reversing the Joint War Committee's (JWC) War Risk Decision in the Malacca Straits: An Interim Review', *Singapore Institute for International Affairs News*, no. 6, March 2006 (http://www.siiaonline.org/?q=reversing-joint-war-committee%E2%80%99s-jwc-war-risk-decision-malacca-straits-an-interim-review; accessed 10 February 2010).

Clark, B., 'Financing Risk in the Capital Markets: Why Bother?', *Hedge Financial Products* no. 2000 (http://www.cna.com/cnare/rescenter/s2k_reports/financing.htm, accessed 10 February 2010).

Clark, G., *Betting on Lives: The Culture of Life Insurance in England, 1695–1775*. Manchester: Manchester University Press, 1999.

——, 'Embracing Fatality through Life Insurance in Eighteenth-Century England', in Tom Baker and Jonathan Simon (eds.) *Embracing Risk*. Chicago: University of Chicago Press, 2002, pp. 80–96.

Clayton, T., 'Companies Expanding Abroad Must Protect Employees', *San Fernando Valley Business Journal* 19 November 2006 (http://www.allbusiness.com/north-america/united-states-california/523842–1.html; accessed 10 February 2010).

Cleirac, *Les Us et Coutumes de la Mer. Divesees en troit parties. i. De la Navigation. II. Du Commerce Naval et Contrats Maritimes. III. De la Jurisdiction de la Marine, Avec un traitte des Termes de Marine, &c*. Bordeaux, 1661.

Connolly, W., *Identity/Difference: Democratic Negotiations of Political Paradox*. Minneapolis: University of Minnesota Press, 1991.

Cooper, M., *Life as Surplus: Biotechnology & Capitalism in the Neoliberal Era*. Seattle: Washington University Press, 2008.

——, 'Resuscitations: Stem Cells and the Crisis of Old Age', *Body Society* 12, no. 1, 2006, pp. 1–23.

CRG, Incident Response website (http://www.crg.com/Default.aspx?page=412; accessed 10 February 2010).

Daston, L. J., 'The Domestication of Risk: Mathematical Probability and Insurance 1650–1830', in Lorenz Krüger, Lorraine J. Daston and Michael Heidelberger (eds.) *The Probabilistic Revolution*. Cambridge, MA: MIT Press, 1987, pp. 237–60.

——, *Classical Probability in the Enlightenment*. Princeton, NJ: Princeton University Press, 1988.

Dastur, F., *Telling Time: Sketch of a Phenomenological Chronology*. London: Continuum International Publishers, 2000.

Davenant, C., *The Political and Commercial Works of that Celebrated Writer Charles D'Avenant*, collected and revised by C. Whitworth. London: printed for R. Horsfield in Ludgate Street, T. Becket and P.A. de Hondt, and T. Calell in the Strand, and T. Evans in King Street, Covent Garden, 1771.

Davidson, E. H., 'The Sea Urchin Genome: Where Will it Lead Us?', *Science* 314, 2006, pp. 939–40.

DAWN Wire Service, 'War Risk Surcharge: Pakistan Likely to Suffer $200m Loss', 8 October 2001 (http://www.lib.virginia.edu/area-studies/SouthAsia/SAserials/Dawn/2001/oct0601.html#warr; accessed 10 February 2010).

De Roover, F. E., 'Early Examples of Marine Insurance', *Journal of Economic History* 5, 1945, pp. 172–200.

Dean, M., *Governmentality: Power and Rule in Modern Society*. London: Sage, 1999.

——, 'Putting the Technological into Government', *History of the Human Sciences* 9, no. 3, 1996, pp. 47–68.

Deleuze, G., *The Logic of Sense*. London: Continuum, 2003.

Department of Health, *Government Response to the Report from the House of Commons Science and Technology Committee: Genetics and Insurance*. London: Department of Health, 2001.

Department of Health and Association of British Insurers, *Concordat and Moratorium on Genetics and Insurance*. London: Department of Health–Association of British Insurers, 2005.

Derrida, J., *Rogues: Two Essays on Reason*. Stanford, CA: Stanford University Press, 2005.

Deuchars, R., 'The Emergence of Statistical Knowledge', in *The International Political Economy of Risk*. Aldershot: Ashgate, 2004, pp. 32–54.

Dickson, P. G. M., *The Financial Revolution in England: A Study in the Development of Public Credit, 1688–1756*. Aldershot: Gregg Revivals, 1993.

Dillon, M., 'Underwriting Security', *Security Dialogue* 39, no. 2–3, 2008, pp. 309–32.

Dillon, M. and L. Lobo-Guerrero, 'The Biopolitical Imaginary of Species Being', *Theory Culture Society* 26, no. 1, 2009, pp. 1–23.

Dodson, J., *The Mathematical Repository*. London: printed for J. Bourse in the Strand, 1753.

Duffield, M., *Development, Security and Unending War: Governing the World of Peoples*. Cambridge: Polity Press, 2007.

Eden, F. M., *An Estimate of the Number of Inhabitants in Great Britain and Ireland*. London: T. Burton, printer, 1800.

Eklöf, S., 'Piracy: A Critical Perspective', *IIAS Newsletter* no. 36, 2005.

——, 'Piracy in Southeast Asia', *IIAS Newsletter* no. 40, 2006.

Engels, J., 'Floating Bombs Encircling Our Shores: Post-9/11 Rhetorics of Piracy and Terrorism', *Cultural Studies–Cultural Methodologies* 7, no. 3, 2007, pp. 326–49.

Ericson, R., 'Governing through Risk and Uncertainty', *Economy and Society* 34, no. 4, 2005, pp. 659–72.

Ericson, R., Barry, D., and Doyle, A., 'The Moral Hazards of Neoliberalism: Lessons from the Private Insurance Industry', *Economy and Society* 29, no. 4, 2000, pp. 532–58.

Ericson, R., Doyle, A., and Dean, B., *Insurance as Governance*. Toronto: University of Toronto Press, 2003.

Esposito, R., *Bios: Biopolitics and Philosophy*. Minneapolis: University of Minnesota Press, 2008.

Ewald, F., *L'Etat Providence*. Paris: P. Grasset, 1986.

——, 'Insurance and Risk', in Graham Burchell (ed.) *The Foucault Effect: Studies in Governmental Rationality*. Hemel Hempstead: Harvester Wheatsheaf, 1991, pp. 197–210.

——, 'Genetics, Insurance and Risk', in T. McGleenan, U. Weising and F. Ewald (eds.) *Genetics and Insurance*. Oxford: Bios, 1999, pp. 17–34.

——, 'The Return of Descartes's Malicious Demon: An Outline of a Philosophy of Precaution', in Tom Baker and Jonathan Simon (eds.) *Embracing Risk: The Changing Culture of Insurance and Responsibility*. Chicago: University of Chicago Press, 2002, 273–301.

Ferguson, A., *An Essay on the History of Civil Society*. Cambridge: Cambridge University Press, 1996.

Ferguson, R., 'Insurance Solutions for Emerging Markets', paper presented at the Economic Forum, London, 5 December 2006.

——, 'Luncheon Speech: The Risk and Opportunity of Climate Change – a Reinsurer's Perspective', paper presented at the Large Cities Climate Summit, Essex House, New York City, New York, 16 May 2007.

Fernandez-Duran, J. J. and Gregorio-Dominguez, M. M., 'Actuarial Valuation of CAT Bond for Natural Disasters in Mexico', *Trimestre Economico* 72, no. 288, 2005, pp. 877–912.

Fleming, C. and Lyons, J., 'Mexico's $160 Million Bond Issue to Insure against Earthquakes', *Wall Street Journal – Eastern Edition* 247, no. 111, 2006, p. C3.

Foucault, M., 'Of Other Spaces', *diacritics* 16, no. 1, 1986, pp. 22–7.

——, *The Order of Things*. London: Routledge, 1989.

——, *Discipline and Punish: The Birth of the Prison*. London: Penguin Books, 1991.

——, 'Governmentality', in James Faubion (ed.) *Michel Foucault: Power, the Essential Works 3*. London: Allen Lane The Penguin Press, 1994, pp. 201–22.

——, *The History of Sexuality*, Vol. 1: *The Will to Knowledge*. London: Penguin, 1998.

——, *Society Must Be Defended*. London: Penguin Books, 2003.

——, *The Hermeneutics of the Self*. New York: Picador, 2005.

——, *Security, Territory, Population: Lectures at the College de France 1977–1978*. Basingstoke: Palgrave Macmillan, 2007.

——, *The Birth of Biopolitics*. London: Palgrave Macmillan, 2008.

FP, 'Key Malacca Strait Route Not a War Risk: Industry', Agence France Presse, 29 December 2005.

Fréçon, E., *The Resurgence of Piracy in Southeast Asia*. Paris: IRASEC Occasional Paper No. 5, 2008.

Fries, J. 'Measuring and Monitoring Success in Compressing Morbidity', *Annals of Internal Medicine* 139, no. 5, 2003, p. 455.

——, 'The Compression of Morbidity', *Milbank Quarterly* 83, no. 4, [1983] 2005, pp. 801–23.

——, 'Frailty, Heart Disease, and Stroke: The Compression of Morbidity Paradigm', *American Journal of Preventative Medicine* 29, no. 5, Supplement 1, 2005, p. 164.

Gamble, A., *The Spectre at the Feast: Capitalist Crisis and the Politics of Recession*. Basingstoke: Palgrave Macmillan, 2009.

García-Márquez, G., *Noticia de un Secuestro*. Barcelona: Grijalbo Mondadori, 1996.

Geneva Association, 'Special Issue on G-20 Summit', *Geneva Association Information Newsletter*, April 2009.

Ghesquiere, F. and Mahul, O., 'Sovereign Natural Disaster Insurance for Developing Countries: A Paradigm Shift in Catastrophe Risk Financing', Policy Research Working Paper no. WPS 4345, World Bank, 2007 (http://www-wds.worldbank.org/external/default/WDSContentServer/IW3P/IB/2007/09/10/000158349_20070910112223/Rendered/PDF/wps4345.pdf; accessed 10 February 2010).

Gigerenzer, G., Swijtink, Z., Porter, T., Daston, L. J., Beatty, J. and Kruger, K. *The Empire of Chance*. New York: Cambridge University Press, 1989.

Glasner, P., 'Beyond the Genome: Reconstituting the New Genetics', *New Genetics and Society* 21, no. 3, 2002, pp. 267–77.

Glass, D. V., *Numbering the People*. Farnborough: Saxon House, 1973.

Glenn, B., 'Risk, Insurance and the Changing Nature of Mutual Obligation', *Law and Social Inquiry* 28, 2003, pp. 295–314.

Godin, B., *Measurement and Statistics on Science and Technology: 1920 to the Present*. London: Routledge, 2005.

de Goede, M., *Virtue, Fortune, and Faith: A Genealogy of Finance*. Minneapolis: University of Minnesota Press, 2005.

——, 'Beyond Risk: Premediation and the Post-9/11 Security Imagination', *Security Dialogue* 39, no. 2–3, 2008, pp. 155–76.

Government of Sri Lanka, 'Sri Lanka to Make Representations against Negative Risk Assessment', *Sri Lanka Current Affairs* 2001 (http://www.priu.gov.lk/news_update/Current_Affairs/ca200108/20010811SL_representations_against_negative_risk_assessment.htm; accessed 10 February 2010).

Graunt, J., *Natural and Political Observations Mentioned in a Following Index, and Made upon the Bills of Mortality*. London: printed by Tho: Roycroft, for John Martin, James Allestry, and Tho: Dicas, at the Sign of the Bell in St. Paul's, 1662.

Great Britain, 'An Act for Regulating Insurances on Lives', 14 Geo III c. 48, 1774.

Greenberg, M., Chalk, P., Willis, H., Khilko, I., and Ortiz, D., *Maritime Terrorism: Risk and Liability*. Santa Monica, CA: RAND Corporation, 2006.

Gregory IX, *Decretal Naviganti of Pope Gregory IX* GREG.LIB. V. TIT. XIX. CAP. XIX, 1236.

Hacking, I., 'Biopower and the Avalanche of Printed Numbers', *Humanities in Society* 5, 1982, pp. 279–95.

——, 'Making up People', in T. Heller, M. Sosna and D. Wellberry (eds.) *Reconstructing Individualism*. Stanford, CA: Stanford University Press, 1986, pp. 222–36.

——, *The Taming of Chance*. Cambridge: Cambridge University Press, 1990.

——, 'Risk and Dirt', in Richard Ericson and Aaron Doyle (eds.) *Risk and Morality*. Toronto: University of Toronto Press, 2003, pp. 22–47.

——, *The Emergence of Probability*. Cambridge: Cambridge University Press, 2006.

Halley, E., 'An Estimate of the Degrees of the Mortality of Mankind', *Philosophical Transactions* no. 196, 1693, pp. 596–610.

——, 'An Estimate of the Degrees of the Mortality of Mankind, Drawn from Curious Tables of the Births and Funerals at the City of Breslaw; With an Attempt to Ascertain the Price of Annuities upon Lives', *Philosophical Transactions (1683–1775)* 17, 1693, pp. 596–610.

Hardt, M. and Negri, A., *Empire*. Cambridge, MA: Harvard University Press, 2000.

——, *Multitude: War and Democracy in the Age of Empire*. New York: Penguin, 2005.

Haufler, V., *Dangerous Commerce: Insurance and the Management of International Risk*. Ithaca, NY: Cornell University Press, 1997.

HCSCST (House of Commons Select Committee on Science and Technology), *Fifth Report: Genetics and Insurance*. London: House of Commons Science and Technology Select Committee, 2001.

——, *Human Genetics: The Science and its Consequences. House of Commons Science and Technology Committee. Third Report*. London: Her Majesty's Stationery Office, 1995.

Heidegger, M., *The Concept of Time*. Cambridge, MA: Blackwell, 1992.

Helfenstein, R. and Holzheu, T., 'Securitisation – New Opportunities for Insurers and Investors', *Sigma* 2007, no. 7, 2006, pp. 1–42.

Hendriks, F., *Contributions to the History of Insurance, and of the Theory of Life Contingencies, with a Restoration of the Gran Pensionary De Wit's Treatise on Life Annuities*. London: C&E Layton, 1851.

Hirschman, A. O., *The Passions and the Interests: Political Arguments for Capitalism before its Triumph*. Princeton, NJ: Princeton University Press, 1977.

Hoover, C. B., 'The Sea Loan in Genoa in the Twelfth Century', *Quarterly Journal of Economics* 40, no. 3, 1926, pp. 495–529.

Hoppit, J., 'Political Arithmetic in Eighteenth-century England', *Economic History Review* 49, no. 3, 1996, pp. 516–40.

Howard, W. M., 'A Note on Mortality Tables and Interest Rates', *Journal of Insurance* 24, no. 2, 1957, pp. 88–92.

Human Genetics Advisory Commission (HGAC), *The Implications of Genetic Testing for Insurance*. London: HGAC, 1997.

Human Genetics Commission, *The Use of Genetic Information in Insurance: Interim Recommendations of the Human Genetics Commission*. London: Human Genetics Commission, 2001.

Ibarra, H. and Mechler, R., 'Innovative Risk Financing Instruments', in *Agriculture and Rural Development – IIASA Conference*. Manila: World Bank–IIASA, 2006.

IISS, 'Chapter Nine: Country Comparisons – Commitments, Force Levels and Economics', *Military Balance* 109, no. 1, 2009, pp. 425–54.

Ingham, G., 'Fundamentals of a Theory of Money: Untangling Fine, Lapavitsas and Zelizer', *Economy & Society* 30, no. 3, 2001, pp. 304–23.

International Maritime Bureau, 'Global Worldwide Piracy Incidents Show a Decline', *Cargo Security International*, 2005 (http://www.cargosecurityinternational.com/chan-neldetail.asp?cid=9&caid=4282,; accessed 10 February 2010).

Jenkins, D. and Yoneyama, T., 'A Scheme for Erecting a Friendly Society for Insuring Lives', in *The history of Insurance*. London: Pickering & Chatto, 2000 (1700), pp. 315–21.

Johnson, D. and Valencia, M., *Piracy in Southeast Asia: Status, Issues, and Responses, Piracy in Southeast Asia: Status, Issues, and Responses*. Amsterdam: International Institute for Asian Studies/Singapore: Institute of Southeast Asian Studies, 2005.

Joint War Committee, 'JWC Hull War, Strikes, Terrorism and Related Perils Listed Areas', *Lloyd's Market Association* JWLA-001, 20 June 2005.

——, 'JWC Hull War, Strikes, Terrorism and Related Perils Listed Areas', *Lloyd's Market Association* JWLA005, 7 August, 2006.

Jones, E. L., *Agriculture and Economic Growth in England, 1650–1815*. New York: Barnes & Noble, 1967.

Jones, G. B., 'Alternative Reinsurance: Using Catastrophe Bonds and Insurance Derivatives as a Mechanism for Increasing Capacity in the Insurance Markets', *CPCU Journal* 52, no. 1, 1999, p. 50.

Kant, I., *Critique of Pure Reason*. New York: St. Martin's, 1965.

——, *Perpetual Peace: A Philosophical Essay*. London: Garland, 1972.

Kantorowicz, E., *Frederick the Second, 1194–1250*. London: Constable and Co., 1931.

Kay, L. *Who Wrote the Book of Life?: A History of the Genetic Code*. Stanford, CA: Stanford University Press, 2000.

Kerridge, E., *The Agricultural Revolution*. London: Allen & Unwin, 1967.

Kirshner, J., 'Preface to Raymond de Roover', in *Business, Banking, and Economic*

Thought in Late Medieval and Early Modern Europe. Chicago: Chicago University Press, 1974.

Knight, F., *Risk, Uncertainty and Profit*. Boston: Houghton Mifflin, 1921.

Knorr-Cetina, K., 'Sociality with Objects: Social Relations in Postsocial Knowledge Societies', *Theory, Culture and Society* 14, no. 1, 1997, pp. 1–30.

Kohn, M., 'Risk Instruments in the Medieval and Early Modern Economy', Department of Economics, Dartmouth College, Hanover, Working Paper No. 99-07, 1999.

——, 'Payments and the Development of Finance in Pre-Industrial Europe', Department of Economics, Dartmouth College, Hanover, Working Paper 01-15, 2001.

Kokna, A. M., 'Piracy and Terrorism Are Joining Forces and Creating Troubled Waters for the Maritime Industry', *Security Management On-line*, June 2004 (www.securitymanagement.com/library/001617.html; accessed 10 February 2010).

Kroll, *Kidnap for Ransom* brochure, 2006 (http://www.krollworldwide.com/library/brochures/Kidnap%20for%20Ransom.pdf; accessed 10 February 2010).

Krüger, L., Daston, L., and Heidelberger, M. (eds.), *The Probabilistic Revolution*, Vol. 1: *Ideas in History*. Cambridge, MA: MIT Press, 1987.

Langholm, O., *The Aristotelian Analysis of Usury*. Bergen: Universitetsforlaget AS, 1984.

——, *Economics in the Medieval Schools: Wealth, Exchange, Value, Money, and Usury, According to the Paris Theological Tradition 1200–1350*, Leiden: E.J. Brill, 1992.

Laster, D. and Schmidt, C., 'Innovating to Insure the Uninsurable', *Sigma* no. 4, 2005, pp. 1–36.

Le Goff, J., *Time, Work, and Culture in the Middle Ages*. London: University of Chicago Press, 1982.

——, *Your Money or Your Life: Economy and Religion in the Middle Ages*. New York: Zone Books, 1988.

——, *Saint Francis of Assisi*. London: Routledge, 2004.

Lemke, T., 'From Eugenics to the Government of Genetic Risks', in Robin Bunton and Alan Petersen (eds.) *Genetic Governance: Health, Risk and Ethics in the Biotech Era*. London Routledge, 2005, pp. 95–105.

LiPuma, E. and Lee, B., 'Financial Derivatives and the Rise of Circulation', *Economy & Society* 34, no. 3, 2005, pp. 404–27.

Liss, C., 'Maritime Piracy in Southeast Asia', in *Southeast Asian Affairs*. Singapore: Institute of Southeast Asian Studies, 2003.

Lloyd's, 'Joint Statement Issued on Behalf of the Sri Lankan High Commission and Lloyd's Underwriter's Association', *Lloyd's Press Releases* LL59/01, no. 17, August 2001.

——, *360 Risk Project: Climate Change, Adapt or Bust?* London: Lloyd's of London, 2006.

Lloyd's MIU, 'Seaborne Trade Accounts for 77% of Total World Trade', *Lloyd's MIU*, 2007 (http://www.lloydsmiu.com/lmiu/article/200174859999/index.htm; accessed 10 February 2010).

Lobo-Guerrero, L., interview with Professor Angus Macdonald, Heriot-Watt University, Edinburgh, 11 November 2005.

——, 'Pirates, "Stewards" and the Securitization of Global Circulation', *International Political Sociology* 2, no. 3, 2008, pp. 219–35.

Lopez, R., *The Commercial Revolution of the Middle Ages: 950–1350*. Englewood Cliffs, NJ: Prentice Hall, 1971.

Low, L., King, S., and Wilkie, T., 'Genetic Discrimination in Life Insurance: Empirical Evidence from a Cross Sectional Survey of Genetic Support Groups in the United Kingdom', *British Medical Journal* 317, no. 7173, 1998, pp. 1632–5.

McCormick, T. G., 'Transmutation, Inclusion, and Exclusion: Political Arithmetic from Charles II to William III', paper presented at the conference 'Without Let or Hindrance': Inclusion and its Subversion from the Medieval to the Modern, Department of History, Lancaster University, 7–9 July 2006.

Macdonald, A., 'How Will Improved Forecasts of Individual Lifetimes Affect Underwriting?', *Philosophical Transactions of the Royal Society* B, 352, 1997, pp. 1067–75.

——, 'Modelling the Impact of Genetics on Insurance', *North American Actuarial Journal* 3, no. 1, 1999, pp. 83–105.

——, 'Moratoria on the Use of Genetic Tests and Family History for Mortgage-related Life Insurance', *British Actuarial Journal* 217, 2003, pp. 217–37.

MacKenzie, D. 'The Material Production of Virtuality: Innovation, Cultural Geography and Facticity in Derivatives Markets', *Economy & Society* 36, no. 3, 2007, pp. 355–76.

McNally, R. and Glasner, P., 'Beyond the Human Genome Project: Genomics, Proteomics and Systems Biology', manuscript, 2007.

Maier, C. T., *Preaching the Crusades: Mendicant Friars and the Cross in the Thirteenth Century*. Cambridge: Cambridge University Press, 1999.

Maritime Institute of Malaysia, 'Combined Navy, Air-Force High-tech Exercise', *Maritime Institute of Malaysia's News Flash* Week 1&2, no. 1, 12 August 2006.

Miller, P. and Rose, N., 'Political Power beyond the State: Problematics of Government', *British Journal of Sociology* 43, no. 2, 1992, pp. 173–205.

Mittra, J., '"Genetic Exceptionalism" and Precautionary Politics: Regulating for Uncertainty in Britain's Genetic and Insurance Policy Process', *Science and Public Policy* 33, no. 8, 2006, pp. 585–600.

More, C., 'Agriculture and Rural Society', in *The Industrial Age: Economy and Society in Britain, 1750–1995*. London: Longman, 1997, pp. 3–11.

Moss, D. A., *When All Else Fails: Government as the Ultimate Risk Manager*. Cambridge, MA: Harvard University Press, 2002.

Multiple Sclerosis Society, *MS and Insurance*. London: Multiple Sclerosis Society, 2006.

Murphy, M., 'Contemporary Piracy and Maritime Terrorism: The Threat to International Security', *Adelphi Paper* AP 388, 2007.

Nabholz, C., Caroll, J. L., Wekwete, C., and Sommerville, K., *Life Risk Selection at a Fair Price: Reinforcing the Actuarial Basis*. Zurich: Swiss Re, 2007.

Neumann-Held, E. M. and Rehmann-Sutter, C., *Genes in Development: Re-reading the Molecular Paradigm*. Durham, NC: Duke University Press, 2006.

Nietzsche, F., *The Will to Power*. New York: Random, Vintage, 1968.

Noonan, J., *The Scholastic Analysis of Usury*. Cambridge, MA: Harvard University Press, 1957.

O'Brien, G., *An Essay on Medieval Economic Teaching*. New York: Longmans, 1920.

O'Donovan, J. L., 'The Theological Economics of Medieval Usury Theory', *Studies in Christian Ethics* 14, no. 1, 2001, pp. 48–64.

O'Malley, P., 'Uncertain Subjects: Risk, Liberalism and Contract', *Economy and Society* 29, no. 4, 2000, pp. 460–84.

——, *Risk, Uncertainty and Government*. London: Glasshouse Press, 2004.

O'Neill, O., *Genetics, Insurance and Discrimination*. Manchester: Manchester Statistical Society, 1998.

Ogborn, M. E., *Equitable Assurances: The Story of Life Assurance in the Experience of the Equitable Life Assurance Society, 1762–1962*. London: Allen & Unwin, 1962.

Paterson, M., 'Risky Business: Insurance Companies in Global Warming Politics', *Global Environmental Politics* 1, no. 4, 2001, p. 18.

Paterson, M. and Dalby, S., 'Empire's Ecological Tyreprints', *Environmental Politics* 15, no. 1, 2006, pp. 1–22.

Perdikas, P., 'Die Entstehung der Versicherung im Mittelalter: Geschichtliche Grundlagen im Verhältnis zu Seedarlehen, Überseekauf, Commenda und Bodmerei', *Zeitschrift für die gesamte Versicherungswissenshaft* 55, 1966, pp. 425–509.

Pesce, P. G., 'La dottrina degli anichi moralisti circa la liceitá del contratto di assicurazione', *Assicurazione (Rome)* 33, 1966, pp. 36–66.

Petty, W., *Political Arithmetick*, London: Printed for Robert Clavel at the Peacock, and Hen. Mortlock at the Phoenix in St. Paul's Church-yard, 1690 (http://socserv2.socsci.mcmaster.ca/~econ/ugcm/3ll3/petty/poliarith.html; accessed 10 February 2010).

——,*The Political Anatomy of Ireland*. London: printed for D. Brown and W. Rogers, at the Bible without Temple-bar, and at the Sun over-against St. Dunstans Church, 1691.

Poitras, G., *The Early History of Financial Economics, 1478–1776*. Cheltenham: Edward Elgar Publishing, 2000.

Pokorski, R. J., 'A Test for the Insurance Industry', *Nature* 391, no. 6670, 1998, pp. 835–6.

Porter, T., 'Objectivity and Authority: How French Engineers Reduced Public Utility to Numbers', *Poetics Today* 12, no. 2, 1991, pp. 245–65.

——, *Trust in Numbers: The Pursuit of Objectivity in Science and Public Life*. Princeton, NJ: Princeton University Press, 1995.

Power, M., *The Audit Society: Rituals of Verification*. Oxford: Oxford University Press, 1997.

——, *The Invention of Operational Risk*. London: Centre for Analysis of Risk and Regulation, 2003.

——, 'Risk Management and the Responsible Organization', in Richard Ericson and Aaron Doyle (eds.) *Risk and Morality*. Toronto: University of Toronto Press, 2003, pp. 145–64.

——, *The Risk Management of Everything: Rethinking the Politics of Uncertainty*. London: Demos, 2004.

——, *Organized Uncertainty: Designing a World of Risk Management*. Oxford: Oxford University Press, 2007.

Pryke, M. and Allen, J., 'Monetized Time–Space: Derivatives – Money's "New Imaginary"?', *Economy & Society* 29, no. 2, 2000, pp. 264–84.

Raeburn, S., 'Implications of Genetic Testing for the Insurance Industry: The UK Example', *Community Genetics* no. 5, 2002, pp. 102–9.

Regenmortel, V., 'A Paradigm Shift is Needed in Proteomics: "Structure Determines Function" Should Be Replaced by "Binding Determines Function"', *Journal of Molecular Recognition* 15, no. 6, 2002, pp. 349–51.

Reuters, 'Insurers Eye Opportunities in Poorest Nations', *Reuters On-line*, 13 November 2006 (http://www.alertnet.org/thenews/newsdesk/WAL343918.htm; accessed 10 February 2010).

Rheinberger, H.-J., *Towards a History of Epistemic Things: Synthesizing Proteins in the Test Tube*. Stanford, CA: Stanford University Press, 1997.

Rice, A., 'Captive Market', *BBC News Magazine* (http://news.bbc.co.uk/1/hi/magazine/4650840.stm, 19 November 2006; accessed 10 February 2010).

Roper, C., *Risk Management for Security Professionals*. Woburn, MA: Butterworth-Heinemann, 1999.

Rose, N., *Powers of Freedom*. Cambridge: Cambridge University Press, 1999.

——, 'Governing Liberty', in Richard Ericson and Nico Stehr (eds.) *Governing Modern Societies*. Toronto: University of Toronto Press, 2000, pp. 141–76.
——, 'The Politics of Life Itself', *Theory Culture Society* 18, no. 6, 2001, pp. 1–30.
——, *The Politics of Life Itself: Biomedicine, Power, and Subjectivity in the Twenty-first Century*. Princeton, NJ: Princeton University Press, 2007.
Rose, N. and Miller, P., 'Political Power beyond the State: Problematics of Government', *British Journal of Sociology* 43, no. 2, 1992, pp. 173–205.
Roseveare, H., *The Financial Revolution, 1660–1760*. Harlow: Pearson Education, 2001.
Rotman, B., *Signifying Nothing: The Semiotics of Zero*. New York: St. Martin's, 1987.
Sabine, G. H., *A History of Political Theory*. London: George G. Harrap & Co., 1961 (1937).
Serres, M., *Statues: le second livre des fondations*. Paris: Bourin, 1987.
Skees, F. R. and Collier, B. 'The Potential of Weather Index Insurance for Spurring a Green Revolution in Africa', paper prepared for the Alliance for Green Revolution in Africa Policy Workshop, Nairobi, Kenya, 23–25 June 2008.
Smith, J. H., *Francis of Assisi*. London: Sidgwick & Jackson, 1972.
Smith, N. and Roberts, N., interview by the author, 2007.
Smith, R. S., 'Life Insurance in Fifteenth-Century Barcelona', *Journal of Economic History* 1, no. 1, 1941, pp. 57–9.
Society for Equitable Assurances, 'A Short Account of the Society for Equitable Assurances on Lives and Survivorships; Established by Deed, Inrolled in His Majesty's Court of King's Bench', in David Jenkins and Takau Yoneyama (eds.) *The History of Insurance*. London: Pickering & Chatto, 2000 (1762), pp. 361–87.
Society of Assurance for Widows and Orphans, 'An Abridgment of the Most Material Things in the Articles of Settlement, Agreed and Subscrib'd by the Several Members of the First Society of Assurance for Widows and Orphans', in David Jenkins and Takau Yoneyama (eds.) *The History of Insurance*. London: Pickering & Chatto, 2000 (1699), pp. 309–14.
Spagnesi, E., 'Aspetti dell'assicurazione medievale', in *Associazione nazionale fra le imprese assicuratrici, L'assicurazione in Italia fino all'Unità: Saggi storici in onore di Eugenio Artom*. Milan: Giuffré, 1975, pp. 3–189.
Steinberg, P., *The Social Construction of the Ocean*. Cambridge: Cambridge University Press, 2001.
Stigler, S. M., *The History of Statistics: The Measurement of Uncertainty before 1900*. Chicago: Chicago University Press, 1986.
Strange, S., *The Retreat of the State*. Cambridge: Cambridge University Press, 1989.
Swiss Re, 'World Insurance in 2007: Emerging Markets Leading the Way', *Sigma* 3, 2008, pp. 1–44.
Taylor, S. D., 'Predictive Genetic Test Decisions for Huntington's Disease: Context, Appraisal and New Moral Imperatives', *Social Science & Medicine* 58, no. 1, 2004, p. 137.
Trenerry, C. F., *The Origin and Early History of Insurance, Including the Contract of Bottomry*. London: P.S. King & Son, 1926.
Tyers, M. and Mann, M., 'From Genomics to Proteomics (Insight Overview)', *Nature* 422, 2003, pp. 193–7.
UK Department of Health, *Government Response to the Report from the House of Commons Science and Technology Committee: Genetics and Insurance*. London: Department of Health, 2001.
UK Government, *UK Government Response to the Fifth Report of the House of Commons*

Select Committee on Science and Technology, 1996–97. London: The Stationery Office, 1997.

United Nations, *United Nations Convention of the Law of the Sea*. Montego Bay, Jamaica, 1982.

United Nations Environment Programme Finance Initiative (UNEPFI), *Adaptation and Vulnerability to Climate Change: The Role of the Finance Sector*. Geneva: UNEPFI, 2006.

——, *Insuring for Sustainability: Why and How the Leaders are Doing It – Inaugural Report of the UNEPFI*. Geneva: UNEPFI, 2007.

Usher, A. P., 'The Origin of the Bill of Exchange', *Journal of Political Economy* 22, no. 6, 1914, pp. 566–76.

Vagg, J., 'Rough Seas?', *British Journal of Criminology* 35, no. 1, 1995, pp. 63–80.

Vedenov, D. V., Epperson, J. E., and Barnett, B. J., 'Designing Catastrophe Bonds to Securitize Systemic Risks in Agriculture: The Case of Georgia Cotton', *Journal of Agricultural and Resource Economics* 31, no. 2, 2006, pp. 318–38.

Velthoen, E., 'Sailing in Dangerous Waters: Piracy and Raiding in Historical Context', *IIAS Newsletter* no. 36, 2005, p. 8.

Virno, P., *A Grammar of the Multitude*. Los Angeles: Semiotext(e), 2004.

Vranckx, A., 'Private Security Services in the Colombian Context', International Peace Information Service, 2001 (http://www.ipisresearch.be/publications_report.php; accessed 10 February 2010).

Wæver, O., 'Securitisation and Desecuritisation', in Ronnie Lipschutz (ed.) *On Security*. New York: Columbia University Press, 1995, pp. 46–86.

Waldby, C., 'Umbilical Cord Blood: From Social Gift to Venture Capital', *BioSocieties* 1, no. 1, 2006, pp. 55–70.

Ward, A. and Hacket, J., 'Piracy and Maritime Terror in Southeast Asia: Dire Straits', *IISS Strategic Comments* 10, no. 6, 2004, pp. 1–2.

Weir, D. R., 'Tontines, Public Finance, and Revolution in France and England, 1688–1789', *Journal of Economic History* 49, no. 1, 1989, pp. 95–124.

Wellcome Trust, *Letter to Second Clerk of the Committee, Science and Technology Committee, House of Commons*. London: Wellcome Trust, 15 August 2001.

——, Responses to the 'Whose hands on your genes?' Human Genetics Commission Consultation, London, 2001.

Wong, A., "Insurers Meet Rising Demand for Kidnap and Ransom Insurance', Columbia News Service, Columbia University, Graduate School of Journalism (http://www.jrn.columbia.edu/studentwork/cns/2004-03-15/644.asp; accessed 10 February 2010).

World Food Programme, *World's First Humanitarian Insurance Issued*, 6 March 2006 (http://www.wfp.org/node/598; accessed 10 February 2010).

Wright, C. and Fayle, C. E., *A History of Lloyd's: From the Founding of Lloyd's Coffee House to the Present Day*. London: Published for the Corporation of Lloyd's by Macmillan and Company, 1928.

Young, A., *Contemporary Piracy in Southeast Asia: History, Causes, and Remedies*. Amsterdam: International Institute for Asian Studies/Singapore: Institute of Southeast Asian Studies, 2007.

Zanetti, A. and Schwartz, S., 'Natural Catastrophes and Man-made Disasters in 2006: Low Insured Losses', *Sigma* 2, 2007, pp. 1–40.

Zeno, R., *Documenti per la storia del diritto marittimo nei secoli XIII e XIV*. Turin: Zeno, 1936.

Index

For Product Safety Concerns and Information please contact our EU
representative GPSR@taylorandfrancis.com
Taylor & Francis Verlag GmbH, Kaufingerstraße 24, 80331 München, Germany

www.ingramcontent.com/pod-product-compliance
Ingram Content Group UK Ltd.
Pitfield, Milton Keynes, MK11 3LW, UK
UKHW022125190926
475702UK00013B/1655
9780415522854